Without a Script

A Memoir

Judith L. Harkness

Without a Script
A Memoir

ISBN: 978-1-5323-7064-9

1. A Memoir

Without a Script

Part 1 Australia

Losses

If I were to define one moment that changed the course of my life, it would be the moment my mother died. Vera was twenty-seven; I was not yet three. The year was 1932; the place was Sydney, Australia. I learned the circumstances of her death by accident when I was in my fifties and thousands of miles away.

Vera's death prompted an official inquiry. My mother's only sister, Edith, and her husband Eric, attempted to gain custody of me but the law favoured my father. Shortly afterwards, at age thirty, he left me in the charge of his mother-my grandmother Lillian- and sailed for India.

****

Early in my grandparents' marriage, a fire destroyed the furniture warehouse my grandfather, Walter Scott Harkness, owned and managed in Oxford Street, Sydney. Undaunted, he came home and asked my grandmother *if she could keep the children on bread and jam for three weeks,* as he thought he could establish a real estate business in that time. The business prospered, and after his death, was carried on by his eldest son Eric, followed by Eric's son Robert, until the early 1970's.

My grandfather acquired several residential and commercial properties and amassed a fortune. To accommodate his growing family, Walter asked his brother Edward to design and build a house on a large lot on Carlotta Road in Double Bay. He named it *Lillianfels*, after my grandmother Lillian. It became a landmark in Double Bay, which lies in the eastern suburbs of Sydney, and when it was no longer our home, served briefly as the French Embassy.

During the Great Depression of 1929, my grandfather often lent money or forfeited his tenants' rent without documentation. Two years later he died, his fortune reportedly in decline. A photograph taken at *Lillianfels* at Christmas, 1925, shows thirty people, mostly family members, gathered on the front steps, unaware of what was to come.

Lillian bore eleven children but I actually knew only seven. Her third and fourth children (sons), born in 1892 and 1893, *died young*. Her sixth child died in 1899, before he was two years old and her fifth child, Raymond, died at age thirty-four in 1929, the year I was born, leaving a wife and five young children. In 1931-the year my grandfather died-my gentle aunt Phyllis (Lillian's seventh child and second daughter) was widowed when her husband Humphrey died at age thirty-one of what then was called *consumption*. Phyllis had no recourse but to return to her childhood home with her two young sons, Noel and Ron.

The following year, when my own mother died, I too arrived at *Lillianfels*.

Retracing these dates through family records, I can begin to understand the enormous losses my family – especially my grandmother - suffered within a few brief years. The Great Depression surely increased her hardship. Now, with her youngest grown, she took me in, a child not yet three. She was about sixty-five at the time.

Discovering the Past

One Sunday in 1959, the Sydney Morning Herald published a list of *First Fleeters* - the name given to the first convicts to set foot on Australian soil- and their descendants. To me, in 1959, the list meant nothing.

High on this list were Anthony Rope, born 1759, and Elizabeth Pulley, born 1757. It wasn't until 1993 when a cousin I had never met before, Helen Harkness, compiled and published a book called *Harkness Heroines,* which has helped me greatly in the telling of my own story. Like me, Helen had seen the *First Fleeter* list in the Sydney Morning Herald in 1959. Unlike me, she recognized the family connection immediately, and like many Australians, was initially horrified, especially since her family was in direct line to those early convicts. As it turned out, so was mine. From Helen's meticulous family charts, I learned that Anthony and Elizabeth were direct ancestors of Helen's great grandmother Adeline, and Adeline's sister - my grandmother, Lillian. I had never heard so much as a whisper of my family's dark past; I think my grandmother did everything to protect me from it. I learned that Lillian's grandfather, James Tobias Ryan, who would later became known for his book *Reminiscences of Australia,* was the son of Mary Rope, eldest daughter of Anthony Rope and Elizabeth Pulley.

Helen launched the book in July of 1993 at a large family reunion, which I attended, on the grounds of the old government house in Parramatta, N.S.W. The reunion was preceded by a commemorative service at St. Mark's Church in Granville where the minister devoted his sermon to Harkness history, of which I knew nothing. Despite a drenching downpour, spirits were high as dozens of family members reunited or met for the first time, and in some cases, the last: my cousin Noel with whom I had shared my childhood at *Lillianfels,* died shortly afterwards.

Wikipedia, which I quote loosely here, says: *Harkness is a Scottish name of hidden origins, perhaps partly old English, first recorded in Dumfriesshire in the 16th century*. But Helen has traced it as far back as 1273 AD, as a place on the border of Cumberland and Westmoreland, so named by one Reyner de Harkness. However, since Helen writes only of family history that is officially verifiable, she begins the Harkness account in the seventeenth century with Adam Harkness, who died in 1657. In the early 1990's, Helen and her husband Eric Ryan visited Adam's estate, *Mitchellslacks,* in Closeburn, Scotland. In her book, a colour photograph of *Mitchellslacks* shows an austere two-story stone house surrounded by stables and outbuildings. It sits isolated on a great sweep of emerald moor at the foot of low smooth hills, above a winding silver river. Until 1906, the house was still occupied by Adam's descendants.

Helen and Eric saw many historic family sites in Scotland. They traced the history of the Covenanters, among them many of the Harkness clan, who refused to swear allegiance to the reigning monarchs of the time. In the largely Protestant Scotland of the seventeenth century, James VI attempted to re-establish Episcopacy, which implied royal control of the church through the bishops appointed by the Crown. When his son Charles I attempted to force a new prayer book on the Scots, rebellion followed and eventually Charles was executed. Without the courage of the men and women who signed the Covenant in 1638, the Presbyterian Church would have expired. Many died for their religious beliefs, others were imprisoned or persecuted. Helen' book is full of related facts and photographs, including a monument inscribed with the names of the martyrs, in Dumfriesshire. In 1684, during a period known as The Killing Times, James Harkness of Locherben, grandson of Adam, led an attempt to rescue a group of Covenanters who were being taken for trial in Edinburgh. James escaped and fled to Ireland but for this act, his brother Thomas was hanged the following year. Other members of the Harkness family migrated to Australia, America and Canada, while some eventually returned to Scotland and England.

In 1879, English brothers Robert and John Harkness established a rose-breeding nursery long considered the finest in England.

The New York Harknesses prospered. Amongst other philanthropic endeavours they founded the Harkness Ballet and the Harkness Foundation. According to an article in the New York Times January 30th, 1940 (*The Man who went to Work on a Yacht),* Edward Stephen Harkness became the sixth largest taxpayer in America, due in part to generous inheritances. He devoted his lifetime to educational and welfare organizations.
He was related by marriage to William Rockefeller.

But that's another story, not mine.

Several family members including myself contributed personal recollections to Helen's book. My cousin Noel, older than I, recalled incidents that I, as an infant still living with my mother and father in Rose Bay, would not have known. Noel wrote of social gatherings in the ballroom verandah of *Lillianfels,* of gaiety and laughter, music and dancing into the early hours. Later I heard stories of formal dinners there for officers of visiting fleets.

But by the time I came to *Lillianfels,* all that had changed.

The Household

Eight of us occupied *Lillianfels* when I began my new life there shortly before my third birthday: my grandmother, her daughter Phyllis, thirty-three at the time, who had returned to *Lillianfels* the year before with her two little boys, Noel and Ron; Lillian's sons Noel and Keith, twenty-eight and twenty-six respectively, and her daughter Edna, who at twenty-three was Lillian's youngest child. My cousin Noel was about five years older than I, Ron about six months older. Although they were my first cousins, we grew up more like siblings, sharing the big house and the life it represented for most of our childhood. As I recall, we all got along well.

I think of my aunt Phyllis as the softness in my daily life at *Lillianfels*. I suspect she was intimidated by her mother. My cousin Noel writes of my grandmother's insistence on good posture in all her children: his mother, Phyllis, told him that when she was a child, Lillian would place a broomstick across her back and under her arms to force her to stand straight. She developed a nervous squint and my father Bruce, three years younger, would run to his mother and tell her *Mumma, Mumma, she's doing it again!*

I recall my uncle Noel as quiet and serious. I picture him most vividly in the music room, lost in the piano. He remained at home until he married in his late thirties but lost his wife to cancer before his three children were grown. *Because the baby punched her in the chest,* Lillian declared.

My uncle Keith was the clown, the one who taught us silly tricks and made us laugh. Once when I was about four, as I fumbled with a button on the side of my bloomers which Phyllis had made to match my pretty pink smock, he knelt to help me. We were in the entry hall, in plain view. Suddenly my grandmother appeared, obviously angry, and told him to get away from me. Although I didn't understand her reaction, I never forgot it. As it turned out, Keith was not the son my grandmother should have been watching.

By the time I was seven, Keith had married and left *Lillianfels*.
Edna was the wild one who managed to get into pubs at a time when only men were allowed. When I was big enough, she let me trail along at the country club where she always seemed surrounded by dapper men with fast little English sports cars. I have an awestruck memory of Edna standing in our entry hall: Jean Harlow in an apple green chiffon gown, a red velvet rose at her waist. I heard stories of how she and Keith, already dressed in their evening clothes, would wait in their beds until my grandmother bid them goodnight, then escape through a window to a dance. Had they asked permission, it most likely would have been denied. My grandmother was a strict disciplinarian; she ruled her children with an iron hand even when they were grown.

Our household included Prince, my beloved Scotch Collie; Cocky, an irrepressible pink galah; a large tropical parrot, and creatures we occasionally rescued, nursed and set free. We also housed several cats over the years, including a pair of kittens I wanted to name Silverfish and Mildew, two of the loveliest words I had ever heard.

Lillian

As the matriarch of this household, my grandmother was the dominant force in my life. She was born in 1866 in Sydney, one of nine children. According to Helen's book, Lillian's father owned a pub in the country, near Penrith. On one particularly busy day when she was eighteen, Lillian pitched in and served beer to a full house of rough, thirsty men. When her father learned of this, he chased her from the pub with a horsewhip, yet later fondly referred to his daughter as *his little soldier*.

In the book, my cousin Noel recounts the day years later when my grandfather had forgotten his office keys. He attempted to climb through a skylight above the back door but slipped and fell onto the sheet glass, severely cutting his back near his kidneys. Lillian, waiting outside by the front door and realizing he was in trouble, somehow gained entry and quite probably saved her husband's life.

I remember my grandmother as square-jawed, sharp-eyed, as solid and unyielding as granite. She believed that children should be seen and not heard, that children should respect their elders and all authority without question. Children were instructed to address unrelated adults as *Mr., Mrs.* or *Miss;* to call them by their Christian names was presumptuous and disrespectful. Children should never question or talk back; such impudence was forbidden. I don't think I was ever bold enough to do so, least of all to my grandmother, but I did make up a sing-song response: *CERTainly your MAJesty!* That didn't last long due to the promise of having my ears boxed. If a child dared ask an adult's age, she interjected with: *as old as his tongue, a little older than his teeth.* We were frequently admonished us to *put on our thinking caps* but dared not to express our thoughts. She cautioned us against *putting on airs* or *getting too big for our britches.* She predicted *if you screw up your face like that, it will stay that way.* Lillian knew a thing or two.

Walter

I was only two years old when my grandfather died, so I cannot claim memory of him. Still, a wistful impression lingers: a small fair-haired child perched contentedly on the knee of a kindly old gentleman with a splendid white walrus moustache. My cousin Noel, seven at the time, may have passed this impression on to me. Like others since, Noel recalled our grandfather fondly as a generous and kind man. Walter loved his automobiles, a Rickenbacker and later, a Silver Anniversary Buick. Noel remembers the Buick, an impressive car with velvet upholstery, interior blinds and polished wooden wheel spokes.

Walter and Lillian seemed very different in temperament and, as I was to learn later, very different in ancestry. How, where they met and what they had in common I may never know, but they stayed together for forty-five years, until Walter's death.

Walter was connected by marriage to the famous navigator Captain James Cook. James had a niece named Hannah who, with her husband and young children, migrated to Australia where their third child, Rachel, was born only fourteen days after their arrival in 1838. In 1854 Rachel married John Harkness, a brilliant mathematician twenty-three years her senior, who had graduated from Edinburgh University. With his family's blessing and money to buy land, he had immigrated to Australia in 1839. John died in Paddington in 1877.

Amongst Rachel and John's five surviving children were my grandfather, Walter Scott Harkness and my granduncle Edward Knox Harkness, three years younger.

Coincidence and Reprieve

In 1768 Captain James Cook embarked on the voyage which led to the discovery of the East Coast of Australia; the West Coast had been sighted and even visited during the previous century-and-a-half by various Dutch navigators on their trade routes. In 1769 Cook carried a group of British astronomers to Tahiti to observe the planet Venus as it crossed the face of the sun. The transit of Venus was first recorded in 1639 and in 1679 an English astronomer, Edmund Halley, had pointed out that these transits could be used to determine the distance of the sun. James Cook was the first to establish this distance. In an era where astronomy was the sister science of navigation, this was a major revelation. Tahiti was chosen because, had the weather been unfavourable in Europe, astronomers would have waited another 105 years.

In 1770, Cook discovered a safe anchorage for his ship, the *Endeavour*, and named it Botany Bay, after its unusual flora. For a week he and his crew gathered plant specimens and observed the Aboriginal fishermen. When he eventually returned to England, his vague and varied reports of that one week prompted the British government to select this unexplored site as a future convict settlement, a dumping ground for England's undesirables, victims of the squalor and oppression behind the gracious facade of Georgian aristocracy. For England, this remote site offered a solution to its social problems at a time when the War of Independence had closed America's doors to English convicts.

And so the future was set in motion.

Never could my grandfather, whose mother Rachel was related to James Cook, have imagined that Lillian, the woman he would someday marry, would never have existed but for Cook's explorations. Had a penal colony not been established upon Cook's recommendation,

Elizabeth Pulley, Lillian's great-great grandmother, would surely have been hanged in England, childless!

Elizabeth and Anthony

My Grandmother Lillian's ancestor, Elizabeth Pulley, had begun a life of crime at sixteen when she stole some clothes. She was acquitted but was arrested again later for *stealing goods,* to which she confessed. She was sentenced to three weeks in Norwich Castle, followed by a public whipping in the marketplace. A year later she was back at Norwich where she served a year at hard labour, again for theft. Then on Christmas Eve 1782, in the small town of Hethersett where she lived, Elizabeth Pulley broke into a widow's shop and stole food: bacon, flour, raisins and a large quantity of cheese which she may have planned to barter or sell. She was tried in March 1783 and sentenced *to be hanged by the neck until dead.*

She was imprisoned in Norwich Castle until November 1786. However, with transportation now a viable alternative to hanging, Elizabeth Pulley's death sentence was delayed. While there is no record of an official reprieve, a paragraph in the Norwich Mercury read: *The Keeper of the Castle received a letter signifying His Majesty's pleasure that Elizabeth Pulley (and two other women) be conveyed to Plymouth and put aboard a ship to be transported to Botany Bay. They were taken from the gaol and seemed not in the least dismayed at the length of their voyage or their future fate.*

This lack of dismay is understandable, considering that women prisoners of Norwich were kept, *sticky and filthy, shackled together in leg irons.* Surely, an uncertain future couldn't be worse. And yet, some prisoners chose hanging over transportation, perhaps due to fear of the unknown.

In 2012, an old family friend, having just discovered his own convict roots, came across mention of Elizabeth on page 72 of Robert Hughes' heartbreaking book, *The Fatal Shore.* After the family reunion, I had searched that book for any mention of my convict ancestor but found nothing. For good reason: there are three recorded variations of the spelling of Elizabeth's surname: *Powley, Pooley Pulley*. Helen's research indicates that *Pulley* is the most likely one. Rope and Pulley: destined?

Robert Hughes writes: *Elizabeth Powley, twenty-two and unemployed, raided a kitchen in Norfolk, took a few shillings' worth of bacon, flour and raisins, with twenty-four ounces Weight of Butter value 12d, and was sentenced to hang; but a reprieve came and to Australia she went, never to eat butter again.*

On a website called *Australian Royalty,* a tongue-in- cheek title for a list of the first convicts, my infamous ancestor, Elizabeth Pulley, reigns at the top.

Meanwhile, in 1785, in Chelmsford, Anthony Rope, at twenty-six, was sentenced to death for *stealing goods to the value of thirty-five shillings.* His sentence was reduced to seven years and then, as part of England's desire to be rid of the *criminal class,* he too was condemned to Botany Bay.

Thus, Anthony and Elizabeth were destined to become *First Fleeters.* In his book, *The Fatal Shore,* Robert Hughes describes the First Fleet as *This Noah's Ark of small-time criminality.* And so it was that from this inopportune beginning, a new country was forged.

In January 1788, only two days ahead of the First Fleet, Captain Arthur Phillip led the advance party into Botany Bay to establish this infamous penal colony. However, he decided that Botany Bay was unsuitable for a permanent settlement and ventured north to a harbour he described as *the finest harbour in the world, a deep sheltered cove in which a thousand ships could ride in perfect security.* He named it Sydney, after the man who had sent him on this mission,

Lord Thomas Townshend Sydney.

Anthony arrived on the *Alexander* and was put ashore on January 26th, 1788. Elizabeth arrived on the *Prince of Wales* and was put ashore on February 9th, 1788. Elizabeth's reputably rebellious spirit probably helped her survive her ordeal. In fact, because she was considered a troublemaker, she was transferred, at the Cape of Good Hope, from the transport ship *Friendship* to the *Prince of Wales.*

Now, after the harrowing voyage, Anthony and Elizabeth were condemned to serve out their sentences in an unknown land, with no hope of ever returning to England. Three months after their arrival, they married and five months later their first son Robert was born, the first white male child conceived and born in the colony. How they connected under these circumstances, one can only guess. In 1791 Anthony and Elizabeth were pardoned by Governor Macquarie and granted seventy acres of land at Birds Eye Corner in Castlereagh, near Penrith. Elizabeth's grave in Castlereagh Cemetery is marked by the official First Fleeter plaque.

Many convicts died during the voyage, others afterwards from illness, disease or old age. Phillip found that very few were capable of hard labour although included in this sorry lot were individuals of talent, including Macquarie's favourite architect, Francis Greenway who had been transported for forging a contract. For the first two years, conditions were bleak and those still alive faced starvation. Eventually, however, under Phillip, the colony thrived.

During the years of transportation, England sent 160,000 (recorded) men, women and children to Australia in bondage. The spreading penal colonies included Point Puer, a penitentiary for children, and the beautiful, historically brutal Norfolk Island, which lies 1,500 kilometres off Australia's east coast. In 1856, descendants of the mutineers of the *Bounty* and their Tahitian women, who had originally settled on Pitcairn Island in 1790, resettled on Norfolk when Pitcairn became too small for their growing population.

In 1979 Norfolk became the only non-mainland Australian territory to be granted self-government. But now this is changing. No longer will Norfolk have its own parliament, its own flag, its own laws; its residents will pay taxes for the first time. Many of Norfolk's 1800 islanders see this as an end to their independence.

The playful uncle Keith of my childhood, since widowed, died there several years ago; his two daughters live there still. Helen visited them once, hoping to add to her Harkness history, but received a cool reception. I never knew why or when they retreated to this insular, exotic place; by all accounts Keith died a changed man, serious and over protective of his daughters. Was this watchfulness a trait learned from his mother, my grandmother Lillian, who guarded me so diligently?

Still, I like to think that Keith chose to retire to Norfolk Island in part to honour his wife's probable Tahitian heritage and that of his daughters.

Lillianfels

Lillianfels was a sprawling Federation style brick house set on a spacious, elevated property beyond double wood gates. A long driveway curved up to a tennis court on one side and a meadow-like courtyard edged with Christmas bush and gum trees on the other. Ron and I often hid beneath the lush passionfruit vine that lined the driveway and gorged ourselves.

In the courtyard, we played leapfrog and practiced somersaults and handstands. Whimsical tropical sun showers teased us in the courtyard yet left our front yard dry. We wondered at this and sometimes tried to out-race them around the house. Christmas bells, flannel flowers, fragrant boronia and waratahs – the state emblem of N.S.W., appeared in spring, wattle brightened winter. In hot December, city florists flocked to *Lillianfels* to harvest our abundant Christmas bush, in high demand during the holiday season. When their lorries headed back down the driveway, they overflowed with fragrant pink wax-star blossoms. Formal brick pillars marked the beginning of a straight brick path beneath a rose pergola, leading to a broad flight of ivy-faced steps to the front verandah and main entrance. Once, on that verandah, I lay on a wicker chaise, my feet blistered from a ballet lesson, and saw one of Edna's admirers - a rather pompous, rotund politician - heave himself onto, and through, a wicker chair, feet pointing skywards. Only his pride was bruised but I was dismissed for giggling. She married him briefly and remained childless the rest of her life.

The entrance hall was spacious and formal. A lamp with an elaborate red silk shade hung from the centre of the high ceiling, casting a warm glow everywhere. Next to a Jacobean bench, a small carved table held a black European-style telephone and to this day, I remember our phone number. A large grandfather clock dominated the hall, equipped with two separate chimes - Dick Whittington and Westminster- and a circular brass pendulum and ornate hands that unfailingly pursued each Roman numeral. The clock was my steadfast companion when I curled up on the bench with my *Golden Wonder Book*. I read Hans Christian Andersen's *The Little Mermaid* and *The Little Match Girl* over and over again, hoping each time that the endings might change. Anne Anderson's delicate colour illustrations pulled me into each story and inspired my first artistic attempts.

Doors on each side of the entry hall led to two master suites. Each had its own verandah, open to the warm night air through lattice for summer sleeping. Each held a large fireplace. In one of these suites I slept in a high four-poster bed, counting plaster cherubs and rose garlands on the high domed ceiling before drifting off.

Beyond the master suites, hallways spread left and right into symmetrical wings. One wing held most of the bedrooms and my uncle Keith's wireless room, where Keith introduced Noel, Ron and me to the mysteries of Morse code. There we listened to the crackling of overseas radio reports from a Europe uneasy since Hitler had acclaimed himself Kaiser, President and Parliament in 1934.

The opposite wing held the dining room, kitchen and remaining bedrooms. The centre of the house held the sitting room and music room, separated by a carved wooden arch. I did not care for the darkly paneled sitting room except in winter when a fire occasionally roared in the fireplace. On the other hand, the music room, which opened through French doors to the back verandah, once the ballroom, was filled with light and often the sounds of the piano. All of Lillian's and Walter's children played a musical instrument of some kind. My cousin Noel remembers that my father, Bruce, would pluck his banjo non-stop, until an exasperated Walter would shout s*top!* My father would then continue to play under his bedcovers. Noel recalls seeing my father sitting on a coil of rope at the bow of an ocean liner, playing his banjo and singing *Goodbye Sydney* as the great ship pulled away from the wharf. I do not know what year this was; perhaps he was on his way to India then.

The verandah ran almost the entire length of the house and faced the lower orchard. The outer wall was of brick arches, open to the temperate climate. When my cousins and I were not outside, we were usually on the verandah, piling chairs and playing house, or dragging one another around and around on oriental rugs over the polished timber floor as fast as we could go. I doubt the adults were aware of this, since at any moment any one of us was in danger of flying off into the brick wall.

I remember eating watermelon on the verandah as my grandmother cautioned me against eating the white of the melon because it was deadly poisonous, or swallowing a seed because that's how babies started. We pretended to be spies and scribbled invisible messages on scraps of paper with nibs dipped into lemon juice. A lighted match held beneath the paper revealed the words as though they had been written in sepia ink.

My cousins and I staged plays on a great heavy table in the ante room between the verandah and the kitchen, using a silk velvet tablecloth as a theatre curtain. We performed music with a makeshift mouth organ made from an ordinary hair comb wrapped in tissue paper. On that same table, we built kites and aeroplanes of balsa wood and tissue held precariously together with flour and water paste. We turned clothes pegs into dolls with painted moustaches and hair and ribbon skirts. In the former housekeeper's lavatory off this room Ron perched and sang *Cu-cucaracha* with gusto. This amused the adults so heartily that once, when he emerged, I went in and tried the same thing. No one was amused. I was pointedly ignored for showing off.

I had my small revenge in a way, at breakfast the following morning. We ate most of our meals in the dining room, at the long table that once had accommodated my grandparents' large family. My grandmother, seated at the head of the table several chairs away, did not notice as I carefully peeled the top half of my soft-boiled egg, quickly ate it, then turned it upside down in the eggcup, deceptively intact. With a furtive glance at my grandmother, I slumped down in my chair and pouted as fiercely as I could. With a sharp glance she admonished me to *eat your egg, Judith!* In a moment of splendid triumph, I turned the empty shell right side up and announced with great self-righteousness that I *had!* With that, I was banished to my room. It wasn't that I felt jealous of Ron; I simply felt *dismissed* by the adults. But I had got even and it was *worth* it!

Much of our life centred around a big green-painted table in the kitchen. Here Ron and I shelled peas into an enamel colander, one of our few household duties. On that same table I counted backwards into an ether haze to have some teeth pulled - house calls were common then. I think our kindly family doctor, Dr. Curtis, may have performed the surgery: in the 1930's, the medical community was not so specialized. It was at that table that uncle Noel once unhappily announced that he had *got the sack.* My grandmother admonished him for such language. She did not approve of *job* or *boss* either; she considered such words to be *coarse and common. Position* and *manager* were deemed more appropriate. Needless to say, during my childhood I never heard words such as *sex* or *pregnant.* Years later, when I was nineteen and a friend of my father's described a neighbour as a Lesbian, I scanned a map of Eastern Europe in my head without success then asked *Where's Lesbia?* I remember the skeptical silence that followed.

Above the orchard was a small gazebo, which we called a summerhouse, a latticed hideaway beneath a cool green canopy of prickly pear vines. A little wooden bridge led to the summerhouse through dense, thorny bush that sometimes snatched us as we ran by. Once, when I was six or seven, a spider crept into Ron's short pants and at the sound of his screams, my aunt came running, my grandmother close on her heels. Before Phyllis could pull down Ron's pants to find the spider, my grandmother dispatched me back to the house, watching until I was out of sight. To her, modesty was paramount; never mind that most Australian spiders are deadly! Happily for Ron this one was not.

The bridge led back to the lower orchard, where blood plums, peaches and apricots grew in abundance, there for the plucking. Terraced steps led to the upper orchard, an undisciplined tangle of natural bush and sub-tropical colour which threatened to overtake the berries, mandarins and crab apples that struggled there. It was the perfect place to build flimsy tree houses and makeshift wigwams and play *Pretend*. The low branches of a huge coral tree by the steps provided a private perch for reading, uninhibited singing and escape from grownups. Sometimes Ron and I amused ourselves by teasing trapdoor spiders from their burrows in the bamboo-shaded banks of the tennis court, when we were supposed to be rolling the lawn court in preparation for the Sydney Racquet Club's Saturday games. Somehow the court was always ready in time, bright white lines staining the brilliant green, the flagpole high-flying the Australian flag by the lower gate where the players entered from the driveway. Near the court, uncle Noel had built a little pond with a rock ledge where we could sit and watch goldfish flash beneath heart-shaped water lily leaves. *Lillianfels* was full of such special places to entertain a child. Nurtured by nature, we learned to be curious, imaginative and creative.

In spring, the lower orchard beyond the brick archways was a glory of deep and pale pinks and delicate white blossoms. My imagination flourished: once I saw a tiger leap mid-air through the latticed fernery by the garden shed, dark stripes flowing, fangs and claws bared. It was a long time before reason convinced me that such a thing was impossible since there *are* no tigers in Australia.

I don't recall ever feeling lonely or bored. When I wasn't with my cousins, I was quite content to sit alone on the verandah at a table piled with paper and crayons and watercolours, the happy raucous din of Australian birds nearby. I awoke each morning to these big, bold, demanding entertainers, to the laughter of kookaburras, the cawing of currawongs and magpies, the shrieks of cockatoos, galahs and rosellas. What better way to begin a day?

We stayed on at *Lillianfels* for about five years after my grandfather's death. Growing up there, I never wanted for anything that money could buy. In fact, money was never discussed, since my grandmother believed that *proper young ladies need know nothing of such matters which were better left to the men.*

Kindergarten

An overgrown corner of the tennis court concealed a little arched wooden door, which led to a neighbour's yard. Mrs. Crawford was an American woman who ran a small pre-kindergarten at her home and it was there that I spent most of my early days. I felt special, a girl with her own secret door to another world. Phyllis made cotton shifts the colour of cocoa for all the little girls who attended the school, each one hand-smocked with pastel thread. I don't remember any boys there. A stone sundial and a birdbath marked the top of the steps that tumbled down through the tangled garden to Mrs. Crawford's house. I can still recall the fragrance of mulberry leaves and silkworms and rabbits and straw at Easter. I looked forward so much to seeing Mrs. Crawford's wire-haired terrier and calico cat that long afterwards, when I was about eight, I wrote a poem about them: *Dinky the Dog and Cheeky the Cat.*

Dinky the Dog and Cheeky the Cat

Said Cheeky to Dinky
You mustn't go away
everyone is out
gone on holiday.

I want to go and look around
said Dinky to the cat
But you mustn't I am telling you
now I want to have my nap.

When Cheeky was asleep
and all was sound and quiet
Dinky crept away
but the people came home that night!

When everyone came inside
they found Dinky wasn't home
I know mewed little Cheeky
he went off for a roam.

When the people all were sound asleep
Cheeky heard a cry
It must be Dinky he purred in glee
he's come home for his nice fish fry!

—Judith Laurel Harkness, about age eight.

It was not until Christmas 2002 that I rediscovered eleven poems I'd written as a child, left forgotten in a box of old family photographs. I remembered then, as I sat on the verandah with my paints and brushes, that Lillian had placed a black leather-bound book, an inkwell and a fine-nib pen before me and encouraged me to record, in my best handwriting, a few poems I had made up.

These early scribbles touched my emotionally fragile daughter. They seemed a special gift because, as it happened, that was our last Christmas together.

When I visited Mrs. Crawford years later, when *Lillianfels* was no longer my home, I opened the little wooden arched door for the last time and was stunned by the sight of our tennis court ablaze with poppies: Anderson Seed Company had leased it as a growing field.

Cousins and Others

Lillianfels always seemed to be filled with people, among them cousins and great-aunts I'd never met before and numerous friends of those who lived there.

Sundays were traditional family visiting days; my uncle Eric was a frequent visitor. He was blind in one eye; someone told me my father poked Eric with a wooden sword when the brothers were playing *Trench War*n at *Lillianfels*. However, given their fourteen years age difference, I find this unlikely.

Eric lived nearby with his wife Peggy and their son Harry in a tall row house overlooking a deep gully of natural bush in Cooper Park. The house was embellished with ironwork called Victorian Lace, popular in Sydney's early days. Fragrant pink and cream frangipanis grew to the upper balcony. Like other houses on Edward Street, it was built by my granduncle, Edward Knox Harkness, for whom the street was named, as were others, including Knox Street and Harkness Street, in Double Bay. There, years ago, I saw the name *Harkness* faded on the old brick building that once had been my family's real estate office.

Between 1880 and his death in 1924, Edward built about four thousand homes in the eastern suburbs of Sydney, including affordable row houses for the average working man in Woollahra and Paddington. Now these homes are desirable, often beautifully restored to retain their historic significance. Edward's grander homes reflected aspects of Victorian Gothic or Federation architecture. Hallmarks of the Harkness style may still be seen in high-pitched roofs and double reception rooms with elaborately molded and vaulted ceilings. Even today, the term *Harkness-built* within a real estate text implies quality.

Edward believed in civic duty: he donated land for small parks that still exist throughout the eastern suburbs, and laid brick footpaths at his own expense in Double Bay. At the time, some predicted they wouldn't last but they still exist; in fact, councils since have voted to lay more.

Lillian's eldest daughter, Violet, whom two year-old Eric immediately dubbed *the bebe,* was known forever after by that name. She and her family were regular visitors to *Lillianfels.* Bebe lived with her husband, three sons and two daughters in the country. When I was in my teens, my grandmother occasionally allowed me to travel there by train with Ron and Noel. We picked fresh lettuce and beetroot, gathered warm eggs from the chickens and plucked sweet grapes from the arbour. Appropriately, in Bebe's front garden, fragrant old-fashioned violets bloomed everywhere. When it rained, we splashed in the mud. Life at Bebe's was less restrictive than at *Lillianfels* and I savoured these small freedoms.

Bebe and her husband often took their five children camping. Whenever they invited me, my grandmother declined because, she said, *ladies don't camp.* I longed for adventure: fishing for trout and frying it over an open fire, running barefoot, sleeping beneath the stars, swimming in a river. Years later when I camped for the first time, reality fell far short of these childhood imaginings.

Bebe's youngest, Jill, a year my junior, occasionally came to Sydney to spend a night or two with us, but always kept me awake, crying for her mother. I thought she was a terrible baby for I, on the other hand, yearned to escape to places unfamiliar. When we both were very young, Jill heaved a half-full tin sand bucket at me, cracking the bridge of my nose. In those days, children were not likely to be rushed to the nearest emergency room; rather, we were admonished to be brave and not cry. To this day my imperfect nose reminds me of those early days I shared with Jill, not always wistfully: I recall one hot summer evening, fragrant with Christmas bush and gum trees, the season for Christmas beetles. I liked to hold them lightly in my palm then cast them skyward: *fly away, fly away home.* When Jill crushed one underfoot, because, she said, *she liked to hear it crunch*, I burst into tears. My memories of Jill after that are elusive.

Jill had a sister Linda, five years older than I but light years ahead in sophistication. As a young woman, she was married briefly to a handsome soldier whose family supposedly had a history of *insanity.* At a time in Australia when divorce was not easily granted, Linda was fortunate: the marriage was dissolved and she later married another. There were three brothers as well. The eldest, Lance, was a naval officer. He escaped death when a fellow officer took over his watch on a ship that was torpedoed during the Second World War. His brother Keith was an Australian Air Force officer. Reported missing in action and presumed dead, he turned up later, alive and well. The youngest brother, Max, was in the army; he too survived the war. Since they were a few years older than I, they live in the outskirts of my memory but I was aware of the joyful relief of their homecomings.

Aunt Ethel visited *Lillianfels* often with her five children. At the time her husband Raymond (Lillian's son) died at age thirty-four, her youngest was only two, the eldest nine. I remember them as tolerant and affectionate. Ethel's only son John, about five years older than I, was a Junior Lifesaver, a traditional role for youngsters of the Australian coast. He was unaffectedly good-looking and kind and I had a secret childish crush on him.

Of the many relatives who came to visit, Aunt Stella was, to me, a bright light. She was the third wife of Edward Knox Harkness and twenty years his junior. She bore him six children and raised seven more by his first two marriages. In 1993 when I first met Helen, who wrote *Harkness Heroines,* and mentioned that Stella was a favourite of mine, she told me that Stella was her grandmother, and that Stella's mother Adeline was my grandmother Lillian's sister. In the book, a beautiful young woman gazes pensively from an old photograph. It is Stella Kate at the age of twenty-five.

Stella was born is 1884. I remember her with flaming henna hair, a full figure and a hearty laugh. One day when I was very young, I burst into a room where Stella was changing. She still wore her heavily boned corset and knee-length bloomers but her pendulous bosom fell unbound. For years I believed that as women grew older, their nipples fell off, since Stella's had fallen out of sight.

I sometimes wondered if my grandmother approved of Stella; she seemed anything but Victorian! But looking back, I realize they must have shared a sad bond as widows raising large families alone in a troubled world at a troubled time. Now, thanks to Helen's book, I am aware of the infamous heritage they also shared.

Eventually, this early convict heritage was to become a source of pride for many Australians. At last the courage and resourcefulness of these early pioneers began to be recognised as the seed from which the unique Australian spirit evolved. It wasn't until about 1960 that Australians seemed to realise they had a history worth telling.

Prior to the 1960's, England's attitude toward its colony seemed, for the most part, condescending; I think Australia suffered a national inferiority mindset which held it blindly faithful to the Mother Country beyond the Second World War. Even the sacrifice of ANZAC soldiers at Gallipoli in 1915 – fourteen years after the Commonwealth of Australia was created – did little to deter this loyalty. Among those lost at Gallipoli in 1915 was Edward George John Harkness, eldest child of my granduncle, Edward Knox Harkness. Like so many Australian women then, young Edward's wife was left to raise their four children alone. In 1918 the infant son of my granduncle Edward and Stella died and in 1924 Edward himself died at the age of sixty. In 1944 Stella's son Geoffrey, an RAAF pilot, was killed in a plane crash just two weeks after the birth of his first child.

It was not until the 1980's, after Stella's death in 1976, while her son Earnest was researching the family history, that her own personal secret was revealed: Stella Kate was illegitimate. In those times, being illegitimate often meant being ostracized but I never saw any indication of that. Stella's mother Adeline - Lillian's sister - was married when Stella was two years old but not to Stella's father. Apparently, he never married and story has it that he never stopped loving Adeline to the day he died. To her husband, Adeline bore eleven more children.

A Proper Upbringing

My grandmother's heritage seemed in direct opposition to my upbringing; perhaps, because of that heritage, or in spite of it, she made sure that I was instructed in *proper* ways appropriate for young girls of the Victorian era although actually I was born at the end of the Flapper era. The two little English princesses, Elizabeth and Margaret, were touted as good examples, especially Margaret Rose whose birthdate I shared, although a year apart. I think my grandmother, like many of her generation, was fiercely loyal to the monarchy. When George V died in 1936, when I was not yet seven, she made us children sit by the radio to endure every sombre detail of the pomp and ceremony that accompanied his funeral. The following year we suffered the scandal of King Edward's abdication of the throne when he chose to marry American divorcee Wallis Simpson.

I was timid and shy, I blushed easily. I was obedient, fearful of my grandmother's disapproval although I do not recall that she ever physically punished me as a child. Still, I was bold enough, when she insisted I wear a wool overcoat outdoors, to discard it as soon as I was out of sight.

I studied ballet, piano and elocution. I read the classics and attended private art lessons in a city park under a giant Moreton Bay Fig tree. On the verandah, I meticulously wrote poems in the black leather book; the eleven fragile poems I discovered in 2002 seem to have been torn from that book. I attended Sunday school every week at St. Stephens Church of England in Bellevue Hill where I had been baptised. I learned to behave correctly in social situations, to drink tea from fine porcelain cups, little finger curved gracefully aloft, knees modestly locked beneath the hem of my frock.

As my grandmother served tea to her guests, I drank in tiny scraps of horror about tidal waves, rats feeding off babies in prams, smallpox, diphtheria, consumption, polio, blue babies and one unfortunate soul's encounter with a steam roller. Lillian was right: *little pitchers have big ears.*

At one time, long after I left, Double Bay was dubbed *Double Pay* because of its transformation from an ordinary neighbourhood to a district of fashionable shops and cafes and a Ritz-Carlton, which a former Prime Minister once called home. On Knox Street, where Edward Knox Harkness and his wife Stella first lived, the quaint row houses he built years before have since become stylish designer boutiques. But when I was growing up, Double Bay was simply a pleasant place to live; we knew the butcher, the baker, the chemist, the greengrocer.

As in most Sydney suburbs at that time, the pub dominated much of one block, a green-tiled monstrosity where only men were allowed. I would hold my breath as I walked by to avoid the stink of beer. There was a newsagent, a tradition that still survives in most neighbourhoods, a place to buy international newspapers and magazines. At the edge of the bay we bought fresh prawns and oysters. In the ice cream parlour on the corner, I met the boy who was to give me my first kiss years later.

In the Town Hall, I took dance lessons from Elsie Leonard. Faded photographs record me in costumes lovingly created by Phyllis on a treadle machine. I was Dutch, I was Russian, I was a gypsy, I was a ballerina. I was elegant in a long black satin sheath with rhinestones everywhere, my long hair swept up into a chignon, as I made my entrance to *A Pretty Girl is just like a Melody.* One enlarged photograph, hand-tinted, shows my dance partner, Phoebe McCartney, and me, poised for a Mozart minuet. Phoebe played the Lady, a ruffled bonnet covering her wispy hair; I the Gentleman, resplendent in pink and green satin and top hat. Closer inspection of the image reveals that the photographer had taken it upon himself to whittle away my plump stomach with a fine blade. I recall the nervous thrill of performing at the Conservatorium of Music in the Botanical Gardens, just one of many young, hopeful ballerinas fidgeting in the wings, sweeping satin toes through resin.

I saw picture shows at the Vogue Theatre where an organist played at intermission, perched off-centre high above the stage. For years, my grandmother allowed me to see only Shirley Temple movies although she approved of films with a moral message: once she and Phyllis accompanied Ron and me to the Vogue to see *The Sign of the Cross,* which, to her chagrin, turned out to be a third-rate melodrama rife with lions nibbling away at comely half-naked Christian damsels. Once outside the theatre, she strode ahead of us all, obviously angry. We didn't know why until later, at home, she accused Ron and me of holding hands. This would have been impossible, since she and Phyllis were seated between Ron and me. *What was Lillian thinking?* But her accusation made me aware for the first time that Ron was not only my cousin and playmate, he was a *boy*. I don't think she thought about the newsreels either, horrifying images of Nazi concentration camps flickering in black and white across the screen, burning into an impressionable young mind.

Until I started school, my grandmother didn't allow me outside the gates of *Lillianfels* alone; usually Ron and I walked together with Prince at our side. No stranger could have approached us with Prince nearby, yet I have seen him harbour a tiny kitten gently between his paws. Prince was particularly distrustful of strangers wearing sandshoes: one day a peddler slipped silent and unnoticed up the driveway to the back door. It was not uncommon for us to offer strangers who were down on their luck a meal of some kind before sending them on their way. This time, however, Prince intercepted the intruder at the door and took a bite out of the poor man's trousers. Phyllis asked the man to remove his trousers so that she could mend them and saw then that

Prince had drawn blood.

So my modest aunt Phyllis tended the peddler's wound, despite its delicate location, and mended his trousers. In retrospect, this episode seems highly improbable in our Victorian household and even less probable in today's world, where people rarely invite strangers into their homes and a dog bite can invite a lawsuit. I admire Phyllis' resourcefulness but I suspect my grandmother remained ignorant of this incident. Prince was not reprimanded, which is as it should be.

My grandmother often sent Ron and me down the driveway to the gates to wait for the horse-drawn carts of the milkman or baker. We would return to the house with full pails of milk or loaves of warm bread. Then back down we'd go – this time to spade the fresh manure from the road into a wheelbarrow and together, huff and puff our load back up the driveway. I thought it odd that while ladies were prohibited from so many things, ladies could spade manure! I never minded; it was a small escape from my grandmother's watchful eye.

Only a few years earlier, spading manure, like the upkeep of the grounds and tennis court, would have been left to Mr. Russell. While I don't remember him, my cousin Noel, in Helen's family book, recalls Mr. Russell well. He was our full-time gardener until The Great Depression changed *everything*. Noel remembers my grandfather rising at six o'clock every morning to cook Mr. Russell a hearty breakfast before leaving for the real estate office. The fernery, with its potting shed, was Mr. Russell's proud domain and a wondrous place for a small boy. Mr. Russell seemed to welcome Noel's obvious delight and curiosity of the seedlings, plants and tools the shed held.

Holidays

During the Christmas holidays, we stayed in a beach cottage in Collaroy. The water stretched pale and shallow for a distance before dropping suddenly into a deep canyon where, we were cautioned, sharks lay in wait for unwary swimmers. But mostly we paddled in the safety of the shallows. When we weren't in the water, we were happily sliding down the smooth white sand dunes.

We spent countless days in the warm waters of Nielsen Park in Vaucluse and, after its completion in 1941, Redleaf Pool in Double Bay. I was twelve then and my memories of Redleaf are tinged with my embarrassment of Lillian's watchful presence and the humiliation of having to wear a singlet under my blue wool bathing suit and a childish sun hat over my eyebrows. My grandmother, of course, was dressed as though she were on her way to the city - stockings, sturdy shoes, hat and all. I was painfully aware of the tanned and stylish adolescents who leaned on the deck rail above the beach, observing, waiting to be observed, and never, ever getting wet.

Like most Sydney bayside beaches, these pools were enclosed by shark-proof netting. Once, I was told, a twelve-foot grey nurse shark broke through the net at Redleaf, scattering alarmed swimmers onto the sand. I recall hearing of one fatal attack on a young woman who was standing knee-deep in the calm shallows of Middle Harbour. And another, at the mouth of the Hawkesbury River, where a young girl wading near the shore was severed at the waist by a great white as her father watched helplessly from the bank. Yet fear never kept us out of the water. I suppose we placed an inordinate amount of trust in the shark-lookout towers that guarded every major ocean beach at that time, as well as the small shark-spotting aeroplanes that buzzed overhead and transmitted alarms to the towers. The sirens would shriek, swimmers and surfers would make a wild dash for the shore en masse.

In defiance of the tenacious Australian sun, my grandmother believed that *young ladies should have pale skin.* Once home from the beach, she scrubbed my face with a half lemon to ward off any threatening freckles. Still, we spent endless hours at the shore. After all, I was an Australian child, living in Sydney, where all children, by legacy, are water babies.

Summer also meant Sunday school picnics beneath the Sydney Harbour Bridge. I remember the agonized anticipation of these outdoor events: would it rain that day? Would I catch measles before then? Would God decide I hadn't been good enough and cancel? But inevitably, the day would arrive, the sun would shine, I awoke unspotted and God was merciful.

Now and then we went to Luna Park where we were swallowed up by the grotesque laughing face that was the entrance. Luna Park opened before I was born and still exists on the north side of the harbour, although it has seen many changes over the years. It seems tawdry to me now but for a child living in Sydney at that time, it was the best fun zone in the world.

Along New South Head Road, beyond Double Bay, lay Rose Bay, where I had lived with my parents as an infant. It was also the site of Sydney's first international airport, established in 1938, home to the big luxurious flying boats that carried passengers between Sydney and England. As children, we were unaware that this was the golden age of aviation, but the flying boats never failed to thrill us as we leaned on the rock wall and watched them alight on the water and take off within easy view.

One summer day a neighbour set fire to a pile of garden rubbish near our courtyard fence. A scorching gust of wind set the fence and the courtyard ablaze. Gum trees exploded fiery missiles across the dry summer grass toward *Lillianfels.* Fire trucks and equipment overflowed the courtyard as curious onlookers climbed our driveway at the sound of sirens. For some reason, I recall the dress I was wearing - a pretty crepe, blue-flowered thing which Keith's wife Lorraine had made for me to match her own dress. Distracted by the frenetic activity around me, I was unaware of firemen shouting at me: unwittingly, I was standing on a fire hose. The rush of water became a dribble just before the hose burst, drenching my lovely crepe dress, which immediately shrank into a soggy pucker. By the time it was over, Edna's latticed sleeping verandah was scorched but the main house was spared.

Because Christmas fell during the hot summer, we always received presents for the beach: surf-a-planes, pails, spades, big colourful balls, parasols, wooden sailboats, sun hats. Father Christmas stuffed most of these things into pillowcases that we had hung on our bedposts on Christmas Eve - never mind stockings! We had yet to succumb to the tradition of a Christmas tree hung with ornaments, or *wrapped* gifts. Sometimes there were hand-knit sweaters, usually pale blue *to match your eyes*, china-faced dolls, wicker prams, miniature doll furniture and tea sets, wooden trains, marbles, tops, yo-yo's and bubble pipes. Always there were wonderful books: The Gumnut Babies, Tales of King Arthur, Winnie the Pooh and colourful pop-up books full of forests, cottages, lost children, castles and knights. And who could forget those miniature Disney flip books that told a story like a black and white movie when thumbed through rapidly? Goofy, as a skyscraper window washer, stepped back to admire his work and plunged toward the pavement below. Flip the pages backwards and Goofy was back up twenty stories! Mickey was in there too, in trouble with Minnie for exclaiming *what a terrible waste* (of water) which she took to mean *waist* (hers).

Still, I longed for a Shirley Temple doll - the rage at the time - and a miniature child-size train complete with steam engine and a string of carriages in which, I imagined, I would carry my cousins and Prince on tracks that would encircle *Lillianfels:* past the tennis court, through the fernery and lower orchard, past the brick arches of the verandah, across the courtyard, then back to the brick pillars where we had started.

Weeks before Christmas, Lillian made two traditional English plum puddings. In a big bowl, she stirred the batter, heavy with dried fruits and pungent with brandy, while Ron, Noel and I dropped in boiled threepences, sixpences and silver trinkets to be rediscovered later. She wrapped the puddings in muslin and strung them above the doorway where they were punched and pummelled by anyone who could reach them. Later they were cooked in the copper - a vessel known in England as a boiler - which sat in its own room, heated beneath by a fire. The copper also served as a laundry vat; a washboard and a strong arm banished stains, a long wooden pole transferred clean sheets outside to the clothesline.

Lillian never revealed her recipe, if there ever was one, but every year the pudding was the delectable highlight of Christmas dinner, borne to the table aflame with brandy, a holly sprig atop, served warm with heavy cream or custard. Instead of turkey, we ate roast beef or lamb with homemade mint sauce. Afterwards, with the temperature outside sometimes near one hundred degrees Fahrenheit, we escaped to the beach and sank into the cool surf.

The next day was Boxing Day, a national holiday that gave coastal Australians another excuse to head for the beach. Boxing Day originated in Britain when alms boxes placed in churches over Christmas were opened and their contents distributed to the poor. In homes much wealthier than ours, families gave small gifts to their servants.

On January 26 we celebrated Australia Day and the landing of the First Fleet in 1788, ignorant still of the very personal significance of that occasion.

On April 25, Anzac Day, we cheered on our veterans with their turned-up Digger hats as they marched past Hyde Park to squawking bagpipes and thundering drums. We were too young to mourn all those young ghosts of Gallipoli and the First World War; the Second World War was still deniably in the future.

On May 24, when the weather had cooled, Empire Day offered the main annual event for spectacular fireworks over the harbour. During the day we cheered on university regattas as we picnicked along grassy banks and after dark, lit bonfires as the fireworks set the night sky and harbour alight. At home later we lit Tom Thumbs and sparklers. In 1966 Empire Day became Commonwealth Day and the date was moved to June 11 to coincide with the official birthday of Queen Elizabeth 11.

Every year my grandmother and Phyllis took Noel, Ron and me to The Royal Easter Show. At the entrance, children received brown paper bags with raffia handles, filled with miniature packages, all exact replicas of grown-up grocery items, and exotically flowered paper parasols from Japan. Sticky with fairy floss, we thrilled to the bagpipes, the sheepdog trials, the merry-go-round, the Punch and Judy booth and the pungent aroma of animal pens. A day at the Royal Easter show was tactile and earthy, alive with colour and noise and the warmth of baby farm animals.

Before we knew that animals should be free, we eagerly anticipated days at Taronga Park Zoo, where we raced from one wild exhibit to another: bears, lions, tigers, apes and elephants, as well as our own native creatures, as Peter's Ice Cream melted from our cones. We reached the zoo by tram or sometimes a small ferry out of Circular Quay that always brings to mind the delightful 1910 painting by Emanuel Phillips Fox, *The Ferry*. Ferries, small and large, have always been a standard means of transportation around Sydney Harbour. Now there are hydro-cats for those in a hurry and more recently, environmentally friendly solar-sailors.

Occasionally during the autumns of those early years, we drove to the Blue Mountains where my family once kept a holiday house. Curled up in a snug cacoon of Scottish wool plaid in the back seat of my uncle Eric's Wolseley, I watched towering gums and pines fly by overhead and eagerly anticipated the promised treat to come: trifle, served in style at the grand old hotel that may still be there, a triumph of sponge cake and lady fingers soaked in sherry, layered with raspberries and jam, rich custard and Devonshire cream, topped with almonds. To me, the Blue Mountains and trifle were synonymous although every New Year's Day my grandmother made one quite as grand, layered in a large cut crystal bowl.

Once, somewhere in the Blue Mountains, we visited relatives whose faces and names I don't remember. In the misty early morning we gathered mushrooms in the woods and returned to the house to serve them, hot and buttery, on toast. I think we were there to comfort the family of a young cousin who was killed when his motorbike crashed on the mountain road.

Sometimes my grandmother took me to tearooms in the city. There, among the potted palms and art deco glass, a maid in black under a frilly white cap tempted us with a tiered silver tray heaped with exquisite cakes, tarts, eclairs and scones. She served tea properly made in the English style, with water briskly boiled for two full minutes, poured over black tea leaves in a teapot kept warm by a pretty tea cozy, steeped for two or three minutes more then poured into fine china teacups. Afterwards, we peered into our empty cups to read our fortunes in the damp leaves. I suspect these outings were intended as instruction within my *proper upbringing* but I enjoyed them, although I have long since abandoned such formality.

I remember childhood birthdays on the top floor of Farmers, a popular department store in Sydney at that time. In my memory, Farmers provided everything to make a small child's birthday an unforgettable event: balloons, clowns, games, cake and candles and paper crackers that popped as we pulled the ends, wincing, to discover the favours inside. These paper crackers, which we called *bangers,* were always part of our table settings on New Years Day as well.

I have a photograph of me taken at Farmers on my third birthday, just three months after my mother's death. A label reads: *Farmer's, the Children's Store, Radio Birthday Club, 1932.* The photograph has been hand-tinted: I am wearing a red sweater over a cream pleated wool skirt and someone has softly rag-curled my hair for the occasion. I am gazing directly into the camera, unsmiling, uncertain.

Reunion

I do not recall seeing my father again until I was about five years old. Now he was in New Zealand and my grandmother and I were to sail on an ocean liner to Auckland to meet him. The Second World War was still beyond the horizon and travel was still gracious. I pressed against the rail, watching a colourful swirl of paper streamers twist from the ship to the dock - the last fragile connection to those left behind - until the liner reversed its great engines and pulled away amid cheers and tears. I still remember the smell and throb of the giant ship, streamers escaping into the blue sky, farewells fading in the wind.

I recall little of that reunion or how long it lasted. However, I do remember soft green hills and sheep almost everywhere as my father drove us through the beautiful New Zealand countryside. As I sat in the back seat gazing out at the passing scenery, a bird crashed onto the windscreen. The sight and sound of the impact, the small limp body falling onto the bonnet amid scattering feathers, shocked me so that I was sick and my father had to stop the car. I remember the hot springs at Rotorua, a treeless landscape of cragged lava rocks and bubbling pools, hissing steam and reeking sulphur. I remember Maoris with alarming painted faces, chanting, swirling, warlike.

Not long after my grandmother and I returned to Sydney, my father followed. He planned to be married there to a woman I had yet to meet. I remember perching on my father's lap in the sitting room at *Lillianfels*, extending my small cupped hand to receive the ashes from his cigarette, as my grandmother admonished me to *stop bothering your father, Judith.*

I have a faded memory of visiting my future stepmother at her parents' home in a small country town north west of Sydney. I remember that her sisters taught me how to churn butter and pat it into bite-size balls with little wooden paddles. I remember my father lifting me onto a horse and later, perching me on a milking stool beneath a cow and instructing me to *milk!* as he aimed his camera. In another photograph I stand in a field of cattle, and in all these pictures, I appear to be quite pleased with myself. Outside of that visit, I have no recollection of my stepmother in my life at all and I have no idea how, where and when she and my father might have met.

My father was obsessed with cameras. A skillful photographer, he recorded my young life in fragments that coincided with his rare visits. One of my favourite photographs, taken a few weeks before his wedding in May 1935, shows me sitting on the curved lid of a Singer sewing machine in the lower orchard of *Lillianfels.* I am wearing a beautiful new satin robe and matching slippers my father has brought me from somewhere; my long light hair falls straight around my shoulders. Even though the photograph is not in colour, I remember the robe's exact shade of pale blue that matched my eyes. I am looking directly into the camera, wearing a small shy smile.

At the wedding, I wore a blue wool coat and blue ribbons in my plaited hair. I remember I had a miserable cold. After the wedding my father once again vanished from my life.

During the next few years, as my father and stepmother traveled the world, packages with foreign postmarks arrived, containing dolls in native costumes. Too fragile to play with, they lived in a locked, tall glass cabinet for me to admire. From France, my father sent me a doll I *could* play with, a life-sized baby with dark lashes and deep blue eyes that opened and closed. I named her *Fifi* and I adored her! Also from France came a very special book: a large, slim volume of *The Lord's Prayer,* with full page illustrations in soft, pale colours embellished with gold leaf.

Once huge wood crates arrived at the house filled with Indian treasures: jeweled daggers, gold-threaded wall hangings, carved tables inlaid with real ivory, wood elephants holding progressively smaller elephants inside, silk saris and embroidered slippers with narrow toes curled like the prow of a Viking ship.

Our reunions, however, were isolated events, like an Empire Day celebration, too fleeting to establish a bond.

My Mother's Family

Some of my happiest childhood memories are of my mother's family. My maternal grandfather, Arthur, died in 1913 when he was forty. His widow, Emily, lived in a simple little row house called *Halcyon,* in Bellevue Hill. Emily had borne four children but one had died at birth. The others were Clarence, Edith and my mother Vera, who was five years younger than Edith. The sisters were inseparable; old photographs show them laughing together, playing the guitar, clowning, sometimes with Edith's congenial husband Eric. It was Edith and Eric who tried to adopt me when my mother died. At that time they had a son, Bruce; their daughter Margaret was born five years later.

Clarrie, as he was called, lived at *Halcyon* as well, with his wife Robin and their son Ian who was about my age. Another son, Peter, had tragically died when he was only four. Believing he could fly, Peter leapt from the edge of the lawn-covered garage rooftop and fell to the concrete footpath below.

I remember that *Halcyon* once sported an outhouse and that my grandmother cooked on a wood-burning stove - very different from *Lillianfels.* But I liked being there. I recall Emily as soft-spoken and kind and was surprised recently to learn that this gentle woman had once travelled a long distance alone on horseback to Sydney, sleeping under a tree at night. She was a mere girl at the time.

I have always associated my visits to Edith's home with sunshine flooding through white French doors and Toby, my cousins' fox terrier. It seemed the good life, it was a happy family and I was happy within it. Much later, far away from everything I had ever known, I lay in a strange bed and night after night retraced my footsteps through my childhood neighbourhood to Edith's house as though I could will myself there once again.

No one ever spoke of my mother. I knew nothing of her. When I was old enough to ask, I was told that she had died of appendicitis. Vera's untimely death had devastated Edith and up to the end of her life she couldn't bear to talk about it. I learned much later that she felt my father was responsible and she never forgave him. But not once did she speak ill of him to me. *No one did.* While I was too young to realize that my mother's death had irrevocably severed ties between my parents' families, both sides took care that I remained unaware of this rift. It is to Lillian's credit that she allowed me to spend time with my mother's family.

Rosalind

In 1936, five years after my grandfather's death, when I was seven, *Lillianfels* was sold and we moved to a much smaller house called *Rosalind* in Bellevue Hill.

Rosalind sat on a hill a few steps away from Cooper Park. Sometime after we moved there, Uncle Noel married, but before then, he built an aviary tall enough to stand in, where he tenderly kcpt little finches, budgerigars, canaries, cockatiels and rosellas. When one of Noel's little birds died, Ron and I gave it a proper funeral over a tiny grave which we covered with flowers and crowned with a little cross made of sticks held together with twine.

On a wattle tree nearby, Noel hung cages for Cocky and the tropical parrot. Every morning at eight o'clock sharp, Cocky *screeched wake up Keith, wake up Keith*. I think by then Keith had moved too far away to hear this personal alarm but I'm sure everyone else did as it bounced about the gully of Cooper Park.

School

Ron and I attended grammar school in Woollahra, I at the girls' school, Ron at the boys', our schoolyards separated by a fence. Each day began outdoors with assembly as we lustily sang *Advance Australia Fair* and where a girl named Pearl regularly fainted in the subtropical heat. We wore school uniforms – those great social equalizers - as do students in Australia to this day. Unlike today's practical uniforms, mine was a box-pleated, navy-blue wool serge tunic, miserably hot in the Sydney summers. Under it, I wore a white shirt with a tie striped in school colours that matched the band of my Panama hat. Black stockings and brogues completed the discomfort; a crest-pocketed wool blazer was added in winter.

We walked to the school up a hill lined with brick houses then down a long flight of narrow stone steps to an open space we called *the mound,* a sort of marshland not far from the lower end of Cooper Park. There we lingered to observe tadpoles, frogs, dragonflies and the ever-present circus of Australian birds. Once I found a bee with a broken wing, which ungratefully stung me when I tried to help it. Sometimes we held a magnifier close to a clump of dry grass until the hot sun sucked a thin wisp of smoke into a tiny flame. Then, feeling we had gotten away with something, we quickly stomped it out with our sturdy shoes.

From the mound we walked past a small cluster of neighbourhood shops where we sometimes bought honeycomb and climbed, fortified, to the top of the steepest hill to the school, leather satchels heavy against our backs.

Once during recess I went to the bathroom across the schoolyard and lost track of time. Perched there day dreaming, I didn't hear the bell that teachers rang to signal return to class. When I emerged, the schoolyard was deserted. Fearing punishment, I went back into the bathroom and hid. When the headmistress, Miss Tully, approached, calling my name, I climbed onto a lavatory seat and curled into a silent ball. To this day I do not remember the outcome of that episode, only my fear of the consequences.

On the playground, we jumped rope and played hopscotch and quoits. Out of the sight of teachers, we amused ourselves by squeezing the breath out of one another to see who might faint first. In class I avoided volunteering answers and fervently tried to be invisible. Once, a classmate's father wrote a song he called *Sydney Harbour,* which lovingly described the harbour's beauty. He had set the words to *The Blue Danube* and when the teacher played it later and asked us to name it, I eagerly raised my hand and blurted out *Sydney Harbour!* I can still see all the faces turned toward me, the *looks*.

Except for subjects related to English, drama and art, for the most part I found school formidable. My teachers - all women - were strict. My second-class arithmetic teacher, Miss Hall - tall, gaunt, red hair tight in a bun- rapped my knuckles with a ruler every time I gave a wrong answer, which was often. Fearful anticipation shut out all hope of learning mathematics.

But I learned to spell, write and use correct grammar. I learned to pronounce my vowels roundly and never to drop my *h*'s nor add them where they didn't belong. I shone in drama and played *Hermia* with abandon. I was encouraged in art and I developed a hunger for reading and writing. Most Tuesdays my form traveled to the Conservatory of Music in the Botanical Gardens, where I had often danced, to observe Sydney Symphony Orchestra rehearsals. We visited city art galleries, museums and libraries. We learned to swim in big pools built into natural rock, constantly refilled by the ocean - most Sydney beaches have these pools at one or both ends. We played tennis, cricket and hockey. When the baker's cart stopped outside the school each day, I spent my big copper penny on a delicious sausage roll.

In those days a student's intelligence was judged by her success in mathematics, science and language. So after grammar school, the *bright* girls went on to schools devoted to these subjects, while the rest of us went on to what then was called Home Science School where we learned to starch and iron curtains, hand-stitch lawn petticoats, de-bone fish and make gruel for invalids. There was little chance of advancing to university. It's different now – Australia is far from the male-dominated Anglo-Saxon society of my childhood. When I left Australia in late 1946, the population stood around seven million. In 2017 it approaches twenty-five million, a diverse, multi-cultural society in a land about the same size as the United States.

Only once during my growing up did I see an Aborigine; he threw a boomerang to amuse the tourists at Watson's Bay. The small Chinese population didn't venture beyond Chinatown and *that* was a world apart. The Italian greengrocer was the most *foreign* member of our community until after the Second World War, when Greeks and European Jews sought refuge in Australia. Some became our neighbours – I sometimes played with a little Austrian boy whose parents had escaped the Nazis by hiding in a secret cupboard. But mostly they kept to themselves, perhaps by choice. Perhaps they felt unwelcome. They *must* have felt displaced.

Later I was to understand the very particular grief that comes with leaving one's homeland and all one has known, all that is familiar, no matter what has been left behind, no matter the promise of what might lie ahead.

Friends

My best friend in grammar school was Patty Hill who lived near Centennial Park with her divorced mother. Occasionally after school, I walked home with her through the park, stopping to watch the elegant black swans glide soundlessly across the pond. Had she known, my grandmother wouldn't have approved of the divorce *or* the park. One day Patty and I encountered our first flasher there. We burst into convulsive giggles and ran as fast as our feet could carry us, without looking back. We never told anyone. Patty and I seemed always to be giggling; we needed only to glance at one another. Once, as our class sang *Good King Wenceslaus* during a Christmas concert rehearsal, we caught
one another's eye and wound up in Miss Tully's office where we were sentenced to *sixers:* six strikes of the cane across the back of the knees as we hung face down across a hard wooden chair. Sixers were always scheduled for Monday mornings, allowing time to ponder one's folly and anticipate its consequences. *Good King Wenceslaus* is still my favourite Christmas carol; it brings back happy memories of Patty and the fun we shared which never failed to outweigh the risk.

Pearl, who frequently fainted in the sizzling heat during school assembly, was a *secret* friend. Her family lived in Paddington, which I recall as a slum at that time, and could not afford to buy her a school uniform, or even shoes. I think she may have suffered from malnutrition - her hair was very thin and her skin very pale. Sometimes I walked with her to her tenement row house on the way home from school and shared a few amiable moments with her large family. As far as I know, my grandmother remained forever ignorant of this transgression.

The War

Ron had graduated to long pants, a rite of passage for Australian boys turning thirteen. There was no such thing as a teenager then; we simply grew up day by day, unclassified. As expected, I moved on to Home Science School.

Within a week after Germany had invaded Poland in September 1939, Australia, New Zealand, Canada and South Africa joined forces with Britain and France. By 1941 the Japanese were fighting the Australians and on December 7 of that year, they attacked America at Pearl Harborur. On December 11, the German Reich declared war on America and that same day, America declared war on Germany.

On February 19th 1942 the Japanese attacked Darwin. It was the first of sixty-four raids, which killed over two hundred people and destroyed the city's oil supply tanks. It was not until August 1945 that VJ Day was declared – six days before my sixteenth birthday, so for over three years Australians lived with the constant threat of attack, sometimes from midget submarines in Sydney Harbour. In 1942 one submarine broke through the shark nets in the harbour and fired two torpedoes. One landed harmlessly on the shore, the other exploded against the seawall and sank an old ferry being used as a barracks. Twenty-one men died and the two young Japanese crewmen perished.

My own life during those war years was relatively unaffected. We all cheerfully adapted to small inconveniences: ration books, coupons, long queues, shortages of meat, eggs, and butter. Sometimes we shared bathwater. Phyllis darned socks and mended clothes as she huddled over a coal fire, trying to warm her chilblains. Sometimes she found remnants of rose crepe and blue Viyella to tuck, shirr and gore into lovely dresses for me. From scraps of brown and orange velvet she fashioned an elegant hood that made me feel like a mysterious heroine from an Emily Bronte novel. We adjusted to blackouts and the air raid wardens who patrolled our neighbourhood every night. By lamplight, behind darkened windows, we played dominoes and worked on crossword puzzles. Like so many Australians, we were conscientious about the war effort; women went to work in factories, schoolgirls knitted khaki wool mufflers and sent care packages to *our boys overseas.* Too naïve to understand the lyrics, we unwittingly sang *Rum and Coca Cola;* we listened to Big Bands and found inspiration in *Mrs. Miniver.*

Rosalind sat on a hill only a few steps away from Cooper Park to which I often escaped in the early morning hours before my grandmother awoke. While dew still clung like diamonds to huge spider webs, as the bush began to stir, I watched and listened and tried to untangle the bewildered longing of my adolescent years. The park still holds tennis courts and a cricket field where I used to watch my cousin Bruce's school team at play. On both sides of the gully, houses still climb steep, densely vegetated slopes that make me think of fresh heads of broccoli.

Rosalind had a quite ordinary yard which tumbled down toward the gully but a massive camphor laurel tree that engulfed the bottom of the yard made it extraordinary. Rain turned its great trunk ink black, its leaves citrus green and orange. Beneath this colour canopy Ron and I harvested leaves from a nasturtium patch for makeshift sandwiches of white bread and Worchester sauce, snatched from the kitchen. Now and then a blue tongue lizard scurried by, big and harmless, as a kookaburra, perched on the clothesline, cocked his head with interest.

Our two parrots seemed mutually disinterested in one another but when the tropical parrot caught pneumonia and died, Cocky, the pink galah, mourned silently for three weeks. This alarmed us since Cocky was seldom at a loss for words, so we were relieved when he recovered his gregarious self. He was a born comedian, feisty and sociable. He often followed us around the house, chattering and trying to nibble our toes. Whenever we sang *Pop Goes the Weasel*, Cocky danced an exuberant jig, bobbing and dipping, swaying like a drunken Cockney. He even tolerated our blue-eyed white cat who wisely made herself scarce when Cocky was about. One day he flew off into Cooper Park and Ron, Noel and I combed the bush, calling his name. A hawk circled overhead and as it dropped lower, we heard a tiny squawk in the thicket. There was Cocky, trembling and humbled and obviously happy to see us. We clipped his wings and he never flew off again. He lived a very long life in Phyllis' kind care but in the end, plucked himself bald. We didn't know then that captivity could be stressful for creatures meant to be free. In our kind ignorance we thought we were keeping Cocky safe.

Uncle Noel liked to make ginger beer, Australia's traditional soft drink. Seated at tea one evening, we were startled by a series of explosive *pops*. Noel had stored the ginger beer in the linen closet to ferment where it burst into a sticky mess. I don't remember my grandmother's reaction but in an era of coppers, stirring poles, wringers and wash boards, she could not have been pleased. Ironing was a chore too: we heated two or three small irons on the stove, switching them as they cooled. We had no refrigerator: mass production of refrigerators did not begin until after World War II. Several times a week the iceman carried a block of ice on one shoulder, up the back steps and onto the verandah and into our wooden ice chest.

Sometimes I stood on those steps and furtively poured senna tea into the bushes. Lillian regularly plied Ron, Noel and me with senna tea, castor oil, and sulphur and treacle. I *liked* the sulphur and treacle.

When Lillian made Irish stew she boiled the mutton bones clean. Smooth and satisfying in the hand, they made perfect Jacks. Sometimes when Ron and I tired of our game, we lifted the metal cover of the gas metre to tease the red back spiders underneath with sticks. When we ventured into the yard at night, we swept the air ahead of us in broad arcs with upside-down brooms to dispatch the enormous spiders in their enormous webs that laced the trees so swiftly after dark.

Having survived deadly spiders all my life, I launched into a mishap-filled thirteenth year. It began with sixty-four ringworms which, I was told, I had caught from a kitten someone had given me for my birthday. I never saw the kitten again. Then I contacted impetigo which was going around school at the time. Twice a day Phyllis scrubbed my skin with methylated spirits and applied a purple dye, which stained me for weeks afterwards. That same year I had my tonsils out and not long afterwards, I severely scalded my thigh when my jumper sleeve caught the handle of a pot boiling on the stove. Phyllis applied butter, the accepted remedy in those days, and my cousin Noel had to carry me around for weeks until I could walk again. I had no sooner recovered when, in an adolescent daydream, I stepped off the curb into the path of an elegant Jaguar convertible. I wasn't hurt - the fender barely brushed me - but I remember the horrified expression of the equally elegant man who was driving. I also remember that I was wearing a light blue hand-crocheted dress. I attribute this total recall of my apparel at significant moments to my yet unrecognized desire to become a fashion designer and illustrator.

My piano lessons continued. I resented them. I kicked the piano as I practiced and it bore the scars forever. I wanted to be outside playing soccer with the boys. My grandmother told me it was important that I learn to play well because people would invite me to parties but whenever I was invited, she didn't allow me to go. I longed for a bicycle but Lillian considered bicycles too dangerous and it was not until I married that I owned my first one. Perhaps Lillian was trying to keep me intact for the time when my father might reclaim me.

Lillian did allow me a scooter that once gathered downhill speed too quickly and hurled me over a low rail fence and onto the cricket grounds at Cooper Park. I wasn't hurt, merely embarrassed, since a match was in progress at the time. I didn't tell my grandmother because I wanted to keep the scooter. It was my only getaway vehicle except for clattering green trams and red double-decker buses, which I rode only to approved destinations such as school.

That same year my grandmother gave me a book called *Marjory and her Mother* along with several small white towels and safety pins. I thought the story silly; I didn't see the point. Phyllis enlightened me only slightly. I thought my breasts might bleed someday and wondered how to attach the towels with those safety pins – I didn't have a brassiere then. At fourteen it all became clear.

Eric's visits became more frequent. At that time Eric was Australia's Poet Laureate; I still have several poems he sent to me as an adult; I find them disquieting. Eric had begun to see me as an easy target for his advances. They never went beyond molestation. I tried to avoid him but he was obsessive, alert to opportunity. He would pull up in front of the house in his sleek blue and grey Wolseley and tell my grandmother he wanted to take Ron and me out for ice cream. Knowing what was coming, I always politely declined but my grandmother would tell me I was ungrateful and insist I go. With my cousin ignorant in the back seat, Eric would start his groping and I would sit frozen, not knowing what to do. Once, in the copper room where we laundered clothes and boiled Christmas puddings, he invited me to reach into his pocket for a shilling. He had cut off the bottom of his pocket. I never told anyone; I knew instinctively I would be blamed because I felt Eric's advances must somehow have been my fault. After all, my grandmother had always taught me that *adults are always right, you do as you are told.*

In my fourteenth year I contracted scarlet fever. I remember feeling ill as I climbed to my arithmetic tutor's house, up steep steps that connect streets all over hilly Sydney. I stopped to pet a goat through someone's fence, trying to ignore my aching throat. The tutor dismissed me and by the time I returned home, I was burning with fever. There were no antibiotics at that time; the only available treatment was sulphur. I remember faces blurred above me as I was loaded into an ambulance and taken to a hospital somewhere down the coast. My family was temporarily displaced when the house was fumigated, while I spent three weeks in isolation, flat on my back. Now and then a familiar face would appear at the tiny window in the heavy door marked *Quarantine:* Ron, Noel, Phyllis. They could do nothing but wave to let me know they cared. After three weeks I was moved from isolation to a room which I shared with another girl. I was allowed to sit up now and could see the long empty stretch of beach beyond my window. My roommate was sixteen years old, animated and talkative. She told me all about *sex.* She told me how babies were made. I was fascinated, I was dumfounded and I didn't believe a word she said.

I recovered well but soon afterwards Prince, my beloved lifelong companion, died. I had never known life without him. When he could no longer climb back from the bottom of the yard, when he was clearly suffering, the grownups decided to put Prince to sleep. Ron, Noel and I were old enough to understand but understanding was little comfort.

My years in Dover Heights Home Science School seem lost in a haze but for a few pleasant memories of tennis lessons on clay courts and trips to the city as part of our cultural education, atop a red double-decker bus. Art, drama and English classes made school bearable. Yet my clearest memory is of my typing teacher, Miss Dougherty. Miss Dougherty was a large and towering presence. She wore men's brown suits and big brown brogues and cut her hair like a man's. She terrified me. I threw up before every typing class and in the end, failed.

Before I turned fifteen, I sat for Matriculation and suffered the agony of waiting for the Sydney Morning Herald to publish the list of those who passed - or failed. I actually do not remember if I passed or not, so overwhelmed was I with fear of failure and the *disgrace* that would follow.

By all accounts I did pass and went on to East Sydney Art School, which was part of East Sydney Technical College. East Sydney Art School was a thriving art institution in the forties, embracing new contemporary ideas brought to Australia by European Jews fleeing the war. By then many brilliant Australian artists – among them Streeton, McCubbin, Rees and Preston - had already captured the country's unique character in various mediums.

During the first intense year of art training, students were not permitted to work in colour or with live models. Instead, we learned to observe with a critical eye, to draw in ink with traditional pens. Our models were classic Greek and Roman life-size statues. I still value this early fundamental training because I believe that drawing is a solid foundation for good painting.

Built in 1841 as Darlinghurst Gaol, the school was a formidable massive stone fortress where public hangings continued to 1852. With my new friend Peggy, I ate lunch high in the gallows where rotted ropes still dangled above the stone floor below. Peggy was sophisticated. Because her ears were pierced, my grandmother would have said that Peggy was a *hussy*. Peggy was fond of saying that the song *Sweet and Lovely* had been written for me. It was Peggy who advised me of appropriate undergarments, having seen me run unbound in a jumper. Until then, my only instruction had been precautionary: to always wear clean, mended underwear in case I were to be hit by a tram. At East Sydney Art School I had a crush on a good-looking boy who kissed me once on a dare. Years later, married and a mother, I was startled to see Rodney's name flash across our black and white television screen as the star of an American television series.

After art school I worked at a publishing firm in the city for fourteen months - my introduction to a broader world. I spent my lunchtimes in the Botanical Gardens happily devouring meat pies or newspaper-wrapped fish and chips bought from a street corner vendor.

One of my co-workers supposedly was related to Walt Disney. He was mentally slow, loveably childlike and a skilled artist in the Disney tradition. Another co-worker - older than I, tall, gangly, crippled slightly from polio - became infatuated with me. I liked him as a person but that was all - his intensity startled me. Later he wrote me ardent letters, which would cause me trouble even though I myself never received them.

And so my life moved forward in its unknowing ordinariness. We listened transfixed to our favourite radio shows like *Speed Gordon* and *The Shadow,* the images vivid in our minds. But when *Deep Purple* and *In the Still of the Night* began to drift from the radio, my grandmother snapped it off because she considered the lyrics suggestive. *Give you an inch, you take a mile,* she said as though we knew what she was talking about. We pored over big books on World War I, the Kaiser, Ships of the Royal Navy and the British monarchy. Best of all were the oversized books full of beautiful colour plates of butterflies and fish.

I cut my hair – thick, straight and so long, I could sit on it. I had endured years of brushing and plaiting and twisting of rags into corkscrew curls. I wanted to look like the other girls and my grandmother eventually relented. Perhaps she was tired of the fussing too.
When we went to buy shoes, we slipped our feet into an x-ray machine that revealed the whereabouts of our skeletal toes inside the chosen pair. Under my grandmother's watchful eye there was no hope of squeezing into something glamorous and painful and so I seemed destined to wear sensible shoes forever.

We went to a dentist in Bondi Junction, who once drilled my front teeth without anaesthetic. He became very annoyed with me because, he said, I was *shaking like a bowl of jelly* and sent me outside to pull myself together. When I returned, he finished his work and sent me home where Lillian inspected my front teeth and discovered that Dr.

Fox had embellished my smile with shining gold. My self-conscious smile stayed with me until, as a young married woman, I had the gold replaced.

Lillian began to allow me to attend school balls or dances at the town hall in Double Bay as long as Phyllis chaperoned me. I have photographs of me standing in long gowns with boys whose faces and names I don't remember, except for Reginald, a nice boy who aspired to be a dentist and who had an unrequited crush on me. Once at intermission, I slipped out with David, a boy I had adored from afar, the boy who was to give me my first romantic kiss – in the moonlight, by the bay, tender, sweet, innocent, as only a first kiss can be. Phyllis, understanding, had pretended she hadn't seen us leave. That night I lay awake and prayed to my own mother in heaven, longing for her to tell me what I should do if that kiss should bring me a baby.

When my cousin Bruce graduated from Scots College, my grandmother allowed me to attend the ball that followed. The school had booked a ferry for the event and for hours we danced our way around Sydney Harbour to a live band. In the early morning hours, the ferry pulled in to one of the many small islands that dot the harbour. There, at a little kiosk set amongst the trees, we indulged ourselves with hot scones, thick cream and raspberry jam. I was heady with excitement. I had never stayed up so late before.

Now approaching eighty and always suspicious by nature, Lillian had become increasingly paranoid. She demanded more and more of Phyllis who was still beautiful: chocolate eyes, pink skin, becomingly premature white hair. Lillian effectively dispensed Phyllis' potential suitors by professing timely asthma or heart attacks. I remember a naval officer who courted Phyllis and I remember her face when she looked at him. Eventually, they both must have realized it was hopeless. I think Phyllis was trapped by her mother's demands, her own kindness and her sense of responsibility.

When I saw Phyllis years later in a convalescent home, when her body and mind had betrayed her, I was struck with the *unfairness* of it all.

I came home from work one day and found my grandmother waiting at the door, hairbrush in hand. She began to beat me about the head, shouting, *You little hussy, I know you've been with that taxi cab driver.* I didn't even *know* any cab drivers. But there was no reasoning with her. Sometimes she wielded the stick end of a feather duster, sometimes a ruler. I don't think anyone ever witnessed these incidents or would have dared to intervene.

More and more I dreaded coming home. I began to leave the bus before my usual stop to seek refuge in All Saints Church. I did not dare to linger long for fear Lillian might be counting every moment I was late as her suspicions mounted. Inside the cool empty gloom, I sat in a hard wood pew and prayed for my grandmother to be in a good mood, for courage, for rescue. Mostly I sat, miserable, helpless and tearful. But I found no comfort there, beneath the vaulted arches and stained glass windows.

As these scenes escalated, I began to write to my father, begging him to save me. I hadn't seen him since his wedding, before I was six, and during that time he and my stepmother had travelled extensively. They spent some time in Africa before settling in Buenos Aires but in 1938, when my eldest brother was about to be born, they fled to New York as Argentina's sympathies with Fascist Germany and Italy escalated. Their second son was born in Massachusetts and their two younger sons, in California.

By the time I was seventeen they had settled in Monrovia, in Southern California. It had never occurred to me to wonder why they had never included me in their new life; I only imagined a perfect family of which I would be part: a mother, a father, little brothers. I pictured white picket fences and maple trees, a Norman Rockwell life in America.

It had been almost two years since I first wrote to my father of my unhappiness and it was almost that long before I was granted a six-month visitor's visa. I do not know who arranged this type of visa for me or why - perhaps, in 1946, options were limited, immigration waiting lists long, post-war international travel still restricted. Or perhaps my family in Sydney believed I would return home in a matter of months.

The day before I was to leave Australia, as I stood in Edith's sunlit hallway for the last time, she said *I have something to tell you.* She hesitated then added *your mother died in childbirth.* I said *but I thought she died of appendicitis?* Then I asked *was it a boy or a girl?* She struggled a moment then replied *it was a boy.* I accepted this and asked nothing further but I wondered about the little brother I would never know.

Three months after my seventeenth birthday I sailed on the *SS Monterey* – a recently converted troopship – for America and a new life. I left Australia with one old trunk containing little but my clothes. My books, my doll collection, even Fifi, stayed behind, lost forever, along with my childhood. Edna sailed with me. She had escaped her mother's restrictions by marrying an American soldier several years her junior. She had lied to him about her age and made me swear not to tell. I never did. They stayed married for many years until his death.

We stopped at Pago Pago, a hilly tumble of tropical flowers set in a crystal aqua sea, and Suva, a busy, steaming mangrove swamp. There the towering grass-skirted police chief came aboard and played Ping-Pong with the passengers. Smiling broadly, he always won.

On November 12th, 1946, I sailed under a Golden Gate Bridge enshrouded in fog, full of idealized misconceptions, a product of my sheltered upbringing.

Without a Script

Part 2 - America

A New Stage

My father met me at the dock, a man I did not know. My aunt's new husband swept her off to meet his genial Italian family who lived in San Francisco's Twin Peaks district. In the San Francisco hotel room where we stayed the first night, my father tongue-kissed me, just once, as I stood frozen. Eric. I don't know what my father was thinking; he never repeated this transgression, nor anything like it, but from that moment on, I would be forever uncomfortable around him. I have a photograph of me taken just before I left Australia, wearing the dress I wore that day: a simple jersey the color of English mustard. I've never worn that color since.

The next day we began the long drive to Southern California where my new life would begin. Along the way we stopped at one of those nondescript truck stops hat dotted the old highways of America then. In the café, my father introduced me to my first shocking taste of buttermilk and told the big blonde waitress that I had just come from Australia. Her mouth fell open. But I thought they were all Aborigines. I did not realize how little the world knew of Australia then. After all, Australia had been my whole world.

Monrovia

At the front door of my new home in Monrovia, my stepmother turned her cheek from my kiss. I had been required to kiss aunts all my life so supposed this was appropriate but her tightened mouth spoke otherwise. She did not hug me or tell me how glad she was to see me. In the living room moments later, my father blurted, You look just like your mother! In retrospect, I think this perceived likeness to Vera might explain his behavior in the hotel room earlier: an unthinking, impulsive reaction. Now, it did nothing to help my initiation into my stepmother's life. It must have been difficult for her: the sudden appearance of a seventeen year-old she did not know must have upset her world; I was not quite seven when we last met and then only briefly, in the flurry of her marriage to my father. Still, I ask myself, why did they not include me then in their new life together? She might have molded me more to her liking, although current statistics suggest that stepparents may be destined to fail with children past four or five.

The three-bedroom house was a moderate post-war tract home set on a corner lot with a lovely old oak tree at the edge of the front lawn. In 1946 housing shortages were acute on the West Coast. For five years all economic activity had been redirected to wartime needs, creating a tremendous migration of African Americans who left low paying agricultural jobs in the South to pursue wartime factory work in California. During the war years, California's population increased by 272 per cent. In a housing market already tight for returning veterans, developers and real estate agents enforced covenants, forbidding homeowners to sell to Blacks, Latinos, Asians and Jews. Racial discrimination thrived.

Whether or not being White gave my father an advantage in this tight housing market, I think he and my stepmother appreciated their home. My father added a breezeway between the kitchen and the garage, creating a pleasant outdoor extension to the house.

In a corner of the garage, he had thoughtfully created a tiny art studio for me. An incinerator squatted at the far edge of the neat back lawn, a common sight in neighborhoods at that time, before anyone understood pollution. I had my own pleasant bedroom next to the third bedroom where my three young brothers slept in bunk beds.
I met my brothers for he first time on the thirteenth of November, 1946. The eldest, Bruce, was now almost nine, John was five, Robert just one and Rodger had yet to be born. I remember them affectionately as happy little boys who got along well together in that small house. I recall Bruce more than the others because he was the eldest. He was obsessed with trains and drew pictures of them constantly and it was no surprise to me that he became a successful artist. John had the same endearing smile he has to this day and Robert was a bright miniature edition of our father.

Debilitating homesickness blurred my vision. I found myself landlocked, away from the ocean for the first time in my life, overwhelmed by a looming barren mountain that cradled smog and blocked escape. I felt I might as well have landed in the middle of the Sahara. The bland neighborhood, where streets were named after citrus fruits rather than elm or maple, bore no resemblance to Norman Rockwell's Saturday Evening Post covers. In reality, Monrovia was a pleasant enough town with an old-fashioned main street that seemed typically American in those innocent mid-century years. But it wasn't my town. I think we all have an environment within us - one we may be born to or one we may choose – a place where we feel we belong. I never felt that way in Monrovia. Whenever I could, I rode a bus for two hours all the way to the beach – any beach – where I would sit for a half-hour under a pier, sea mist cooling my skin. Then I would take the long bus ride back to the house on East Lime Avenue.

Sometimes I hiked up into the Sierra Madre foothills alone, ignorant of possible dangers – of falling, of losing my way, of mountain lions or people looking for trouble. Typical of me then: I did not think about it. I did not think.

These excursions provided an escape from the tension I felt in the house. Nothing I did pleased my stepmother. I wanted to have her acceptance and approval, if not her affection but I felt only her resentment and contempt. At the time, I didn't understand the complex emotional issues that helped shape her attitude toward me. The fact remained that I was another woman's child and a daughter at that. Years later Edna told me that my stepmother, at her wedding, when I was six years old, told my father that she was not going to raise someone else's child. I don't know if that is true; perhaps they decided their anticipated travels might be hard on a child or that I might be better off with my grandmother at Lillianfels. All I knew then was that my father had left me when my mother died and that he was leaving me again.

Within weeks of my arrival, my body spun out of control. I couldn't stop eating – a loaf of bread at a time – and I quickly gained weight. I couldn't stay awake. When I was awake, I was depressed. I cried myself to sleep every night, retracing my steps through my lost neighborhood. My stepmother called me lazy, but I was powerless to change. When she finally took me to see her doctor, tests revealed that my thyroid level had suddenly dropped drastically.

About a week later, my stepmother told me the doctor had called with my test results and had said two things: that I would be in a mental institution within a year and I would never be able to have children. She did not add anything, she did not sympathize. It didn't occur to me to question – I believed her. After all, I had been raised never to question adults. It was not until I was twenty-one, when I went with my future husband to see this same doctor that I learned the truth. By then my father and stepmother had left America.

With the proper medication, my body regained its biological balance. My emotional balance, however, was fragile. I was self-conscious and insecure, haunted by the doctor's supposed predictions. Sometimes I would lock myself in the bathroom and stare intently into the mirror, searching my image for signs. Would I know if I were going insane? Did crazy people believe they were normal?

At a time when a telephone call to Australia cost about eleven dollars a minute, my only connection to my distant family was by boat mail. I wrote long letters home, which cheerfully described my neighborhood, my little brothers, the weather, the mountain – anything but my unhappiness. I felt ashamed of my misery, especially since I had begged my father to rescue me from my grandmother. I desperately missed my aunt and cousins. But when my grandmother died less than two years after I had left Sydney, I guiltily felt little grief or sadness, even though her death sealed off any hope of my return - or so I thought. By then my aunt Phyllis and her sons had moved onto different stages of their lives, less restricted, free. How might I fit in? I felt I no longer had a home to which to return, although no one ever knew I longed to.

The years have softened my memories of my grandmother. Looking back, I see that she tried to raise me in a way she believed best for me, a proper way. But proper is not necessarily right. I doubt her own childhood offered the advantages I experienced. She exposed me to some of the finer things of life - music, art, ballet, literature - but took care to protect me from the common mainstream. (I doubt she ever suspected her eldest son's advances toward me.) In a way it was an unrealistic upbringing that did little to prepare me for the real world but in truth, I do not regret it, although some lessons have come hard and late. I wonder how my father could have abandoned his own responsibility to place the burden of a small child on his sixty-five year old widowed mother who had already raised eleven of her own?

When I tuned the radio to the familiar classical music of my childhood, my stepmother, perhaps thinking it made me melancholy, changed the station. She was probably right: When Walt Disney's Fantasia was released, I sat in a darkened theater time after time, weeping self-indulgently through its sweeping score.

I must have been exasperating to live with: a moping, depressed, dispirited seventeen year old. I didn't stand up for myself; I didn't talk back. Instead, I continued to try to gain my father and stepmother's approval by acquiescence, which likely made them respect me even less. I don't think they really believed I was as innocent or as ignorant as I appeared but I truly was. I was, indeed, the product of my upbringing. Looking back, I can't altogether blame them; now I myself would be skeptical of such naivete.

To make matters worse, the man I knew at the publishing house in Sydney sent me apparently fervent love letters. I never read the letters – my stepmother confronted me, torn envelopes in hand, and accused me of lies and deceit. I had had no contact at all with the man since leaving Australia.

This incident was one of many checkmarks my stepmother added to an invisible scoreboard. My father never defended me. I think it was easier for him not to. Sometimes he echoed her ridicule. I recall a time I mowed the lawn – we had a simple push mower then – as my father watched from the kitchen window. When I finished and came inside, he said, If you can't do something right then don't bother doing it at all. He did not explain what I had done wrong.

I remember the day he was to return from a three -week business trip to New York. My stepmother began to scrub the kitchen floor on her hands and knees. I said, I can do that. She retorted, You are a stupid girl, you can't do it right. The floor was still wet when my father opened the back door from the carport. My stepmother told him to wait outside until it dried. Once he came in, he said, Why didn't you get Judith to help you? She replied, She wouldn't help, she's too lazy.

Another time – perhaps it was my stepmother's birthday or Mothers Day – I prepared breakfast-in-bed for her. I made hot cereal (porridge) and tea and placed a rose in a little bud vase on a tray. She said, This porridge is too thin. You can't do anything right. My father stayed quiet.

My father of the restless feet and jingling pockets, big talk and ethnic jokes and Johnny Walker Black. A cocky little man, cheerful, fit and handsome, quick to show off his flexed muscles; a personable character, one of a kind, whom people found amusing and entertaining. Life of the party who liked to impress people, played his banjo at the drop of a hat, treated strangers in pubs to free beer, was passionate about his American cars, thought the grass was always greener somewhere else, that wherever he had been or wherever he might go was better than where he was at the moment.

For all his brash bravado, I eventually began to understand my father but it would be years before I could face up to him.

A few days after I came to Monrovia, my stepmother walked with me along our street to meet my new neighbors. One remarked that we bore a resemblance, we could pass for mother and daughter. My stepmother seemed offended; she retorted that she was too young to have a daughter my age, when actually she was only six years younger than my father, three years younger than my own mother. In reality, we bore no resemblance. She was an attractive woman, small and fine boned, with hazel eyes and dark hair, while I was blue-eyed and fair-haired. But my prevailing image is of her tight smile tinged with the resentment she felt of my presence. Of course, that was my experience of her; she clearly doted on her little boys. I don't recall that she was ever cross with them. To her credit, she never laid a hand on me. Nor did my father. But there are more effective ways to reduce youthful self-confidence.

She was monetarily wise but extremely frugal. She wore the same multi-colored housedress every day and scraped the last bit of lipstick from its tube with a toothpick. She did not indulge in many clothes or give into trends, but occasionally ordered a custom-tailored wool suit from Hong Kong, in good classic taste to last for years, along with fine leather shoes. She would extend a slim leg, point a narrow foot and solemnly declare that she had the ankles of a fine racehorse.

My father, on the other hand, spent money freely. He loved any new gadgets and had to be the first to own them. I suspect my stepmother's frugality was in protest of my father's excesses, locking them in some neurotic tug-of-war. I saw little warmth or affection between them but my ongoing presence was no doubt inhibiting.

My stepmother was an obsessive housekeeper. Even with the responsibility of a fairly large family in a rather small house, she kept all forms of dust, dirt and disorder at bay. Once, when a few of my parents' friends were gathered in our living room, a careless Australian acquaintance named Darcy, busy relating a gutter-level joke, spilled cigarette ashes on the polished floor. My stepmother rushed to retrieve her Electrolux and with lips pursed, vacuumed up the ashes as Darcy turned mute and withdrew his feet. For years after I was married, I cleaned my house with vehemence, my long-departed stepmother on my shoulder, judging.

Growing up at Lillianfels, I had few household responsibilities. While I thought I kept my room in Monrovia clean and neat enough, my stepmother disagreed. Often, after I left the house, she checked my closet and rummaged through my dresser drawers. She didn't attempt to conceal this invasion of privacy but confronted me later with a list of offences: I had left dirty socks on the closet floor, my clothes were not folded correctly, I had not dusted, or I had set something on the dresser without a doily. I can still recall her exact words: You are a filthy girl; no man will ever want to marry you.

Once, in an attempt to please her, I carefully scraped discolored caulking from the kitchen sink, not understanding its purpose. I can see why my stepmother thought me stupid; I never seemed able to do anything right. I was painfully self-conscious. Early one Sunday when, as usual, I was about to accompany my father to the local Episcopal Church, I realized that my appropriate white crochet cotton gloves were soiled. I washed them, hoping they would dry in time. I still cringe when I recall the startled expression on the minister's face when his hand came in damp contact with mine.

Sometimes I babysat for some neighbors, earning twenty-five cents an hour – a fair price back then. Some of these neighbors became my friends. I asked one once why my stepmother treated me as she did and she replied, Don't you know? She's jealous! This had not occurred to me and I found no solace in it for I understood then that I could never please her: I was a constant reminder of my father's first marriage and I was powerless to change that.

A good friend now in her nineties was a young bride when she met my father and stepmother in Pasadena. As exiled Australians, they shared a common bond. She told me that she and her American husband were having dinner at my father's house in Monrovia one evening when my father casually remarked that his daughter was coming from Australia to live. My friend remembers that they had just begun the first course - my father's excellent Indian curry, which he claimed was taught him by a Maharajah - and that she almost dropped her fork in surprise. She and her husband had known my father and stepmother for three years and had never heard I existed. I don't recall having seen any photographs recording my life in Monrovia, either, although surely my father, an enthusiastic photographer, must have snapped some.

In the Long Island Sunday Press February 20th, 1938, there is a photograph of my father and stepmother. She cradles my eldest brother, born less than two weeks before, shortly after they had fled Argentina. My father tells the reporter that he will have a happy reunion with his eight-year-old daughter, Judith Lorelei, who is coming all the way from Sydney with her grandmother to visit him in his Kew Gardens apartment. Wherever he happens to be in the world, he calls her every few months and sends her dolls from different countries. She has 130 of them now.

I remember the dolls – fewer than a dozen - but I do not remember the calls. I never went to Kew Gardens. As for my name: on one of two different birth certificates, my father has crossed out my middle name Laurel and written in Lorelei.

He claimed he had lived in almost every country in the world and I believe that he once held a record for air miles long before most people even thought of getting on a plane. In later years, he traveled to Japan and became enamoured with its culture and traditional hospitality. He was restless to the end.

Edna

Occasionally I visited Edna at Pete's family's home in San Francisco. I don't recall flying there; I think perhaps my father dropped me off on his way to some business appointment. He thrived on travel, he loved to drive, he loved his American cars.

Pete's house always seemed bursting with Italian exuberance. His family had a small holiday cabin in the Santa Cruz Mountains with no electricity, where the nearest neighbor was miles away and the outhouse a perilous journey down the mountain. I was happy there, in the woods, away from tension. We spent our days at the beach, sunbathing or dodging one another on paddleboats. At the Santa Cruz boardwalk, we swam in the Plunge, rode the merry-g-round or Big Dipper and laughed at our distorted images in the trick mirrors of the fun house.

Sometimes Edna's brother-in-law took me flying in his Piper Cub, doing loop-de-loops above the patterned fields of San Jose. In the Twin Peaks neighborhood of San Francisco, Edna and I took our precious silk stockings to be invisibly darned – even in America there still were post-war shortages. We spent lazy afternoons at Fisherman's Wharf, stuffing ourselves with fresh crab and shrimp. It was there that I smoked my first cigarette and tasted my first sip of beer. Although Edna and I had never been close, we shared a common bond as exiles in a strange country.

She seemed happy then, in her new household, so different from Lillianfels. But after my grandmother's death, she began to change. Edna, the wild one, who had divorced a politician years before, who had had an abortion, became a vehement Jehovah's Witness. She told me that I had caused her mother's death, that my grandmother had died of a broken heart because I had left her. She told me I was selfish, something I had heard since I was six.

When she and Pete moved out of his parents' home and away from San Francisco, we lost contact but for an occasional card or note - little more than a formality.

School Revisited

My father had decided to send me to school. I was dismayed; I thought I was through with all of that. I don't know what I had expected to do with my new life; I hadn't thought about it; I had always let life happen to me. In January 1947 I enrolled at Pasadena City College as an art major and met my first friend in America: Mary, also an art student, six feet tall next to my five foot two. Classmates dubbed us Mutt and Jeff. We stayed friends until her death, even though our lives took different directions. Mary's widowed mother ran the Admissions office at the college; later, she and Mary were to play an important role in my life.

To my surprise, I enjoyed school. The curriculum, the teachers, the casual freedom bore no resemblance to my experience in Australia. I did moderately well in most classes although American Institutions stopped me in my tracks: in Australia I had studied little American history. At PCC it was a required course and I would never have graduated had not an understanding teacher given me a passing grade, which I didn't deserve. I remember sitting up late at the kitchen table, trying to cram dates and presidents and the US Constitution into my tired brain and seeing my father at the door, telling me to shut off the light, that I was wasting electricity.

Psychology 101 fascinated me. It was all new to me, my first small window into human behavior. Watercolor portraiture and fashion illustration excited me and my teachers encouraged me. I remember a particular portrait I painted of a fellow student, an attractive Black girl, which won an award. Later, newly married, I threw it away along with all my other paintings, believing I should put aside childish dreams and aspirations. I did not know who I was - I simply took on the roles that life offered me, discarding those that came before.

To avoid attention, I worked on losing my Australian accent. Some students guessed I was from Texas, some guessed Boston or the South. No one ever guessed Australia.

I blushed at easy compliments; I often felt they were insincere, my uncomfortable responses equally insincere. Easy flattery had not been part of my Australian experience where compliments were rare because they could go to your head.

I found the jocks and their cheerleaders baffling, unlike anyone I had known in Australia. I felt more comfortable with my fellow art students, many of whom were returning GI's. They were tolerant and good-natured toward the unworldly rest of us and they were all in love with a beautiful, likeable art teacher named Emmie Lou. Emmie Lou was married to a fighter pilot whose plane crashed while I was at PCC. Her graceful dignity as she continued to teach through this tragedy was not lost on us.

One GI nicknamed me Hashmark because I could never eat a hamburger without smearing my lipstick across my chin. Another took us joy riding now and then in his jalopy, at a time when few students had cars. I remember once being wedged into the jump seat with a gay friend named Jimmy as the car out-raced an oncoming train. It didn't occur to me that we might all have perished - the thrill of danger was new to me; risk was a heady experience. When a group of us went to the Long Beach Pike, I rode the roller coaster over and over and over again while Mary waited patiently below.

Every year, shortly after the Pasadena Rose Parade on New Year's Day, all Design students were assigned the challenge of designing floats for the following year. I was not good at this but the best students saw their sketches become reality on January first. I liked New Year's Eve best when, with dozens of fellow students, I spent the night in a vacuous, unheated metal building, attaching fresh flowers to float skeletons and gulping bitter hot coffee to stay warm.

Every day after school I worked at The Broadway Department store in Pasadena. I earned seventy-five cents an hour and cleared seventeen dollars a week, nine of which I gave to my stepmother for rent. With the rest, I paid for schoolbooks and supplies, bus and streetcar fare, green Jello fruit salad in the school cafeteria and anything else I needed. I rode the bus to school and returned home on the streetcar late at night after the buses had stopped running. I got off on the other side of the tracks - literally - and once I ran all the way to the house with an aging derelict Black man on my heels. I told my father but I continued to walk home alone late every night. I felt no thrill of danger then.

One of my classmates was a blind boy who had suddenly lost his sight at age fifteen when a baseball struck him in the head as he was at bat. He was smart and likeable and did not seem embittered by his misfortune. We became friends – nothing more – but I think my father and stepmother felt this friendship should be discouraged. My stepmother arranged a date for me with a neighbor's son. Jack was tall and thin and wore horn-rimmed spectacles that gave him a scholarly appearance. I thought him far too polite to adults; I did not like him. But I succumbed to parental pressure and went out with him once. Parked outside my house that night, I had to fight my way out of his car. It was my first encounter with unwelcome male persistence. Even if I had found him attractive, my grandmother had taught me that a young lady's purity must be preserved at all costs.

Then I had a crush on a boy with a beautiful black Buick convertible. David was good looking and worldly and obviously had no romantic interest in me - he treated me more like a kid sister. When we went cruising in his elegant car, its top open to the California sunshine, I was breathless with the glamour of it all. He took me home to meet his Danish family, blonde, blue-eyed, unlike David. I had never thought about it: David's skin was light olive, his sandy-brown hair curly and close cropped. My father told me he did not want David coming around anymore, that David was a Negro.

Sometimes, however, my father made decisions that were in my best interest, like the time I wanted to spend Easter week on Balboa Island with a school club. I just thought how wonderful it would be to have a week at the beach. Of course, my father said no.

Later, when I heard of the malicious mischief that eventually led local authorities to ban Bal Week, I was glad he had.

Getting Away

At the end of my first year at PCC I found a summer job as nanny for a little girl whose wealthy parents summered regularly on Balboa Peninsula Point. This took me away from the suffocating inland summers when public swimming pools in local parks were clogged with bodies trying to keep cool. Every summer, in an era of iron lungs and leg braces, the threat of polio was on every parent's mind. The world had yet to hear of Dr. Jonas Salk. My friend Mary had polio when she was fifteen but suffered no apparent disability until years later when she developed symptoms of post-polio syndrome.

That summer at the beach provided me with an escape from the increasing difficulty of living at home. While I was on duty twenty-four hours a day and was responsible for all my young charge's needs, I managed and I was happy. At night I could climb through my bedroom window directly onto the sand and hear the ocean crashing nearby. Each day I took my young charge to the quieter bayside where she could paddle safely.

At the bay I met four girls my age from wealthy families who owned waterfront summer homes on the peninsula. We spent hours talking and perfecting our tans. Sometimes when I had an evening off, we all walked to the Pavilion where, frozen bananas in hand, we took in the razzle-dazzle of the bustling Fun Zone and watched the colorful splash of sightseers spill from the little ferries. Sometimes we danced to Stan Kenton at the Rendezvous Ballroom, reminding me of the community dances I went to in Double Bay. Sometimes we sailed across the bay in little snowbirds or Lido 14's. Growing up in Sydney, I was a water baby; I rode the harbor ferries often but I had never sailed. Away from parental authority, I was heady with new experiences.

With the end of summer came my return to Monrovia. I resumed school and my job at the Broadway. I formed new friendships and deepened old ones, and immersed myself in my art studies. Life at home had not eased much but my expanding life outside made it more bearable. At school, I found I was liked. I began to gain more confidence. Perhaps by then, I had succeeded in blending in - I wore bobby sox and saddle shoes, Peter Pan collars under lambs' wool sweaters, and straight long skirts that hobbled my footsteps. I was aware that lambs' wool sweaters represented a lower social status than cashmere but I did not care. I was invited by a girl I admired to join her prestigious sorority and I declined. I knew instinctively that I would not fit in, that I was not a joiner. I recognized an element of snobbery in these clubs: I saw that certain girls were excluded because they were not pretty enough or lived in the wrong neighborhood. I think I was invited because I was different, an oddity from an unfamiliar world. A beautiful dark-haired girl named Lorraine was not rushed because another girl had spread a rumor that she was part Negro. Racism still prevailed, even among the young.

I returned to Balboa Peninsula the following summer to baby-sit once again for the same family. My stepmother never objected to my summer escapes: most likely she was relieved to have me out of the house. I was reunited with the same girls of the previous year, all home from their prestigious private schools. That summer drifted pleasantly on, much the same as the one before.

Halfway through that summer, two boys rowed across the bay from Balboa Island and joined our little group. They told us they were staying on the island for a month. One was talkative, the other one very quiet. I was drawn to him because he seemed so shy. He said his name was Fred Harris, that he attended Cal State Long Beach and was on the basketball team there. He said his father was in the oil business in Long Beach. Every day from then on Fred and his companion rowed across the bay to our beach. After three weeks Fred Harris invited me to a movie.

He picked me up in a big blue Buick sedan and took me to a drive-in movie, which I had not expected. When he pulled a six-pack of beer from under the back seat, I said nothing, but when he opened a second bottle, I asked him to take me home. He cursed at me but after a few moments we left the theater. But instead of taking me home, he turned south on coast highway and picked up speed. As we took the curve at Emerald Bay I saw that the speedometer needle was well into the red. I kept begging him to slow down, to turn around, to take me home, but he kept driving fast in the wrong direction, swearing at me. Somewhere near Laguna Beach he turned off the highway and drove high into the hills. I think we might have parked at what is now known as Top of the World, when it was a scrubby, barren plateau, long before anyone lived there. I remember looking back at the lighted string of matchbox cars far below on coast highway. When he stopped the car, I tried to open the door and realized with a shock that there was no door handle. He told me the car was rigged, that I could only get out when he wanted me out. I don't know where I thought I would run once out of the car; beyond it there was only the endless empty black of the night.

We struggled, I fought. I somehow ended up halfway beneath the steering wheel, trying to kick off the weight of his body. When his hands encircled my throat, I knew I was fighting for more than my virginity.

My mind went suddenly dead calm. I willed myself to go limp; I pretended to pass out, which actually was a very real possibility. He relaxed his grip on my throat and in that moment, I clawed his face as hard as I could.

I will never understand, as long as I live, why he stopped his assault then. He put a hand to his face, scored by my nails from eye to chin, shoved me toward the passenger seat and turned the key in the ignition.

He drove back up the highway to Balboa Peninsula, flinging insults, cursing, telling me that I thought I was a princess, I thought I was too good for him. He kept up this tirade all the way to the alley behind my employers' oceanfront house where, without completely stopping, he opened my door from some unseen control and pushed me out onto the pavement. As he sped off, I picked myself up and stumbled into the house. I had no idea how much time had passed. My employers were waiting up for me. They took one look at me and called the police.

An officer took a report and asked me to come to the station the next day. By the time I got there they had checked the apartment Fred and his friend had rented. Although I had not been there, I knew from Fred's description which building it was, close to the ferry. The police found it vacated and no sign of the blue Buick. I had never noticed a license plate let alone recorded the number. The police also told me they had checked out Fred Harris - student, star basketball player at Cal State Long Beach, whose father worked in the oil business. There was no record of any such person. Because he apparently had woven a network of lies, the police believed that he was psychotic and had set out to target a potential victim. They were certain that he would attack other women. They asked me to testify against him once they caught him and I said I would.

They asked me for my home address and I begged them not to contact me there, not to let my father and stepmother know what had happened. Because I was already eighteen, they agreed and I told them they could reach me at my employers' Pasadena address. I never heard from the police again.

For a full month after the attack I was afraid to stay at the house alone. I was even afraid to be in a room alone when others were in the house. I kept my bedroom window-on-the-beach locked at all times and when I had to leave the house with my small charge, I watched nervously for blue Buicks. For weeks, ten blue-brown prints on my throat recorded my ordeal. One late afternoon at the end of summer I walked alone to the Pavilion on an errand for my employers. An old drunk staggered from a bar and grabbed at me. As I began to run panicked back toward the house, a car full of boys, seeing what was happening, pulled up alongside and offered to take me home.

Fear overcame reason and I climbed into the car then quickly realized these boys were looking for some fun. But when they saw how frightened I was they drove me straight home. It was the nearest I ever came to hitchhiking.

The thought later struck me that I had no opinions of my own. Without opinions, how could I make wise decisions? I wondered how one formed opinions. Would better judgement come with time?

Summer was drawing to a close and I would have to go back to the smothering inland heat. I longed to take one last swim in the surf but conditions were dangerous - red flag warnings were posted. I couldn't resist dipping my feet into the boiling shallows, not intending to venture further and the next thing I knew I was being sucked into deeper water. I did everything wrong: I tried to swim against the current only to distance myself further from the shore. At some point I found myself tumbling breathless inside a white cauldron, not knowing up from down until I thumped violently on the rough sandy bottom. When a towering wave tossed me onto the beach, I lay there, gasping and grateful, only to be dragged back in by another wave. A lifeguard spotted me then and ran into the water. When he couldn't reach me, he left, apparently to seek more help. I thought I would drown. But another wave flung me onto the beach and this time I clawed my way up the sand cliff carved by the pounding surf, to helping hands.

I had been in the ocean for almost an hour. At some point my employers had walked down the beach to remind me of the time; I was supposed to have been home much earlier. Not realizing the trouble I was in, they kept waving at me, motioning me to get out of the water and when I didn't, they left.

At summer's end we parted amicably. They had introduced me to another family whose two little boys I cared for briefly in Pasadena before returning to Monrovia.

While I missed the beach, I was happy to be back at PCC among familiar faces, focusing on my art, being involved with school activities. Once again, I worked after school at The Broadway. I had a brief crush on a redheaded boy named Ladd who regarded me with kind indifference; when I think of that old song Whispering, I think of Ladd. But then songs often trigger old associations although I don't recall a song for the Ohio State football player, in town to play in the Rose Bowl, whom I met at a school gathering. He was short and thick and really didn't appeal to me but he was attentive. When my stepmother and father interrogated me about him, I indulged in a rebellious teenage moment and told them I might just marry him – the last thing I wanted to do. They were properly exasperated.

In 1949 my fellow students chose me to represent the art department in a contest for queen of a carnival organized by the Order of the Mast and Dagger, an honorary men's service club on campus. I did not volunteer for this, in fact I was reluctant; I felt exposed and uncomfortable. But each of the five candidates was selected by popular vote and I could see no graceful way to decline. Our larger-than-life photographs were hung in the main lobby of PCC and votes were cast.

On the day of the carnival I went to work after school as usual, a newly sprouted fever blister on my lip. I was nervous, not because I wanted to win, but because I dreaded standing on a stage, facing public scrutiny. That night, in my strapless navy and white Swiss organdy dress, I was proclaimed queen. Among my four princesses were Lorraine, the dark-haired girl I liked, and Priscilla, who had spread the Negro rumor about her. I had hoped that Lorraine would win. Three of my four princesses seemed pleased for me; Priscilla was not; she continued to pout throughout the evening. My father and stepmother were there. Afterwards, below the stage, my stepmother whispered, They picked you because they felt sorry for you. In my heart, I felt she was right.

Why should that memory have held so much power when, on opening my 1949 yearbook for the first time in over fifty years, I found so many affectionate, congratulatory notes from my fellow students, boys and girls alike? How could I have forgotten that my fellow students had selected me as president of the Art Council and vice-president of Zeta Gamma Phi, the honorary art service club?

The scrawled offerings of my three forgotten PCC yearbooks reveal much about who I was at any given time. Yet those yearbooks tell much more, of events larger than my own life. In 1949 it snowed in Pasadena - a rare and exhilarating occurrence. Even the school administrators took time out to throw snowballs. But I will remember 1949 forever as the year that a very popular boy named George was crushed to death by a stock elevator at his after-school workplace. At his funeral - the first I had ever attended - the church and sidewalks overflowed with grieving students. For someone like George to die so young, in such a terrible way, made no sense to me. I began to explore different religions, drifting from one church to another and finding no answers.

I spent one last full summer at the beach, caring for the two little boys from Pasadena. At summer's end, while their parents were off partying, I threw a small impromptu party of my own and allowed my friends free access to my employers' generous liquor supply. I didn't discourage them; I suppose I didn't want to be the spoilsport. Fortunately, everyone lived within walking distance and no one lost control. My employers, regular drinkers themselves, were amused and at the close of summer, I stayed on for a while at their Pasadena home. During that time, a boy I knew only casually from PCC brought a friend to meet the sweet, shy Australian girl he remembered. They arrived on their motorcycles - few students could afford cars then - when motorcycles were considered square. Summers spent among the easy rich with their convertibles and sailboats, exclusive clubs and endless parties had given me a misplaced confidence. Perhaps I was becoming one of those girls I disliked – a snob. I will never forget the disappointment on that boy's face and his embarrassment in front of his friend for my flippant behavior, for being so wrong about me. To this day I wish I could apologize to him, but I don't even remember his name.

Out of the Blue

I returned to Monrovia once again. On day, as I stood beneath the old oak tree in our front yard, I heard the sputtering of an engine and looked up to see a small plane spinning out of the sky. I ran toward the terrible sound of the impact and was one of the first to find a small crumpled mass nose down in the street. There were no flames. I approached the front cockpit and saw that the pilot was dead. I had never known before that severe impact can force the eyeballs from their sockets. A woman in the rear cockpit was unconscious but when the ambulance arrived moments later, there was little the medics could do. To my right a man stood silently with his arm around his fifteen year-old daughter. Suddenly the girl howled in anguish – she had suddenly realized it was her mother who lay dying in the rear cockpit.

The Future

When I graduated, I told my father that my teachers had encouraged me to apply to Chouinard Art Institute in Los Angeles, the place to go in those days to prepare for a fashion design and illustration career. Edith Head had studied there before she moved on to Paris. n a way I had been preparing for this all my life – I can see it in my childhood fashion sketches. I admired the elegant fluid style of Eric whose fashion art dominated fine magazines during the forties and fifties. For once I saw my direction clearly.

My father said, No, girls learn to type and get married; artists live in attics and starve. There was no arguing. I suspect now that the money was not there for my advanced education and I had not yet learned to be resourceful: I had no knowledge then of how to apply for a scholarship or financial aid or even if they existed. And had I known, I might not have qualified because I was an alien, in America on a temporary visa.

I began to suspect then that my father valued education for boys more than for girls, that he believed a woman's place was in the home. I think he was not alone; to many people then, advanced education for a girl seemed a waste of money unless college might provide an opportunity for her to find a suitable husband. A woman still unmarried at twenty-two often was viewed with suspicion as was a married woman still childless a year or two after her wedding vows. What was wrong with her?

Resigned and disappointed, I found a so-called advertising job at J.C. Penney. In reality I sat alone at a big table in the windowless basement of the Pasadena store, clipping glossy black and white sketches of beds, shoes, pots and pans from an enormous heavy book, then pasting them onto pages the size of the local newspaper. Heating

pipes and vents hovered above me; boxes, crates, packing materials and merchandise surrounded me. The job paid very little and it was pure drudgery but I did not think of quitting. Nor did I think about the future - the future would simply happen to me, as it always had.
Life was no better at home. The breaking point came one morning when my stepmother noticed I had placed a first class stamp on a postcard. She called me wasteful. As usual I did not reply, wanting only to flee from confrontation. In an obvious attempt to diffuse the situation, my father asked me some casual, irrelevant question. Before I could answer, my stepmother said, Why are you asking that stupid girl anything? She is stupid, stupid. With that she turned to her little sons who were eating breakfast at the kitchen table and began to conduct a singsong, inviting them to join in - Judith is stupid! Judith is stupid! Isn't she, boys? Sometimes I wonder if my two older brothers have any recollection of this.

I said nothing. I went to work as usual and called Mary and asked her if I could spend the night. Then I called my father, taking care to keep my voice neutral, not wanting to raise the issue of the unpleasant scene earlier. I told him that Mary had invited me to stay overnight. Immediately he shouted, If you don't come home tonight you needn't come home at all! I knew then that he felt guilty- my stepmother's spiteful attack was indefensible yet he had not defended me. I saw that the tension that had prevailed since my arrival was too much for him. My presence caused conflict within his marriage and within himself. I think he really tried to do the right thing but it was beyond him. He must have felt overwhelmed and helpless, feelings perhaps alien to him.

I stayed with Mary and her mother for ten days. Then, one afternoon as I worked on a deadline in Penney's basement, my stepmother called. She quietly told me, If you are not home by six o'clock tonight, we will call D.L. (a business acquaintance of my father) and have him cancel the ten thousand dollar good-behavior bond he put up for you when you came to America. Since I had entered the country on a temporary visa, cancellation of this bond would mean immediate deportation, or so I thought. Perhaps, since my father was not an American citizen and therefore not eligible to act as my sponsor, D.L. had agreed to support this affidavit. Now it seemed in jeopardy.

I felt confused. I felt I had no choice but to return home that night. I had no money for a plane ticket, my home in Sydney as I had known it no longer existed. To complicate matters, I realized I was beginning to adjust to my new life in America – beyond the walls of the house in Monrovia - and wondered if leaving it after almost four years might even invite the nightmare of homesickness again. For I had become a different person, I was now part American, simply by virtue of living in America. I was torn, I felt as though I had one foot inside each country, a feeling that has never quite left me. Staying in America seemed the easiest avenue to take, for I would not need to face the uncertainty of change again.

That evening, I reluctantly gathered my belongings from Mary's house and returned to Monrovia. Nothing more was mentioned of the good behavior bond.

Shortly afterwards, my stepmother received devastating news: her sister, a doctor in her thirties, had died suddenly of a heart attack. I heard my stepmother tell my father that she would never forgive him if her parents died before she returned to Australia to live. I didn't blame her. Shortly afterwards they began to make plans to leave America and made no mention of including me, not that I wanted to continue to live with them anywhere. I knew I would miss my little brothers but thought that somehow I would see them again soon. I had no idea as to where, when and how; as usual, I would just let life unfold.

They left the month I turned twenty-one, when my youngest brother was six months old. For my birthday, I bought myself a simple gray corduroy dress with my employee discount. Even then, as we were about to part, my stepmother told me what a selfish girl I was, thinking only of myself, spending money foolishly. Her words stung but I said nothing. Years later my friend Ruth reminded me that when I called my stepmother years later as she lay dying, she admonished me for wasting my money on an overseas call. How sad, I thought, to pick over money at the end of life.

Mary had persuaded her mother to take me in. I packed my old trunk with my clothes and a few personal belongings; it never occurred to me to worry that I had so few worldly possessions. My father drove me to Mary's house in Pasadena and as we parked outside, he said, Be careful. When I asked him what he meant, he replied that my stepmother had told him about all the boys I had been with. I don't know why I was surprised. Still, this was an especially blatant lie. I tried to defend myself but I saw that my father was uncomfortable. I knew he would not believe me no matter what I said, for if he believed me, he would have to face up to the possibility that my stepmother had lied about me and not, perhaps, for the first time.

He pulled out his wallet, handed me a twenty-dollar bill and drove away. I did not see him again for about three years. By then I was married.

The House on Rose Villa

Mary's mother was widowed; Mary was ten when her father, a university professor, died suddenly. Mrs. E, as she was known, ran the admissions office of PCC and rented rooms in her home to students. A married couple and a quiet, serious girl from the desert lived upstairs. Mrs. E and Mary's older sister Margaret, a librarian who was crazy about baseball, had rooms downstairs. Nearby, Mary and I shared her room. I was neat, Mary was not, but we got along. We enthusiastically painted her room gray with one dark green wall, punctuated with cretonne curtains, which Mary had sewn, in a big tropical watermelon and lime print. A bamboo bucket chair held a matching cushion. We were very aware of being in style.

Mrs. E was an intelligent, down-to-earth Midwest woman, not given to outward expression of emotion, yet fair and perceptive. You always knew where you stood with Mrs. E. She told me she found me easy to have around because I was cheerful and helpful, I ate everything she cooked and I did not complain. I valued this new perspective of me.

In the dining room we all played canasta into the small hours. In the sunny breakfast room off the kitchen Mary encouraged me to sew. In Sydney, my gentle Aunt Phyllis had made all my dresses on a treadle machine but I had never learned, beyond hand-stitching fine French seams on useless lawn petticoats in Home Science School.

The house was big enough to accommodate individual needs and life was agreeable. Sometimes Mary's brother and his wife joined us. Every New Year Mary's eldest sister drove from Utah with her husband and numerous children. On New Years Eve, all the children camped overnight on Colorado Boulevard, huddled in piles of blankets and pillows, safe in the complacency of those days. At eight o'clock New Year's morning, the adults strolled the few blocks from the house on Rose Villa to Colorado Boulevard and watched the Rose Parade from the front row. No matter how threatening the weather may have been earlier, January 1st invariably dawned crystal clear and crisp over the snow-dusted San Gabriel Mountains. After the parade we gathered around Mrs. E's tiny black and white television to watch football in the Rose Bowl. Later we drove to the end of the parade route to admire the floats up close. There was always an abundance of good food and good company at the house on Rose Villa. For years afterwards, on New Years Day, I took my own children there, leaving home well before dawn to make the long drive up from the beach where we now lived. It became a tradition for many years until Mrs. E died and the house on Rose Villa sold. By then, life had changed; life had changed us all.

Fate

I had been living at Mary's house for a few months when one day, just as we all were leaving to hike into the Sierra Madre foothills, the telephone rang. It was an old school acquaintance of the married couple. He was going through a divorce from his first wife; he had called because he was depressed and lonely. They invited him to join us.

There was something familiar about him, something elusive and vaguely disturbing. Years later I realized he reminded me of Lillian: set jaw, tight lips, steel eyes. I did not particularly like him but I was drawn to him as to the edge of a precipice.

Donald managed a drive-in theater. Born in Los Angeles, he was an only child, almost four years older than I was. His parents lived nearby but he did not get along with his father. He attended PCC before I went there but had not graduated. He had served in the Coast Guard for a while and had been unable to find a good job since. He volunteered with a Boy Scout troop sponsored by the local sheriff's department.

Before long, he was frequenting the house, joining the group there and, in a way, courting me. He worked nights, I worked days, so we began to meet around midnight.

We would go to some cheap all-night drive-in for a hamburger or just drive around in his old Ford coupe. Sometimes we parked and talked. He said his wife had treated him badly. He complained that she had taunted him in lacy black underwear when she knew he had to go to work! Their marriage had endured less than six months. He slept in the theater because he could not afford rent.

I felt needed because he shared his misery with me. I listened, I empathized with the misunderstood victim in him. He was a large man with a softly undefined body, well over six feet tall. I perceived his size as strength. I saw a man who would take care of me, protect me, understand me, cherish me and make wise decisions for both of us. At last someone wanted me. He called me Mouse, which I thought endearing. I was compliant and agreeable because I wanted to please; to displease meant silent disapproval, which I could not bear. Worse still was to suffer a muttering retreat out the door. Having no strong sense of myself, I was whatever I thought was expected of me. I was easily manipulated and did not know it. I surrendered my virginity and was startled to realize that a lifelong lack of sexual education had allowed me pleasure, for I held no preconceived notions and therefore, no inhibitions. I mistook all these things for love.

Lack of sleep caught up with me and I fell ill. Because I suffered blinding pain in one eye, my baffled general physician sent me to an ophthalmologist who prodded my eyes and only intensified my suffering. Eventually a third doctor diagnosed me correctly with mononucleosis and told me that I was one for the textbooks because my symptoms were not typical. I was flat on my back for two weeks, in and out of involuntary sleep, temporarily paralyzed. Mary and the others watched over me; Donald visited often. I lost weight, and because I was unable to work for several months, I also lost my job at Penney's. During that time Mrs. E never pressed me for rent.

In the meantime, Donald found work as a technician at the Jet Propulsion Lab in Pasadena. We became informally engaged. Informal, because there was no ring, no announcement, no lavish wedding plans. I did not care about these things; I was in love. We set a date but had to postpone when finalization of his divorce was delayed, intensifying my own insecurities. Our relationship was often dramatic, which I saw as romantic, lacking lightness and laughter. To me, marriage was a serious matter and it was forever; no one in my large family had ever been divorced except for my cousin Linda, whose unusual circumstances had justified it, and my Aunt Edna, married briefly to a politician years ago.

The System

Every six months since my arrival in America, I had dutifully renewed my temporary visa until the day I received a notice in the mail from US Immigration, informing me that I could no longer continue to extend my stay. Deportation proceedings had begun. I could apply for American citizenship but there was no guarantee it would be granted. Although I did not want to renounce my Australian citizenship, I had no choice if I wanted to marry Donald. Marriage alone did not protect me from deportation or grant me automatic American citizenship.

I set the naturalization process in motion and tentatively planned a new wedding date: December 1, 1951. Just one day before, I received notice that deportation proceedings against me had been suspended.

Once again, as with the death of my mother, one moment had changed the course of my life. Had I been deported, had I returned to Australia, I would have become a different woman, living a different life. But on December 1st, 1951, eleven months after Donald and I first met, a minister we did not know married us in Mrs. E 's dining room. Only his parents and a few of my friends were present. Donald joked about the advantage of having in-laws so far away.

As I descended the stairs of the house on Rose Villa, the sounds of a baseball game from Margaret's bedroom radio intermingled with the strains of the wedding march from a borrowed vinyl record. I wore a simple gray suit and a white velvet hat. Afterwards, in a blinding rainstorm, we drove to Laguna Beach for a brief honeymoon at a motel that still exists. As I climbed from the car, my lovely white velvet hat fell into an oily rain puddle and for a fleeting moment, it felt like an omen. When we returned home three days later to a tiny apartment in South Pasadena, we learned that Donald's check to the minister who had married us had bounced. Years later Mary told me that her mother had been very worried that I was marrying Donald although Mrs. E never said anything to me; by nature she was not an interfering woman. I doubt I would have listened anyway. I wonder if she felt similar concerns for Mary whose husband eventually went to prison for sexual offenses, toward his own children and those of others. He and Donald seemed to recognize something in one another and the four of us often double-dated, although I always found the man sinister.

I didn't understand then what my grandmother had meant when she said, A man might be judged by the company he keeps. Donald never had true friends; sometimes he brought someone home from the scout troop but they all seemed odd somehow and I was uncomfortable around them. He had a few buddies from the sheriff's department who seemed to share his cynical attitude toward the public, but never a close confidante. He fenced verbally with jokes; I think he feared emotional intimacy.

A Step Up

I found a new job at Bullocks Pasadena, titled Junior Interior Decorator, assistant to Ruth, a young Jewish woman from Philadelphia who was to become a lifelong friend. Reflecting back on my earlier jobs, I can't remember if I ever applied for a work permit or if it ever occurred to me that as an alien I might require one. Now, at least, I was legal. I officially became an American citizen on April 24, 1953.

I earned basic wages at Bullocks, where most employees were required to wear dark, dignified clothing and to stand at all times. I felt sorry for those aging women behind the hosiery counter, furtively perched on small stools sneaked from the stockroom to rest their swollen ankles, ever alert for sharp-eyed managers.

Employees were required to attend periodic meetings, which were usually held before regular store hours, without compensation. I recall one meeting that addressed Social Security. As I entered the room I realized that no men were present. Social security turned out to be a lecture on the propriety of wearing a latex girdle. Even baby powder didn't ease the body-wrenching contortions required to tug the thing on and off every workday.

Despite all the rules, life amid the furniture was less rigid than in other departments although I quickly became intolerant of demanding customers who expected decorators to make free house calls for lampshade advice. I preferred setting up model rooms to selling, where I could indulge my stifled creativity by choosing pieces and colors that pleased me. Ruth and I used any excuse to drive into the Robertson/La Cienega district of Los Angeles where the showrooms of top designers were located, filled with stunning fabrics and furnishings not available to the general public.

Tree House

We had found an odd little shack, a house of cards, part of the attic of an old home, cradled in the branches of an ancient oak tree in South Pasadena. Rickety wood steps clambered through a leafy tangle to a door, which opened to a small, bright room. A twin bed hugged one plywood wall; opposite was a makeshift counter/kitchen with a single hot plate and tiny refrigerator, almost reachable from the bed. Donald's taste seemed limited to corn flakes, hamburger patties and mashed potatoes, so cooking in these conditions required little effort. Two steps led up to a simple bathroom with a primitive shower that often ran out of hot water. A clothes rod in the dark heat of the attic beyond served as a closet. I remember red linoleum and grass matting and my delight in waking up each morning in a sunny tree house, my new husband beside me. I thought it was romantic. It did not take long before rotting wood and peeling paint lost their appeal but we stayed because it was cheap.

We had lived in the tree house seven months when I awoke screaming one morning before dawn, not knowing why, until I realized our house of cards was swaying back and forth. Fourteen people died in the 7.7 Tehachapi earthquake, fifty miles north of Los Angeles, on July 21st, 1952. When I went to work at Bullocks that morning, almost everything that had been hanging on the walls had fallen to the floor. I had never experienced an earthquake before. This one prompted us to move to a bland one-bedroom apartment in Altadena at the foot of Mount Wilson in the San Gabriel Mountain range.

Most of the time, the mountain was veiled by pollution, but when the hot Santa Ana winds roared through the canyons, it suddenly emerged, looming. Sometimes the heat was so oppressive, we slept naked beneath a fan, windows wide, abandoning modesty. Our only escape came on occasional weekends when we drove down Beach Boulevard to the ocean and Balboa Peninsula beyond, where we huddled in sleeping bags on the cool patio of the house where I had cared for two little boys earlier. We watched the children as their parents played. It was an agreeable trade.

Our first Christmas had fallen only a few weeks after our wedding and I spent my meager Bullocks paycheck recklessly on gifts for Donald. My astute friend Ruth cautioned me to be practical but a Bullocks credit card, my employee discount and blind faith in my new husband's earning potential emboldened me. Actually, Donald made little more than I, even at a time when men earned more than women simply because they were men, a reality that continued to affect me for much of my working life in male-dominated workplaces.

Through these early extravagances I learned that living beyond one's means brought misery although this realization required several unhappy lessons. I learned to hate our white wool Scandinavian sofa when the payments came due. The thrill of a nearly new black Ford convertible with white top and red leather seats faded quickly with threatening late-night calls from the Los Angeles used car dealer. While I lay awake at night, worried to the point of panic, Donald seemed unperturbed. Whenever I raised the issue, he became irritable and I backed off. Certainly, we never worked out a budget together or discussed possible solutions to our financial woes let alone our financial future.

Still, I never regretted the very first purchase I made for our home: two dramatic watercolor prints by John Sessions, one of a perilously tilting deck of a sailboat in a ferocious storm, the other a tranquil scene of a small rowboat beneath a looming rusted hull at dock. I had them framed at Bullocks in rough linen and wormy chestnut and felt pleasure each time I passed the wall where they hung.

I had no money sense. In fact, my grandmother had knowingly shielded me from all financial concerns. When I came to America at seventeen, I had no idea how much a car, for instance, might cost: one hundred dollars? One thousand? On my way to school on the bus or streetcar, I was struck by the casual way my fellow passengers spoke of the cost of things. It seemed to me that Americans were obsessed with money, whereas I had been raised to believe that money was a private matter, best left to men. I suppose my grandmother had expected me to marry well.

I never drove the convertible. Donald did not want me out on the road, he did not want anything to happen to me, because he loved me. This was flattering at first but soon I began to realize that there were many things I could not do because Donald loved me.

Once my hairdresser cut my hair too short, leaving me in tears, for I felt I looked so unfeminine. Donald went to the man's shop and threatened him with a loaded 38 Smith and Wesson revolver. Apparently the incident went unreported for we never heard from the police, but I had to find a new hairdresser. I began to learn that some experiences were best not shared with Donald, for, in the name of love, he would pursue conflict on my behalf. He considered me incapable of standing up for myself and he may have been right. For a while his loving protection seemed admirable until I began to recognize it as a form of control. He told me quite seriously once that I was his possession, since he had paid two dollars for a marriage certificate. In time, I came to understand that to some, a marriage certificate is a license for ownership, to be renewed with each successive union, should earlier ones fail.

In Laws

Sometimes we visited Donald's parents who lived within walking distance of our apartment but the tension between Donald and his father overshadowed these visits, as Donald's mother, Anita, and I attempted to a appease both men. While Donald's parents appeared to live well, it was Anita's father who supported them. Donald's father was hopelessly alcoholic and had never worked a full day in his life. He was the most depressed – and depressing - individual I have ever met. He was completely devoid of humor, toward himself and others. Even in a simple card game, he pondered each move grimly at length as though his life depended on it. Always, hatred between father and son hung like a poisonous fog in the room.

Anita's tyrannical German father (whose middle name was Adolph!), dominated every aspect of her life and frequently reminded her that she should have been a boy. I don't think he ever forgave his wife Laura for this transgression, nor did they have more children.

Anita told me once that she had been in love with a man whom her father forbade her to marry. Although she did not love Donald's father, she agreed to marry him because her father approved of him (he was English and well read) and because she thought their mutual love of books might be enough to hold them together.

When we had known one another many years, she confided that she and her husband had lived as brother and sister throughout their marriage and slept in separate bedrooms. Her son had been somewhat of a miracle and she spent her life catering to his every whim, appeasing, soothing, overlooking, rationalizing and forgiving. But I sensed she found practical parenting difficult. Rather, she expressed her maternal affection through sentimentality: Donald's gilded baby shoes graced the mantle alongside dozens of baby photographs and a satin-bound baby book; baby clothes were lovingly preserved. It was as though she needed to prove her love with material objects, perhaps even to herself. I think she was afraid of her son, or at least of his displeasure, and this we had in common.

Sometimes Anita would lift her skirt and dance a little jig and say, I'm just a little girl at heart! At the time I found this embarrassing but later I realized she tried very hard to put on a cheerful face.

The Visit

When Donald and I had been married about two years, my father called. I had not spoken to him for nearly three years, although I had written dutiful letters to him and my stepmother regularly.

It was three o'clock in the morning. He announced he was at the Constance Hotel in Pasadena and why weren't we up? Donald was annoyed and I didn't blame him but I tried to pacify him because I feared conflict at their first meeting. My father made infrequent business trips to America in the years following and always he turned up unannounced, keeping me off-guard. Perhaps these trips were valid, but I think he took every opportunity to visit America because he missed it greatly. I have since learned that life had not gone easily for him after he returned to Australia in 1950.

He invited us to breakfast at the hotel on the following Sunday. When we arrived, he was nowhere to be found. We waited in the lobby for over an hour as Donald seethed. I began to cry. From home, I called the hotel several times but he had not returned. I wondered if he might have been in an accident – I was in his car once as he sped down the wrong side of a busy divided street.

I called again around dinnertime and caught him in his room. When I asked why he had not met us, he said he had gone to his old church in Monrovia and had run into a business acquaintance there. I decided to have breakfast with Clive instead.

This blatant declaration of my worth was like a physical low. Still, I did not confront him, partly because I lacked the courage, partly because I did not want to fuel Donald's overprotective outrage on my behalf. And when my father asked me to buy several pieces of lingerie for my stepmother and her sisters, I relented. That week I spent my lunch hours selecting intimate wear from my father's list. I paid with my Bullock's credit card and my twenty-percent employee discount and had each item gift-wrapped.

Saturday, knowing he planned to leave the following day, I took them to the hotel. He was not in his room, so I left them at the desk. On Sunday morning, when my father still had not called, Donald and I went unannounced to his room, where he was entertaining four of our old Monrovia neighbors over fine Scotch. I introduced my husband to everyone, including my father. After a while, when I reminded him of the bill, he scanned the receipts and said, It couldn't be that much. He resisted paying me until the woman who had pointed out my stepmother's jealousy years earlier, began to tease my father about being cheap. The others playfully joined in until he relented and pulled a roll of bills from his pocket and asked if I had change. I don't think it ever occurred to him to suggest I buy something for myself for my efforts or even to thank me.

Having kept quiet in the room, Donald fumed all the way home, only adding to my misery. I was emotionally undone, feeling rejected and worthless. At work at Bullocks the next day, Ruth asked, Why do you care what your father thinks? Write him a letter and tell him how you feel once and for all.

That night I sat down and vented my feelings on paper. I recall how the letter began: Dear Father, why should I call you that? You have never been a father to me. I wrote that he treated me like an amoebae. I recall little else except that this letter sprang unedited from my hurt. I never intended to mail it. Two weeks later I -read it again, slipped it unaltered into an envelope and sent it off.

Weeks later an old friend of my father's turned up from Australia. She told me how much my letter had hurt my father and that he had sent her to talk to me. Judy was the colorful wife of Darcy of the foul mouth and offensive cigarette ash incident. I always thought of her as an amusing tart although I admired them both in a way, for their uninhibited brashness. Judy often insinuated that I was named after her for some reason I didn't understand, but I never believed it. I don't know what she might have reported back to my father, but he did not contact me himself and for the rest of his life, never mentioned my letter to me.

The Unexpected

When Donald and I had been married little more than two years I became pregnant, although we had not planned to have a child for another year. So much for diaphragms. I worried about money; Donald worried about loss of attention; he told me that he hated women who neglected their husbands when they had a kid. Morning sickness plagued me through most of my pregnancy; for a while I tolerated little more than unbuttered mashed potatoes and dry bread. In the hot summer, I walked in the early morning, before the sun became unbearable. It was a relief to enter the air-conditioned environment of Bullocks.

I wanted to continue working up to two weeks before my due date. But at about five months the personnel manager called me into her office and told me that in my condition it was best that I quit. I refused and was immediately removed from my position as interior decorator and shifted from one department to another, always behind the scenes, never in clear view of the public who might find my condition offensive. Each new assignment was more disagreeable than the last. Realizing the personnel manager's intent was to force me out, I became more determined to stay.

My most distressing assignment was in the gourmet food section where I stood in a windowless, unconditioned, narrow wedge of space behind the stock room, and hand-packed imported edibles of one kind or another. The air was stifling hot. The rich smell made me sick. Still, I would not give up.

Early in my seventh month I was summoned once again to personnel. I was told to quit or be fired. I was fired. When I was denied unemployment benefits, I appealed and a hearing date was set. There the personnel manager blatantly lied, claiming that I had come to her office in tears, admitting that I was ashamed to be seen in my condition. I was denied benefits. That was 1954; I'd like to think that now the outcome might be different, that women could continue to work as long as they were able, that society at large would be more tolerant. Certainly, I would fight harder for what I believe is right.

At home fulltime now, I continued to be the wife I thought I should be. I made no demands on my husband, I didn't complain or raise issues that concerned me. We never argued: I dreaded conflict and did all I could to avoid it. I simply acquiesced. Donald said he hated bitchy women and so I did everything to prove that I was not. When he made coarse sexist or racist jokes, I pretended to find them amusing. I never denied his requests to tickle his back as he watched Dragnet on our little black and white television; I knew if I got up, he would be irritated. I rationalized my marriage into an acceptable package: if I admitted I was unhappy, I would be. I couldn't be unhappy – I would soon have a child to care for. If I ever voiced my real feelings, I could no longer deny them. More than that: I did not even acknowledge my true feelings to myself, for I sensed at some level that to do so would open Pandora's box; I would have to face up to my weaknesses and failures and admit that I was living a lie. Little wonder my husband didn't understand me: I never allowed him to know me for fear he might find me lacking.

The Patriarch

Every year we were required to spend Thanksgiving and Christmas, as well as frequent Sundays, at Anita's parents' home in Beverly Hills, arriving early and leaving late.

Anita's father - Donald's grandfather - was well off, and used his money to hold his family hostage. His house was filled with expensive Oriental rugs and fine European furniture, although I found it dark and oppressive. On one wall hung an original oil painting of the family castle near Koblenz, among vineyards on the Mosel River. Although spotlighted, it too was dark and oppressive. At that time two elderly cousins lived there but during WW2 it had been taken over by Hitler. After the war, too expensive for the family to maintain, it became a winery, open to visitors. It was held in permanent trust for male descendants who could live there but could never sell. Anita had stayed there; she showed us photographs of its vast stone hall and said that it was bitterly cold.

I liked Donald's grandmother Laura. She stood less than five feet and despite her domineering husband, she did not lack spirit. I wonder if she knew that when Donald was a small boy, his grandfather would place some promised toy on the mantle, out of reach, and hours later tell Donald, I was going to give this to you if you had been good, but now you can't have it.

When I told the old man I was pregnant, he said, If it's a boy, I'll pay you one hundred dollars. I responded defensively: And what if it's a girl? He laughed but did not reply. Later, when we took five-week-old Katy to his home for our mandatory Christmas ritual, he handed me a sealed envelope, which contained a note written on plain white paper. It read, Better luck next time. There was no gift, not even a card.

Motherhood

After twenty-seven hours of labor, ten hours of which she stayed in limbo as though unwilling to enter this world, Katy was born on November 16th, 1954. I had requested mirrors in order to watch her birth but missed it as I slipped into an exhausted sleep, having briefly noted that she looked like Donald and his mother and was apparently healthy. Donald was not there because, in those days, fathers were not permitted in the delivery room.

I was badly torn and required multiple stitches. At home, because walking was painful, I crawled from room to room to care for my child and myself. People brought flowers and food but what I longed for most was a helping hand during the day and a few hours of uninterrupted sleep at night. I was too proud to ask; my close friends worked full time, had demanding husbands, problematic children or serious health issues. I suppose I presented a capable face to the world, for Mary told me years later that she had felt jealous of me because I always appeared so efficient and well groomed. Donald's mother, living nearby, did not offer help, although she thought Katy a dear little thing.

Katy was a restless infant with erratic sleep patterns. She rejected my breast and her pediatrician prescribed formula. Even then, when I held her, she stiffened and thrust out her tongue to reject the bottle. Irrationally, I wondered how I could manage her until she was old enough to leave home. My guilt was boundless. I could not please my husband or my child - whenever she cried, at any hour, Donald would tell me to shut that kid up. He did not offer to feed or change his daughter, or comfort her during the night. Every morning the cross-tempered spinster who lived above us knocked on our door to tell me, Your baby's been crying all night. As if I hadn't known it.

I fell into a deep depression but told no one. When Donald came home from work each evening, I forced cheerfulness. Since he hated women who let themselves go, I took care to keep up my appearance. Sadness kept me slim.

This charade came to an end one day when a casual acquaintance called and caught me sobbing. When I blurted out my misery, she laughed and told me that nothing was wrong with me except postnatal depression. I asked her what she meant. She described the symptoms and told me that it was quite common. Because I was so overwhelmed by guilt, I had sought no help for my symptoms and had fallen into a prolonged dark state.

Odd as it was, her amusement at my ignorance brought me great relief. I had finally unburdened myself - it hardly mattered to whom. When I saw my doctor again, I asked him why he had not warned me about postnatal depression. He replied that he had not wanted to put ideas into my head.

I have a photograph of Katy at four months lying on a pretty rose-sprigged comforter on our living room floor. She is alert and active as we wait for a friend who will drive us to her routine pediatric checkup.

The pediatrician notices fine blue veins on her delicate eyelids and tells me I need to take her to a neurologist immediately. He makes several calls, trying to line up a same-day consultation. Eventually he succeeds and within the hour, Katy is being examined by a neurosurgeon who looks more like a USC quarterback than a doctor. He is abrupt and, I feel, unnecessarily rough with Katy, then tells me to get her dressed and meet him in his office. There, with my friend by my side, he bluntly states that nothing can be done, that Katy will be retarded by age two.

I flee the office, numb, and ask my friend to drive us back to the pediatrician. He makes some more calls and we are on our way in the late afternoon sun to a second neurosurgeon. Gently, he explains that Katy has congenital hydrocephalus, a buildup of excess cerebrospinal fluid in the brain, present at birth. I wonder to myself if twenty-seven hours of labor could have caused this and what I could have, should have done sooner.

Early treatment by three or four months is important to prevent or limit brain damage. Methods have greatly improved since 1955. Nowadays a shunt would be inserted into the brain permanently or a surgical procedure performed in which a small hole is made to allow drainage.

Katy was already almost two weeks past four months. I had noticed, just after she was born, that her forehead seemed particularly high but her head was not abnormally large as is usually the case with congenital hydrocephalus. The neurosurgeon inserted a syringe into my daughter's tiny brain to extract fluid, without success. He took x-rays but they revealed nothing, although he told me that sometimes a tumor at the base of the skull could go undetected. The next step would be exploratory surgery, which he scheduled for the following day.

Early the next morning, because he still didn't allow me to drive, Donald drove me to the hospital himself. There, Katy's small body was wheeled into surgery as the doctor explained that she had a fifty-fifty chance of surviving and that there was a risk of brain damage. As the surgery doors closed behind the doctor, I turned to see Donald's back retreating down the hallway to the exit. He didn't look back.

As I sat and waited outside surgery, I was dead calm. This response to crisis has helped me through some traumatic situations, like the Fred Harris incident, but once the crisis is over, I find myself trembling.

Katy never had the exploratory surgery. Before cutting, the neurosurgeon made one final attempt to draw fluid from the brain, this time with a longer syringe. It produced a fountain. When she was wheeled out of surgery, her little head wore a bandage turban almost as tall as her body. I slept on a cot in her hospital room and checked her often to be sure she did not raise her head – it was essential she remain flat. Periodically a nurse changed her drenched bandage. A friend brought me the few personal items I needed, using the door key I had given her to enter the house while Donald was at work. In the three days I stayed at the hospital, I didn't see him. Nor did he call.

A photograph snapped by the neurosurgeon shows one-year-old Katy in my arms, recovered and apparently healthy. I was grateful that, temporarily at least, I was a stay-at-home mother, because she demanded all my energy.

Not long after Katy's ordeal Ruth left her job at Bullocks. She had acquired a snappy little MG roadster and a very spoiled poodle named Pierre. Ruth loved to drive, I had yet to learn, and I was hopelessly housebound. Soon the four of us could be seen tearing about town, MG top down, Pierre's ears flying, Katy snuggled in her bassinet in the back. I remember that we laughed a lot. I think that Ruth may have saved my sanity.

Before she was seventeen months old, Katy had disassembled her playpen, crib and the folding gate Donald's mother claimed had corralled him until he was almost four. In the time it took me to shower one day, Katy had climbed onto a chair and slipped the extra safety bolt we thought was too high on the door for her to reach. Hearing giggling, I looked out the bathroom window to see my daughter tripping along the street, very pleased with herself. I hastily wrapped myself in a bath robe and ran after her to the home of a very bewildered elderly lady who no doubt wondered where this small fair-haired child had come from. More than once, in a store, I turned to see that she had wriggled from her stroller harness and escaped. As a toddler, she slid from laps, resisting hugs. She was fearless, willful and bright and it seemed a miracle that she had beaten the odds of her birth.

Donald's Father

On one of the rare occasions that we visited Donald's parents, I turned from my conversation with Anita and Donald to see Donald's father across the room, kneeling near Katy, offering her something in his outstretched hand. Instinctively, I moved swiftly and saw that he held tiny shards of broken glass. I gathered up my child and made some excuse to leave. I do not remember if I told my husband about this. I doubt it, because telling might have led to violence. I never returned to that house again but as events would have it, there was little need to.

Shortly after this incident, a distressed Anita turned up at our apartment. Donald's father had tried to attack her with a kitchen knife and she had escaped through a window. She also told us that he had recently tried to push their car over a cliff while she was still in it. On both occasions, he was too drunk to succeed. I urged her to stay with us and call the police but she refused, unconvinced her life was in real danger. To my knowledge, Donald never confronted his father on his mother's behalf. It wasn't long before she filed for divorce, after thirty-six years of marriage. Her husband received a generous cash settlement, got drunk, bought an expensive car and awoke the next morning penniless, apparently the victim of theft. He rented a room not far from us and repeatedly asked us for money, which we did not have. He lived there to the end of his life, which came soon afterwards. One day I opened my door to a sheriff who told me that Donald's father was found shot dead and that they suspected murder, because heroin and drug paraphernalia were found in the room. But when they found a roughly scrawled note on a dirty scrap of paper, they realized his death was a suicide. The note read, To my son, I leave NOTHING! It was the man's final legacy of hate to his son.

My Father Returns

My father turned up again about this time, again unannounced. He made no mention of our last meeting, or my damning letter since. Conversation with my father was, for me, always superficial, about highways and buildings or the weather, peppered with his awful ethnic jokes about kikes, dagos, chinks, abos and the pope. Paradoxically, he attended church regularly and admonished those who did not. We danced around one another in an emotional standoff, avoiding intimacy at all costs. Yet one remark he made during that visit still, to me, seems remarkably perceptive. He asked, Does he treat you right? My father had recognized something in my relationship with Donald that I would fail to acknowledge for a long time. I remember that I answered brightly, and quite sincerely, Oh, yes! I had become skilled at the art of rationalization.

Sorrow and Comfort

One terrible day Anita called to say her parents had been in a serious accident. Her father already had several violations on his record and may have been driving with an expired license. Apparently he ran a stop sign and an oncoming car crushed the passenger side. Laura suffered head injuries and was not expected to live. When Donald and I saw her in the hospital, a tiny pale woman bruised and bandaged, she whispered, I'm going to outlive the old bastard.

She came home and lived to share another Christmas with us. I was sitting next to her on the sofa when her husband said, When Laura dies, I'm getting myself a younger woman. She died within the year, bedridden toward the end, as Anita nursed her. She did not outlive the old bastard but she tried. I felt perverse satisfaction later when he tearfully claimed he missed his wife. He died in 1961, a lonely old man.

Anita eventually remarried. Ed was a bachelor, a good man who had loved her in silence for years and could provide for her very well. She asked my advice; I responded, Do you love him? I did not understand then that a woman in her sixties might have a broader, more practical view of relationship than I. She outlived Ed but I think their years together were probably some of her happiest. She had waited a long time for affection, kindness and respect and I was glad for her.

The Beach

When Katy was seventeen months old, we moved to Balboa Peninsula Point, to a small, dim one-bedroom apartment of minimal charm. Donald now had a job at North American Aviation in Downy. It still was a long commute but at last we were at the beach, with its sights and sounds and smells I had so sorely missed. I could not have been happier.

Balboa Peninsula Point had changed little since my summers there a few years earlier. It was the ideal beach neighborhood then: friendly and safe, a healthy place for families. We lived in swimsuits, always ready for the ocean or the bay. For a while I lived an idyllic life. I bought my first bicycle from one of the girls of my summer escapes. Each morning I strapped Katy into her child's seat and peddled to the bakery, the library or the five-and-dime where I once saw June Alyson and her husband Dick Powell. He was friendly, she less so, possibly because she may have been embarrassed at being caught in pink plastic hair rollers. It was not unusual to run into movie stars in Newport: Rita Hayworth, Jeannie Crain, Buddy Ebsen, John Wayne, amongst others, all crossed my path. Once I collided with Rock Hudson in Richard's Lido Market; I hadn't realized how tall he was. Growing up, I had never been star-struck; to me, actors were the characters they played: Shirley Temple was Heidi, Elizabeth Taylor was a girl with a wonderful collie, like Prince, although I envied her beauty.

Katy and I spent much of our time at the bay, where I taught her to swim. Sometimes we walked to the little park near our apartment or to the broad ocean beach and the Wedge, known for its occasional mighty waves and adventurous surfers. Most of Balboa Peninsula Point is only two or three blocks wide and I delighted in the luxury of trying to decide each morning bay or ocean. At night I lay listening to the clang of the bell buoy near the entrance to the harbor, the forlorn moan of the foghorn or the barking of seals. I had good friends and neighbors and all of these things made my marriage more tolerable.

Donald and I still had never sat down together to work out a budget, so if his paycheck fell short of our expenses, it could only be because I mismanaged. He said, No wife of mine is going to work, and I make the money; it's up to you to handle it. Looking back, I believe Donald felt justified in his logic of all the responsibility, all the blame. If I managed things, it could only be my fault if things went wrong. This applied to everything in our marriage, from the upbringing of children to the cost of living.

Although we had medical insurance, it did not cover all our lingering medical expenses from Katy's ordeal or the cost of moving. Returning to the workplace was the last thing I wanted to do; I wanted only to be a mother and homemaker. But when we could no longer ignore our financial plight, Donald convinced someone at North American that I had qualifications as a technical illustrator, which was not really true. I had worked briefly part time after school at an engineering firm in Pasadena but my knowledge was limited.

I began my new job when Katy was 21 months old. I dreaded leaving my small child with strangers. I lay awake the night before, wishing unreasonably for an earthquake - not enough to hurt anyone, just enough to close the roads.

At North American Aviation, I sat with a hundred other people, mostly men, in a cavernous sort of aerodrome, all lined up on high stools at drafting tables with unfamiliar mechanical equipment. I had never seen a Leroy template and scribe before but I had to catch on quickly if I were to survive there.

Early each morning we drove an unhappy child, disturbed from her sleep, to the only nursery school - near North American - that accommodated working mothers at that hour. Guilt weighed on me for leaving my child all day; good mothers did not deposit their toddlers at nursery school; I felt I was wearing a scarlet letter. There, Katy contracted red measles although the women who ran the nursery school insisted it was German measles. At risk of losing my job, I stayed home with her, nursing her back to health through frightening convulsions. I was not paid for my time off. In a male dominated industry, maternal absenteeism was not well tolerated. Women knew better than to complain.

Chronic infections that followed made it necessary for Katy, not yet two, to have a tonsillectomy. Her health improved afterwards but I longed for us to somehow be able to stay home, to start her day in a swimsuit, ready for the bay, instead of the little starched cotton dresses the nursery school required and I spent hours ironing.

When the Navajo missile, mainstay of North American's defense program, was put on hold, a massive layoff – nine thousand workers in a single day from the division where Donald and I worked – caught my husband in its net. Such a large dismissal of so many people stunned me. I had assumed that if one performed one's job conscientiously, one could expect to collect a gold watch. I was kept on as part of a skeleton crew and promoted to supervisor, with no pay increase. To protest might mean I'd lose my job; now, with Donald out of work, my meager paycheck was essential.

An outspoken male coworker asserted that I was pregnant. I knew immediately he was right: I had rounded out but had been too tired and distracted to acknowledge it; my menstrual cycles were irregular anyway. Soon afterwards, I miscarried in the women's bathroom at North American then returned to my desk. My pregnancy had barely begun and I did not mourn. In fact, given our s financial plight, I was relieved.

I managed to arrange a shared ride to work, which included Katy. At last, in 1956, determined to drive, I persuaded Donald to teach me but his belittling impatience turned me into an incompetent nervous wreck. A friend taught me quickly but Donald was reluctant for me to drive our car. This seemed reasonable enough, since he himself needed it but I also suspected that it was his way of keeping me isolated. Without a car, I could not even shop for groceries on my own.

Whenever people asked if I liked my job, I replied, Oh yes! in much the same way I had responded long before to my father's question regarding my marriage. I knew that if I admitted that I was unhappy, I would be: a self-fulfilling prophecy.

Meanwhile Donald went through a succession of unmemorable jobs. I recall he was laid off six times during the course of seven years, at least once for attitude and more than once for sick days. Finally, he found a job as technician at the new Ford Aeronutronics facility in Newport Beach, close to home. He joined the Newport Police Department as a reserve officer, at a time when psychological screening was not required. Sometimes he was paid but most often he worked voluntoarily. I realized he was in his element there; I saw that the uniform gave him a sense of power.

We had little social life. I met two of Donald's coworkers when they stopped by the house unexpectedly. They asked me why I didn't want to attend any of the company social activities, which included family picnics and barbecues. I had heard nothing of these events. The men said that Donald had told them that I didn't want to socialize with anyone from his work. They said they were surprised I was so nice.

I wanted to have a second child and in late 1957, in the decade of the hydrogen bomb, I decided to take advantage of North American's health insurance plan while I still could. Given the unstable climate of the aerospace industry, this was a gamble but I won. Unlike Bullocks,

North American allowed me to work through my eighth month. My son was born in August 1958 and my working days were over. Later that year the Navajo project was finally abandoned altogether.

My second delivery went well. That night I lay awake with joy; I now had a daughter and a son. In the hospital room later, Donald, wearing his police uniform, strode directly to the window and stood silently, staring out. I asked him if he had seen his son. Without turning around, he muttered, Yeah, he looks like Mickey Cohen. He left without touching me.

Early in my pregnancy, my father had visited us once again. A creative amateur photographer, he captured Donald and me in a photo I still have, taken outside our apartment on the peninsula. Donald stands with thumbs hooked into the gun belt of his police uniform. I smile into the camera, still small-waisted in my black dress. The woman in the picture is a stranger to me now.

During that visit, my father also captured one of my favorite images of a small Katy in a pink dress, laughing over her shoulder as she runs barefoot from an approaching wave.

Shocked Awake

I experienced none of the postpartum depression that had afflicted me after Katy was born. But when Scott was three weeks old I suffered a severe breast infection. I called my doctor who told me I must get to the hospital immediately; he would meet me there. He emphasized that I must not nurse again and arranged for our pediatrician to have formula waiting at the hospital. My infant son was already overdue for his feeding.

Donald was not home; he enjoyed spending his Saturdays browsing through hardware stores and visiting the police station. He could be gone for hours. Living on the peninsula, I was stranded without a car. I changed the baby, dressed Katy and waited for him to return. I was relieved when I heard his car. As he came in the door, I explained why I needed to get to the hospital right away.

With his hand still on the doorknob, my husband said, in a low, level voice, You are a goddamned inconvenience. Then he turned and left, slamming the door behind him.

I will never forget that moment when my whole world crashed in on me, seven years of marriage just a pile of rubble. A neighbor happened to stop by and found me lying on the kitchen floor, hysterical. She gathered my children and drove us to the hospital. She stayed and fed my son and watched my daughter while I was being treated, then she drove us home again.

Donald was not there. I was hurt and fearful. I did not want to face him and I did not want to face the implications of the future. When he finally returned, he acted as though absolutely nothing had happened. And although devastated, I did not confront him. The reality of my situation had struck me like a thunderbolt: I had nowhere to turn, I had no family in America, I could not adequately provide for two small children or myself. I didn't even own a car. I was trapped.

I felt there was nothing to do but make the best of it. I resorted to my old skill of rationalization; I told myself that no one, after all, had a perfect marriage and that young children needed a father. I told myself many things but all love, or my naïve illusion of love, was gone and along with it, trust and respect. Yet rationalization helped me keep the terrifying specter of divorce at bay and with it, my paralyzing fear of the unknown. I even tried to convince myself that Donald might change.

Rationalization also helped me to emphasize the positive. Donald, motivated by his contempt of his drunken father, did not drink. Drug use never entered our suburban consciousness (although Donald, whom I saw as a hypochondriac, often relied on prescription painkillers). He did not womanize. He was almost obsessively neat and I never had to pick up after him. He recorded much of our lives with a keen eye and a good camera although his images of family did not always reflect the truth of the moment. I am glad, however, to have fallen heir to them: they can trigger a torrent of memories. I was especially grateful he did not want me to work even though I knew the reason: my working might reflect negatively on him as a provider. I used that to my advantage to justify staying home with my children not only because I wanted to but because the cost of childcare would make an outside job impractical.

My son was a few months old when our landlord served us notice. He had joined the growing trend toward converting year-round beach rentals into vacation properties. I was heartbroken about leaving the peninsula and its simple pleasures.

We found a pleasant two bedroom pink duplex on the bluff above the harbor. A small patch of lawn in an enclosed yard made it ideal for small children. The owners, a pleasant older couple, maintained the property well and respected their tenants' privacy.

We had lived in the pink duplex a few months when my mother's sister Edith and her husband visited us during their retirement travels. I was happy to see them; they had been an important part of my growing up, and visitors from Australia were a rare treat, especially family. They made no mention of my father, from whom they had been estranged since my mother's death. I never saw my uncle again after that visit; he died of a brain tumor not long after they returned home. I don't know what they thought of Donald; they made no comments and asked no questions. I think he was civil during their brief stay.

The Wives Club

Feeling it my wifely duty, I went to an Aeronutronics Wives Club meeting at a home in an upscale neighborhood of Newport Beach. Our hostess, whose husband was a top executive, served tea and asked us each to state our names and our husbands' job titles. I was startled; I felt we were being defined according to our husbands' salary levels, not as individuals. I caught the eye of a woman across the room and I sensed she felt the same. Norlene was bolder than I; she approached and asked me if I wanted to leave. Later, over coffee, she expressed her indignation at what we agreed was snobbery. Her husband was making good money as an engineer, a title that would have afforded him and his family respectability and acceptance. But Norlene was a confident woman with very clear values; she knew hypocrisy when she saw it. It was only by chance that they had bought a house, sight unseen, in a desirable neighborhood. New to Orange County, they had no idea of a certain local obsession with the right address. At that time Newporters called Costa Mesa Goat Hill, a term meant to be derogatory. But Norlene had come from a down to earth working class family in Buffalo. She was only ten when falling steel beams crushed her father at the factory where he worked. She had to grow up quickly to emotionally support her distraught mother and younger brother.

Until I met Norlene, I had never left my children with a baby sitter since those pre-school days at North American. She introduced me to a remarkable woman who was to become a trusted guardian of my children and a friend. Now in her sixties, Anne had been widowed as a young bride when her fireman husband fell through the roof of a burning house, leaving her nearly penniless. She lived in a small trailer near Coast Highway and drove an aging little pink Nash Rambler. She survived by caring for other people's children and was a firm but fair disciplinarian.

Norlene declared we would have one day out every week, just the two of us. Every Wednesday, smartly dressed, we drove the freeway in Norlene's little robin's egg blue Volkswagen, to Fashion Square in Santa Ana where we browsed through Bullocks and ate thirty-five cent salads at the Jolly Roger and talked tirelessly over coffee refills. A little guiltily, I squeezed money from my housekeeping budget to pay Anne for her six-hour watch. I always made sure I was home long before Donald. Thanks to Norlene, I began to move beyond my insulated little world.

When Donald realized that these excursions were likely to be regular Wednesday events, he began coming home from work just as Norlene arrived, claiming to be sick and expecting me to stay home with him. At first I almost gave in but Norlene would have none of it; she saw that Donald was trying to isolate me. He knows what he is doing, she said. From then on, he took every opportunity to discredit her in my eyes. While I did not openly defend her, I had no intention of giving up her friendship.

Norlene and I never returned to the Wives Club. We developed a bond that influenced my life for many years.

Banished

Donald's naps had become a regular part of his weekend routine and lasted two or three hours. Because he refused to turn off the bedroom extension phone, I felt I had to stay home while he slept so I could reach the phone before he insulted unsuspecting callers. At the same time, it was up to me to keep the children quiet.

My attempts to keep the peace were futile: one Saturday afternoon, our next door neighbor's telephone rang several times. Apparently she was not home and when the phone rang again later, an irritated Donald got up and left the apartment. He returned a few minutes later and told me that he had fixed her: he had cut her telephone line, a skill he had learned once from brief employment at the Telephone Company.

Within hours, the owners served us an eviction notice. They were apologetic to me but said they found my husband's actions reprehensible. Without a referral from our landlords, we would have difficulty in renting again, and as it was, not everyone was willing to accept children.

First Home

In late 1959, on the abandoned runways of the former Santa Ana Army Air base, the first phase of a new housing tract was under construction. At the time of our eviction, the modest homes were selling for less than twenty thousand dollars. They might as well have been a million, for we had no savings. I was humbled when Anne offered me the required small down payment. I also was reluctant – borrowing had brought me too many sleepless nights - but seeing no other way out of our predicament, I relented. When I told Donald, he did not object; it was up to me to figure out how to repay Anne.

Our house was the second to the last, set at the edge of the abandoned airfield, on hard dirt that became a mud swamp when it rained. Cockroaches and field mice, evicted from their natural habitat, found their way into the house, which I tried hopelessly to keep clean, imagining my stepmother's disapproval. But improvements could wait until we could repay Anne, who never pressured me or reminded me of her generosity.

Shock of the New Neighbors

On the day we moved in, I introduced Katy, Scott and myself to my next door neighbor. She responded, If your kids come on to our property, we'll sue you, a threat she was to make frequently. It was an unhappy introduction to our new neighborhood.

One day as I watched little Scott from our bedroom window, absorbed with his Tonka trucks beneath our evergreen pear, I noticed the neighbor's youngest boy slithering on his belly toward our yard. Suddenly he lunged and bit Scott's thigh hard. Immediately I took a crying Scott to the neighbor's door. She retorted, Your kid must have started it and slammed the door. Katy and Scott liked two of the little girls but the eldest boy tormented Katy at every opportunity.

This woman once told me that the only time she felt like a woman was when she was pregnant. By the time we moved away, she had produced nine babies. Because she was so obese, I couldn't tell when she was pregnant, so each new infant caught me unaware. She seemed so ignorant that I was convinced she had grown up in the backwoods somewhere. Then one day I met her mother: slim, well groomed, articulate, a successful interior designer who had raised her daughter in this same county. The contrast was incomprehensible.

Locked out of their house, her children ran wild while she visited neighbors, including a couple who lived directly across the street from us, known for their drunken physical arguments on their front lawn in the small hours of the morning.

The neighborhood seemed always in transition. In the few years we lived there, three different families occupied the other next-door house: a swinging bachelor, a strict religious family, who wouldn't allow their two daughters to attend Katy's birthday party on a Saturday and a couple whose open marriage allowed drunken late night trysts in their swimming pool. I distanced myself from these people and was labeled a snob. It didn't bother me; I immersed myself in my own life and gradually found people I liked.

I met Jeannie and her little daughter one day, walking with their magnificent Greater Swiss Mountain Dog, Beowulf. Jeannie and her husband Larry were well educated. They guarded their privacy but invited me to their house one day to meet a few of their friends. Our friendship was cut short by tragedy. On a Los Angles freeway, en route to the Music Center, a drunk driver hit their car head on. Jeannie was injured but survived. Larry was killed instantly, a smile still on his face, she told me later, as a bystander snatched his watch and his wedding ring, while Jeannie lay there helpless. Her profound grief was inconsolable. She told me she intended to return to Berkeley to continue her studies and left the neighborhood soon afterwards. I never heard from her again. I had the feeling that she wanted to erase all associations with this terrible time in her life.

I became friendly with a woman from Oklahoma who lived on the next street. Doris was married with three children, older than my two. I introduced her to Norlene and the three of us became friends. But it was Norlene and I who spent hours at the edge of the surf with our four children, all close in age. Even though she and I had grown up in very different places, we shared a great love of the coast, a love that my children inherited.

We also shared enthusiasm for the music of that time: Sergio Mendez and his Brazil 66, Astrud Gilberto and her Girl from Ipanema, Herb Alpert's Tijuana Brass – happy and upbeat, with lyrics we could understand, rhythm we could dance to. And we had Henry Mancini, Sinatra, The Beatles, Andy Williams, the music of Camelot and Sound of Music, Victory at Sea, Breakfast at Tiffany's. The music of that time seems so original and eclectic to me, before heavy metal and lament and rebellion took over. Still, for me, classical music is my daily bread.

My obese neighbor reported Doris and her husband to the police because she had peered over their high fence and seen them swimming naked in their own backyard pool. She wanted to sue them for indecency and invasion of privacy, although her vantage point must have required considerable effort, since their yard was not directly behind hers. The police told her it was a civil case and she got nowhere, despite mentioning that her husband was a county sheriff. When someone said they had seen her husband in a bar with another woman, she sued for slander. The judge admonished her and threw the case out. The rumor turned out to be true.

At Aeronutronics, Donald had learned how to use explosives. When these unsupervised children played in their makeshift fort next to our bedroom wall early weekend mornings, Donald bragged that he could blow them up and not leave a trace of evidence.

I tried to ignore the chaos next door but for all the years we lived in our first home, I was constantly on guard, not only for what the neighbor might do, but for what Donald might do, as well.

The Mission

One day, as I was in the middle of painting Katy's bedroom saffron yellow, the doorbell rang. Dripping paint roller in hand, I opened the door to find Edna standing there. She declined my offer to come in. I listened obediently as though still a child, as she declared she was in my neighborhood for a Jehovah's Witness conference and I was her mission.

I was uncomfortable with her fervor but I remained polite – and inwardly resentful. She persisted for months afterwards with phone calls, letters and religious brochures until I finally gathered the courage to tell her to leave me alone.

After that, whenever I knew her whereabouts, I sent her bits of family news and photographs, but neither of us made any real attempt to stay connected.

Power

Donald left the Newport police department and began working as a reserve officer in Costa Mesa. This closer proximity to home meant he might turn up at any moment, keeping me on edge; more than once he had been curt to neighbors he caught me talking to. Sometimes he arrived with the police siren on, to give the kids a thrill, he said but I thought it childish.

He continued to push the limits of his badge. I heard him tell the next door neighbors – the ones with the open marriage - as they backed out of their driveway, that he would get them out on the highway (with a ticket) and no one would believe them because he was a cop.

He bragged that as a cop, he could walk a fine line between the legal and illegal and not get caught. When he wanted a new paint job on his car, he deliberately drove through an industrial area during paint spraying then made an insurance claim. When he wanted a dented door replaced, he clipped the opening door of a parked car, citing negligence on the part of the other driver. Our insurance agent, a neighbor I knew well, told me he knew exactly what Donald was up to but settled because it was easier.

The Family That Plays Together

Now and then we drove somewhere nearby for a family outing. I did not look forward to these excursions because they usually ended unhappily. I have a favorite photograph of the children and me, taken by Donald in Irvine Park, where there were monkeys in big cages and ponies to ride. The children are in the branches of an old oak tree, as I stand close beneath. It is a beautiful image but none of us are smiling. Donald had made a scene of some kind moments before that had left us three miserable. As if to balance this memory, I recall how we laughed later that same day when an unimpressed Scott fell asleep on the back of a pony as it trotted around the ring.

As for vacations, I remember only two during our marriage: the first when Katy was about a year old (the only time Anita ever baby-sat for us), when Donald and I drove to Tijuana for a weekend. I looked forward to sharing a small adventure, exploring a different place and another culture but when we reached the hotel, Donald wanted only to have sex and take a nap. By the time he woke up, the afternoon had gone. We went out for dinner then back to the hotel and bed. The next day was much the same and I remember thinking that I never wanted to take a vacation with Donald again.

The second trip years later was to Yosemite with the children. We drove there from Southern California in our little Volkswagen, over The Grapevine and into the Yosemite Valley. It was early May and record rainfalls had turned the place into a verdant paradise, the waterfalls so thunderous, they made conversation impossible. I remember walking across a lupine meadow where elk and deer grazed, toward a large pond that vibrated with the din of croaking frogs. Alone for a moment, I felt deep joy.

Donald took some wonderful photographs of Katy and Scott perched on rocks at the edge of a raging river but none of those images tell of the smacks on the back of their heads or Donald's seething impatience.

Ordinary Lives

Katy started kindergarten. On her first report card, her teacher wrote that Katy's eyes are pools of mystery. In a family of blue eyes, Katy's were green. Early on she had a way of lowering her flaxen head and looking up through dark lashes, a hint of a pout on her lips. Her teacher reported that Katy was inattentive and might have a hearing problem but I knew better: I could almost whisper lemonade from the back door and Katy would hear me over the chatter of her playmates. At the end of the year, her teacher recommended that Katy repeat kindergarten. However, her new teacher thought Katy a bright child who simply was bored and needed challenges; in her classroom, Katy thrived. She introduced Katy and Scott to a litter of Siamese kittens; we adopted two brothers and called them Nip and Tuck. Katy claimed Tuck, the prettier of the two and Scott was left with Nip, who turned out to be the funniest, most personable and affectionate one. He and Scott were inseparable until Nip died at thirteen. Tuck, always a wanderer, was struck by a car one day as he crossed our street and lived three terrible days while the veterinarian assured me he would recover. I have always regretted that I didn't follow my own gut feelings to have his suffering ended immediately.

After we repaid Anne, Donald bought a 1952 MG-TD in original British Racing Green from a family friend for less than it was worth. It was slow to climb the hill to Aeronutronics but Donald didn't seem to mind. Nor did I: although he never let me drive the MG, I now had use of our 1961 ragtop Volkswagen - and new freedom.

My home became my creative focus. Every morning I awoke eager to drive to the local nursery where a gentle Scotsman guided me through a maze of glorious green things. As he helped me choose the right plants for our unforgiving soil, I found myself attracted to him; we talked easily although neither of us spoke of our personal lives.

Trip after trip I overloaded my little car with plants, including seventeen small trees, their crowns waving in the wind above the open ragtop of the Volkswagen. I always bought small plants because they were cheap, they fit in the car and I could plant them by myself. With care they grew: evergreen pears, a Monterey pine and several eucalyptus as well as ferns, azaleas, baby tears, gardenias, jasmine, strawberry, Xylosma. I fed and deep-soaked them along with the scraggly Brazilian Pepper that had come with the house. Soon after we moved in, Donald had scattered dichondra seed in the front yard and fed and mowed it regularly. He organized an efficient workbench in the garage and enjoyed tinkering. I believe he took pride in our new home then.

I designed side and back patios in charcoal gray concrete with redwood headers, leaving open squares for evergreen pears. I planned a reflection pool outside the living room glass doors, shaded by a high wood partition, which Donald built and I painted, to create a climate for Australian tree ferns, baby tears, camellias and azaleas. A corner of the back yard became an uninhibited place for children to build forts or play Pretend, as I once had at Lillianfels. Donald added an old wood rowboat he had found somewhere. For months our patio and garage overflowed with neglected furniture discovered in the attics of friends' parents as well as pieces Donald's grandfather had brought from Europe years before. I scraped, sanded and refinished and was pleased with the results. I painted raw shutters and bare walls, sewed slipcovers and Roman shades. I made stylish dresses for Katy and myself in quality fabrics, when fine fabric stores still existed and homemade cost less than store-bought. I designed my own originals after Audrey Hepburn and Jackie Kennedy; Katy was one of the best-dressed girls in school and when he was still too small to object, Scott wore outfits I had made in fabrics that matched his sister's.

I decided our street needed trees. I wanted Camphor Laurel because I had grown up with one at Rosalind. I went from door to door with a petition and told all my neighbors that everyone else favored Camphor Laurel. No one objected, except one man who told me he hated trees. The City approved my choice. The last time I was on our street, the Laurels had grown tall, their rosy-green foliage as beautiful as I remembered. A new owner of our house had cut down the Monterey Pine and all the eucalyptus but the Brazilian Pepper had spread its lush foliage over the entire driveway. Before I became aware of Rachel Carson's 1962 bestseller Silent Spring, I had sprayed that tree regularly with some toxic liquid, drenched and unprotected in shorts and bare feet for hours, until I had stuffed clippings into bags and swept and hosed the garage and driveway. The caterpillars never had a chance, and despite my ignorance, I survived. People referred to our yard as Little Vietnam, a green oasis on a bland brown street.

As part of settling into this suburban life style, I joined a local church, known for its liberal young minister. By then I had explored many religions and connected with none. Now, every week my children attended Sunday school while I was in church. Donald declined to go, even at Easter or Christmas. I didn't mind.

I volunteered at a local hospital, which cared for mentally handicapped people of all ages. My nights became restless, the day's images became nightmares. Donald said I was depressed and he was right. One day a young professional Asian couple reluctantly gave up their severely retarded four year-old son because they could no longer care for him. I witnessed their anguish and knew I didn't have what it takes. After six months I quit, feeling inadequate and guilty.

I became an expert at stretching Donald's paycheck. I got away with a lot by not telling him what I was up to; deceit was easier than conflict. I simply went ahead and did what I wanted, as long as I paid the bills. I painted the thirsty stucco exterior of our house – it was a dismal gray-green when we bought it with a pseudo-Chinese architectural theme which I eventually modified. Norlene and I custom-mixed the exact shade of rich off-white that I visualized - the artist still was alive and well in me - and I managed to paint the back and two sides before Donald noticed and by then it was too late to stop me. I didn't mind completing the work myself, away from Donald's belittling criticism, and I enjoyed my own sense of accomplishment. There were advantages to Donald's insistence that I be responsible for our budget. I make the money, you make it work!

I learned to be secretive in other ways: I believed that parents should work together regarding their children but I soon realized that Donald was quick to inflict corporal punishment for childish misdemeanors. By now I had seen enough of his controlled anger: if the children did not move through the doorway of a restaurant quickly enough, he clipped them smartly on the backs of their heads or gripped their arms too tightly.

These aggressions were administered covertly and I don't think he ever left bruises. He rarely raised his voice but his words, delivered in a low, vehement tone, were intimidating.

Sometimes he was not so subtle: once when Scott did not move his new bicycle from the driveway quickly enough, Donald picked it up and threw it into the garage where it lay, its bent wheel spinning. His simmering anger exploded to the surface one day when, in front of his small son, he impaled a gopher with a sprinkler rod.

He smashed a little antique caned bench his mother had given me because he didn't want it in the entry hall. I kept an impossibly neat home but one toy left on the floor triggered tight-lipped fury. I always tried to look pretty for him because I had read, in some women's magazine, that wives should make apples of their cheeks by pinching, in order to glow for their husbands. If he caught me unexpectedly sans lipstick, he accused me of letting myself go. When I wore makeup he'd say, Why do you wear all that stuff?

Donald often said, I'm not such a bad guy and I think he believed it, just as he believed he had a great sense of humor even though his jokes were invariably ethnic, chauvinistic or at the expense of others. One old family friend dubbed him the SS Trooper. In her nineties, she still recalls the panic she felt in being late for a barbeque at our house in the early sixties - she had experienced Donald's seething fury before. She saw him as sadistic: she never forgave him for banging on the door of heir beach vacation rental very late one night, stern and official in full police uniform, knowing she was anxious about her teenage daughter, out in a new beau's car for the first time. It was Donald's idea of a joke.

Once, when Norlene was visiting, he left the room abruptly, returning a while later in his police gear. Standing tall in the doorway, legs spread, he shifted his gun belt and said, The police department needs me. As he left, Norlene said, There he goes in his Mickey Mouse outfit and we burst into convulsive giggles. By then, all respect for my husband had flown.

More serious things were happening in America then. In April of 1961, the unsuccessful Bay of Pigs invasion resulted in the Cuban missile crisis the following year. Some people talked of bomb shelters, others of hoarding. I remember driving to the local Stater Bros. market with my children and finding the shelves bare. I picked up the few canned foods I could find and left. Distracted by the tension in the air, I placed my wallet on the roof of the Volkswagen as the children clambered in, and drove home. The wallet was found later in a nearby trash can, minus cash and credit cards. As my grandmother Lillian often said, Haste makes waste. Yes, Lillian knew a thing or two.

The Season to be Jolly

Early in our marriage, I eagerly anticipated Christmas. I made wreaths and ornaments. I shopped for special wrapping paper and gifts that seemed perfect for their recipients. I sewed Christmas dresses for Katy and me; I made trifle and baked gingerbread men.

But as the years wore on, I began to dread the holidays.

Weeks before, Donald would tell me to make a list of the things I really wanted. Every day he'd say, I'm going to get you something really special! Almost always, on Christmas morning, I would find something I had never wanted and could never use, let alone anything on my modest wish list. I couldn't return these things for fear of offending him.

Yet I began to suspect that his inappropriate choices were perversely intentional, for I recalled a time much earlier in our marriage, when he impulsively stopped by a roadside stand after work and bought me a small bunch of fragrant old-fashioned violets. I love violets, like those that grew in my Aunt Bebe's garden when I was a child, so I told Donald how thrilled and touched I was. He never bought me violets again. From then on, he didn't bring flower at all, except for an occasional bunch of dyed carnations, lacking fragrance.

The weeks before Christmas rankled with Donald's resentment of the season, beginning with shopping for the tree. Transporting it, setting it up, stringing the lights, were accompanied by curses, leaving the children in tears, and me with a cold, sick knot in my stomach. Invariably, between Thanksgiving and New Years, I came down with strep throat, a manifestation of seasonal misery.

Like Christmas, birthdays had become something to dread. For days before my birthday, Donald would claim he was going to buy me something nice. One year he told me to have the children ready and in the car at 8:30 a.m. and I made sure I did. About ten minutes before, he began ranting that we should have been ready earlier. This was not unusual; I had long realized that when it came to Donald, I could never get things right, no matter how right I was. We drove to Bullock's, three of us unhappily silent. There he led us to the jewelry counter, although jewelry did not interest me. He stood, arms folded, and told me to hurry up and make up my mind. When the children became restless, he administered his well-practiced clip to their heads. Sometimes I chose anything just to get the ordeal over with; sometimes I went home empty-handed.

On my next birthday, a repeat of those before, I bought a large bottle of cheap wine, locked myself in the bedroom and got fairly drunk. This must have startled Donald because we didn't keep alcohol in the house and we rarely drank. Nor had he ever seen me so openly rebellious. He left me alone to sleep it off and had no recourse but to watch the children himself.

Our eleventh wedding anniversary followed less than four months after that birthday. On the afternoon of our anniversary, during Donald's Saturday nap, Doris called to recommend a new restaurant she thought we might like. Donald answered before I could and told her, We don't want anyone interfering with our young lives, and slammed down the receiver. This was a term he flung frequently at people, including his own mother. I have seen her eyes fill with tears although she never rebuked him- I was like her in that way, suffering the hurt in silence, until Norlene said, Don't be hurt; be angry! I have seen the stunned look of teachers, school principals and neighbors, wondering what hit them. He delivered these insults swiftly and unexpectedly and retreated before the recipients could recover. Yet Donald himself was hypersensitive even to perceived criticism. Touchy, my friends said.

Norlene labeled these attacks hit and run. Exasperated, she told me, not for the first time, to stop defending him; he knows exactly what he is doing. From then on, upsetting as it was, I did not defend him as his insults found their mark. Norlene and Doris told me they would no longer come to our house or invite Donald to theirs. After that, I met my friends elsewhere.

Anita often said, At least Donny always apologizes. I thought, but why do something in the first place that you need to apologize for? As far as I was concerned, apologizing only justified repeating the offence again and again, just as confession, for some, might wipe the slate clean until the next time.

Donald had inherited a Mason ring from his grandfather, which he had coveted for years. As our marriage disintegrated, he told me he was going to have the diamond reset in a ring for me for our anniversary. I told him no, because by then I knew I would someday leave him. Perhaps sensing I was slipping away, he had the diamond reset in a ring for me anyway. The following year I forgot our anniversary altogether.

About that time, Norlene and I discovered Erich Fromm, best known for his book The Art of Loving, written in 1956. But it was his earlier book, Man for Himself, on humanistic versus authoritarian ethics that excited me most. Reading it, I felt as though Fromm had been a fly on the wall of my life. For the first time, I could define my relationship with Donald and understand how earlier relationships had prepared me for it. It seemed I had been a masochist and where there was a masochist, there probably was a sadist. Fromm told me I was a victim. I resolved to change.

Emboldened by this new awareness, I signed up for an evening art class, two nights a week at nearby Orange Coast College, and persuaded Donald to put the children to bed those evenings. When I came home after the first class, he demanded to know where I had been in the twenty minutes since the class ended. I explained that I was trying to get out of the busy parking lot. After the second class, he complained that the children had behaved badly and he had put them to bed early. I found them awake and upset. I gave up the class; Donald knew all the ways he could control me.

Tragedy

In November of 1963, the year when Scott began school, my father visited us once again. This time my stepmother accompanied him. I hadn't seen her for thirteen years. She seemed impressed with my immaculate home and garden and my beautifully dressed children - as though I were a different person. I suppose I was; now that I was an adult with my own family, she and I could meet on common ground and be comfortable together. I doubt if she saw beyond our façade of the perfect little family; as long as Donald behaved, I could almost convince myself.

They went on to visit old friends and neighbors in Monrovia and Pasadena, all of whom I had invited to dinner later that week. Then on November 22nd, the terrible news of John Kennedy's assassination broke, a day when it seemed to me that the world had turned black. I was overcome by grief. Donald called me from work to chat, not yet having heard. He often phoned me in the middle of the day – I suspect to check on me – and spent more time making sexual remarks his co-workers could overhear than actually talking to me. He was genuinely shocked when I told him the news, then went on to say he had had an accident on the way to a job site at the El Toro marine base.

He had collided with a car carrying two people; he or the other driver had taken a curve on the narrow road too sharply. He was not hurt and our 1961 ragtop Volkswagen, which he drove that day, was unscathed. He laughed. You should have seen the other guys! I hung up and thought uncharitably, Why a man like Kennedy and not you? It seemed to be one more thing that God had got wrong, just as he had got Laura wrong.

My father, my children and I were walking by a fleet of television sets in White Front in Costa Mesa when we heard the shots that killed

Harvey Lee Oswald as he was led from a prison cell, and we turned to see him fall. Everyone came to dinner as planned, but the mood was somber.

In February 1964, the same year the Surgeon General issued his warning on smoking, the Beatles invaded America. Crew-cut Donald derided their haircuts, I appreciated their originality and America was momentary distracted.

That same year a neighbor who was involved with the Republican presidential campaign asked if he could hide Barry Goldwater's limousine – a large Chrysler Imperial hard-top with a tire on the back trunk- in our garage for a day or two. Donald, a Republican, agreed and I, politically ignorant then, enjoyed this small flutter of excitement in our ordinary lives. We never saw the senator; the limousine protruded from our small garage so much that we couldn't lower the door. It scarcely mattered: who would expect to find a prominent politician, or his car, in such a modest neighborhood? The neighbor took the car to its next campaign destination and Goldwater lost the election to Democratic incumbent Lyndon Johnson.

Life went on. I raised my children by unreliable instinct, in some ways misguided by my own upbringing and the advice or opinions of others. In those days little information about parenting was available and Dr. Spock was my main map. I tripped along the path I believed best and came to regret some of the turns I took. The children said their prayers every night, Katy joined the girl scouts, Scott Indian Guides and I held meetings, baked cookies, worked at school carnivals and made posters, like other suburban mothers. Scott recently recalled something that I had managed to blot from my memory: as he waited eagerly at home in his buckskins and feathers, his father went to Indian Guides meetings alone. Some of the other boys told him that their dads found this weird. Apparently Donald told the group that Scott wasn't interested.

When we moved to the beach, Donald became involved with a Sea Scout group. Those weekends he didn't spend at the police department, he took other boys camping to places like Catalina Island, although he never once took his own children camping. They pleaded and he deterred them with empty promises. Someday, he would say. Someday. I began to suspect that these hours spent with other peoples' sons enabled him to feel like a hero, no emotional investment necessary. Why else?

Scott also told me that sometimes, when I was out of sight, Donald handcuffed him until he cried. Then came the swift clip to the head: What's the matter with you, you baby; I'm only kidding. Once, when Katy ran home from the nearby fairgrounds stables, sobbing because a horse had kicked her in the nose, he delivered his well-practiced head smack and taunted her, Little princess, you think you're a little princess.

My stifled emotions manifested themselves physically. A mysterious lump grew rapidly in my jaw. A biopsy forwarded to the Mayo Clinic proved inconclusive and I was scheduled for surgery. The lump was removed from the inside of my jaw without incident and proved to be a harmless benign tumor. Donald told me later that the doctors, not knowing what to expect, had given me a 50/50 chance of survival because of the potentially dangerous location of the growth. It's to Donald's credit that he withheld that information from me until I was safe, but by then I'm not sure I would even have cared.

One Sunday, as I shook hands with the minister on the church steps, I exploded into tears. Startled, he asked me to go behind the church where I waited, mortified, as he greeted the last of his parishioners. When he ushered me into the rectory afterwards, he was clearly uncomfortable. He told me to kneel and pray. I wanted to spill out my misery and receive some comfort and helpful advice but there was none forthcoming. I rose and left as quickly as I could, ashamed for having lost control. A week passed with no word from the minister, his wife, his secretary or any other church member. I felt abandoned by the church. As usual, I found my support in my women friends.

During the infamous Watts riots in the summer of 1965, Donald donned his uniform, loaded a .38 Smith and Wesson, told me to keep it under my pillow, and if any niggers come to the door, shoot first, ask questions later. When he left, I unloaded the gun and went to sleep. A fervent member of the NRA, he kept fourteen loaded guns on the top shelf of our bedroom closet, including a .57 Magnum which, he claimed, could kill an elephant. I refrained from pointing out the obvious shortage of elephants in Costa Mesa.

He bought a new Ford station wagon that year. Sometimes when he came home from work he drove the car directly into the dim garage, dropped the tailgate and unloaded things that appeared new: tools, tires, odds and ends I didn't recognize and once, even a small rowboat. When I asked him where they had come from, he said off handedly, It was stuff the company didn't want anymore. Even then, I could see that seven year-old Scott knew this wasn't true.

In November, following the Watts riots, as my marriage became increasingly intolerable, Donald's work sent him to Nevada for three weeks. I drove him to the airport and sang out loud all the way back home. That night, the children and I played Catch in the dark, happily chasing one another through the house until Scott, laughing over his shoulder, ran into a corner of the wall and required a trip to Emergency. The damage to his forehead was minor but our change of mood was not. Until that night I had not fully realized how oppressed our three lives had been or how depressed I had become. It was as though a great dark cloud had lifted.

Donald came home for Thanksgiving weekend. A cab dropped him off around midnight when the children were asleep. He wanted sex immediately and for the very first time, I told him we needed to talk first. He was furious. He slept in the den as I spent a restless and fearful night in our bed, trying to hang onto my resolve. In the morning he rose early and used the shower next to the bedroom as I feigned sleep. When he left the room, I cautiously opened the bedroom door and listened. The children were already up, watching cartoons on the den television. I heard them say, Hi Daddy! To which their father replied, You goddamned little bastards, get the hell off my back. The back door slammed, rubber peeled out of the driveway.

I found my small son sitting rigid on the edge of the couch, tears streaming down his face. My eleven-year-old daughter sat beside him, dry-eyed and calm. She said, Mother, we're better off with him gone. It was a defining moment for me. I knew then that I could no longer claim to remain in this marriage because of the children, no matter the dictates of society.

I've often thought since that if Donald had been kind to his children, if he had been an involved, loving father, I might have stayed until Katy and Scott were grown, knowing I would escape soon afterwards.

When Donald returned later that day, he acted as though nothing had happened. Once again he demanded sex. I gave in to keep the peace until I could drive him to the airport the following morning. On the way there, with the children in the back seat, he moved his hand up my thigh and said, See? All you needed was a good lovin'.

When he called me that night from Nevada, I told him I wanted a divorce. There was a small silence before he said, This isn't your idea; it's those friends of yours. They put ideas into your head. He did not believe I had the courage to make such a major decision, let alone act on it. But when he realized I meant what I said, he told me he wanted me to come to Nevada so we could talk. He would arrange a flight. He would book a room for me on another floor of the hotel; we would meet on neutral ground. He would not press me for sex. I was reluctant but felt I should at least hear what he had to say. I asked Anne to care for the children for a couple of days.

When Donald called me back with my flight plans, I took a deep breath and asked if he had booked a separate room for me. He exploded. Goddamn it, you're my wife, you're going to sleep with me!

I hung up and called a lawyer.

Donald returned home a few days later, the Nevada project over. I told him I had talked to a lawyer but that I would delay filing if he agreed to counseling. I made a lunch-hour appointment with the same minister who had let me down, thinking he might be more at ease seeing us as a couple. At the last minute Donald called to say he couldn't get away from work. I saw the minister anyway but found his grasp of my situation still lacking. I never returned to church.

Next, I arranged an appointment with a county family counselor. This time Donald came with me but toward the end of the session, the counselor asked Donald to wait outside. As the door closed behind him, she said, I cannot deal with that man. I'm sorry.

I called a well-known Newport psychiatrist – our health insurance covered most of the cost. Donald did not show up and I met with the psychiatrist alone. I made five appointments altogether and each time Donald failed to appear. I had been keeping a daily journal, recording words and actions as they happened. After five sessions, the psychiatrist said, While I am not supposed to tell a patient what to do, I will be very frank with you because I am about to retire to Panama. I believe your husband is psychotic, a classic case of arrested emotional development at about age fifteen. He will not change; indeed, his behavior will only intensify.

I protested, believing this man held the key that would unlock the door to Donald's mind and help him to see the light. The psychiatrist said, If he looked into himself, he might very possibly attempt suicide. That stunned me, because I had not told the psychiatrist that Donald's father had taken his own life. He shook his head and said, You are an intelligent woman. You need to get out of this marriage now. It will only get worse. I left, feeling I now had clear permission to file for divorce. I also felt boosted by the psychiatrist's assessment of me: I was intelligent! No one had ever said that to me before.

When I told Anita about the divorce, she burst into tears and threw her arms around me and exclaimed, Oh my dear, he is just like his father! I think that was the most genuine moment we ever shared. We stayed in close touch for a while but I think, as Donald's mother, she felt conflicted, unable to divide her loyalties.

For a while, she sent occasional cards and little notes to Katy and Scott but these soon stopped; I suspect that Donald objected to this contact. She was a good woman and had always treated the children kindly. Scott, as an adult, recalls her as being affectionate and I am glad of that. When my children were older, they made some effort to visit her. When she was hospitalized at the end of her long life, Katy was living hundreds of miles away but Scott carried a big bundle of balloons to her room. She had told both children as young adults that that she was leaving them some money but I think she trusted Donald to fulfill that promise, something he would never do. It's not surprising that Donald, who had often treated his mother hurtfully, became suddenly attentive when she was dying. Ah, the smell of money!

I knew when I filed for divorce that Donald, who never had money, would eventually inherit a considerable sum. As an only child, Anita would inherit her father's substantial estate and her future husband would leave her financially comfortable as well. I knew, if I stayed, I might share in that good fortune but I felt my physical and mental health would suffer in the meantime. My children were already suffering; I had already waited too long.

I wrote to my father and stepmother – two airletters, marked A and B, explaining why I was divorcing Donald. I felt ashamed of divorce, of my own failure. I wanted them to understand and I hoped for their emotional support. My father didn't reply but my stepmother wrote a terse note that said, You made your bed, you lie in it.

Divorce

Because I had met Ruth's divorce lawyer years earlier and found him to be a monstrous tyrant who made her life miserable, I was determined to find a gentler, more ethical representative. I chose an elderly lawyer who advised me to change your door locks and find another man while you still have your looks.

Norlene, who was my witness, was a rock throughout. I remember, on the day that Donald and I were to face one another in court, Southern California experienced torrential rains. Norlene's Volkswagen floated cockeyed through intersections, windshield wipers flailing helplessly against the downpour. To make matters worse, I was sick with Hong-Kong flu. No wonder: I had felt sick with fear every morning for most of that year; I was physically and emotionally depleted. It didn't help that, in the courtroom, Donald contested the divorce.

I fumbled through with little legal help and after fourteen years of marriage, settled for one hundred and sixty-five dollars alimony each month for four years and eighty-two dollars per month for each child to age twenty-one. Even back then, it wasn't enough to survive on and I had no real working skills. But Donald was threatening to leave the state to avoid paying support and I didn't have the stomach to fight him anymore. Later I read in the local newspaper that the elderly lawyer had been sued for incompetence.

On our first Christmas apart, Donald sent Katy and Scott each an 8x10 color photograph of himself, standing stiffly in full police uniform before an American flag. He signed it Love, Dad.

Before our divorce became final, Donald called to say he wanted to spend time with the children. I suspected an ulterior motive because he'd had little contact with them since our day in court seven months earlier, even though he lived nearby. Sure enough, he told me he had changed his mind about the divorce; he wanted to reconcile. He said he had turned to take a second look at an attractive woman on the street then realized it was me; he wanted me back. Difficult as my life was, I knew that I did not want to reconcile. Yet I felt that if I were so sure, I should put myself to the test if only to honor fourteen years of marriage. I agreed to have dinner with him. We went to one of those dim, pedestrian places with red plastic booths and tough steak. There was little for either of us to say. But then, we never had really talked, a failure for which we both were to blame. I couldn't wait to escape.

For a while, Donald continued to take Katy or Scott on alternate weekend afternoons. Following these visits, Scott simply sat on the sofa and stared into space. When Donald took Katy to a movie, she told me, I don't want to go with Daddy again. When I pressed her, she said that Jayne Mansfield was in the film and that Donald had said, I'd like to get my hands on those big tits.

Just before the final decree in February 1967, Donald called to say he had leukemia and had three weeks to live. I did not believe him. I hear he went through a western phase of jade, silver and spurs, bought a pig farm then was born again.

Once our marriage ended, Donald rarely attempted to see his children. Still, believing that divorcing parents should try to be civil for the sake of the children, I explained that Daddy loved them, he was just tired or overworked or very busy. Finally, Scott's teacher told me that I was sending mixed messages: while I was telling my children that their father loved them, they were not feeling that love and were blaming themselves. I was relieved that Donald did not pursue his visitation rights; the few hours he spent with the children left them unhappy and confused. Besides, it was easier to be the sole parent because I could avoid him and therefore avoid conflict. I tried to be both mother and father and found myself lacking.

Donald never hit me although he told me years later that he had wanted to. I almost wish he had, for that would have been clear proof of abuse and the end of our marriage. But his emotional abuse was less definable and always administered in the name of love; his manipulation of me was successful and complete. He believed that our active sex life proved his love while I hungered for tenderness and respect. Increasingly, our sex seemed impersonal: I felt I could have been anybody. Fantasy made it tolerable; I gleaned what I wanted from it by thinking of other, more likeable men. Perhaps he knew this at some level, for he often told me he would kill me and anyone he caught me with. He need not have worried; he did not understand me well enough to know my insular upbringing excluded any possibility of infidelity. While I had grown up with no clear examples of bad marriages (it never occurred to me to wonder about the private lives of my various aunts and uncles) I'd had no clear examples of good marriages either. My preparation for relationships was a void. I've heard that our love maps are charted early in life; perhaps later I unconsciously looked for those things that had been lacking: my mother's support, lost through death; my father's support, lost through absence.

When my divorce was final, I gathered enough courage to invite the lovely Scotsman from the nursery for a romantic dinner. He declined and when I pressed him he told me he could not be with a woman. Not understanding, I said, Oh no, were you injured in the war? He had no recourse then but to tell me the truth: he was gay. Later I saw his partner, flagrant and affected, and wished that things could be different. I still cringe at my naivete - at age thirty-seven! After all, I had worked comfortably with gay interior designers at Bullock's but it had never occurred to me to reflect upon their personal preferences. I simply saw them as different but then, they were more overt than the lovely Scotsman was.

Challenges

An observant man at a single parent Thanksgiving dinner suggested that eight-year-old Scott was dyslexic. I had never heard of dyslexia, now loosely labeled ADD/ADHD. Little was known about it then and children who suffered were cruelly labeled neurologically handicapped. Hyperactivity is common. More enlightened studies show that dyslexic individuals often have above average intelligence and tend to be more creative and less structured in their thinking than most; they include many well-known successful people who think outside the box, names you would recognize, like Richard Branson and Charles Schwab, among others.

In retrospect, I could see certain incidents, which I had attributed to normal little boy behavior, in a new light. When he was four, in the few minutes it took for me to whip up a Fruit Flummery for dessert, Scott pulled a chair to the hallway thermostat and found the hidden carpenter's nail we used as a key for the locked bathroom door. He unlocked the door, dragged the chair to the bathroom counter, clambered up to the medicine cabinet and swallowed a handful of orange-flavored baby aspirin - candy to Scott. In the emergency room, Scott had his stomach pumped.

Fruit Flummery, for those of a different era, consisted of Cool Whip and Jello beaten into a tasty froth of no nutritional value, a fact that never occurred to us then. We thought that Metracal was healthy too. When I awoke to chocolate-colored stains on the white hallway carpet and a mysteriously diminished quart of the stuff, I realized that Scott had raided the refrigerator during the night.

One day in Sears, Scott dove headfirst into a trash barrel next to the cash register to retrieve a dollar bill he had spotted. Back on his feet, he found himself face to face with an amused John Wayne and was duly impressed.

It was no surprise then, while Donald I were still together, that Scott tied a noose on a branch of the Brazilian pepper tree, just like John Wayne. When Donald and I heard strange choking sounds coming from the front yard, he dashed out one door, I another. When Donald reached the tree, Scott was clutching the roped branch above him with one hand while trying to free himself from the makeshift noose with the other.

From an early age, Scott was a perfectionist. I expect this offered him some form of order and control over his distracted mind. Sometimes, while the rest of us slept, he re-folded and rearranged his clothes in his dresser drawer, unlike Katy, whose idea of hanging clothes was to shove them under her bed.

Dyslexics perform best in calm environments devoid of sensory excess. This explained why Scott seemed overwhelmed in shopping malls: too many people, too many objects, too much color, too much activity, too much noise. At times his energy could disrupt a classroom. Often dyslexic children are regarded as incorrigible, rebellious and unruly when in reality, they are frustrated by their own learning disabilities, which even today are often misunderstood. Early recognition and specially trained, empathetic teachers are essential.

The observant man at the Thanksgiving dinner was involved in dyslexia research. He suggested I have Scott tested by a group of physicians in Orange County, pioneers in this then uncharted field. Scott was tested physically and psychologically and was diagnosed as moderately dyslexic. These doctors told me that this condition was more common in boys than girls and was usually inherited from the father.

In retrospect, this explained a lot about Donald's behavior. Still unconvinced however, I found a second group of specialists. When they completely concurred with the first diagnosis, I called Donald, hoping he would help pay for the costs, which were not covered by insurance. When I told him that Scott would require professional help, he said, That's your problem and hung up.

For a year, Scott went through therapy that included trampoline work: up/down and catching: left/right; dyslexic children invariably get them backwards just as they get words backwards. I once read in a medical journal that it's as though, in the dyslexic brain, the wires are crossed.

No wonder Scott resisted reading. I didn't know then that his first and second grade teacher frequently made him stand before the class as he struggled to read each page, backwards, from the bottom up because he thought that was the way it was done. She was relentless: Keep reading, keep reading as the other children laughed. I don't know how a teacher could be so unkind or why I hadn't known.

Trampoline therapy can also help dyslexic children judge relation of height to ground. I looked out the kitchen window one day to see a triumphant Scott, oblivious of danger, at the top of a very skinny thirty-foot eucalyptus tree as a circle of awestruck friends gazed up in admiration from the concrete patio below.

Another time I opened the back door and was startled to find a dead rattlesnake convincingly coiled on the doormat, as Scott giggled around the corner. He had found it in the nearby field and thought he would play a joke on me. Was he sure the snake was dead? I found his joke creative but worrisome.

When I could no longer afford special help, an empathetic teacher arranged a six-month reading scholarship at The Reading Game in Huntington Beach. Several evenings a week I drove Scott there to spend an hour working with a young woman named Tony on a computer ahead of its time. Scott responded well to Tony's tutoring and his reading level jumped two grades. Then our school district decided to remove dyslexic students from the regular classroom and sent Scott to a school across town, where, in a special class, separated from his friends, he struggled, miserable. Some of his new classmates were severely dysfunctional or mentally handicapped. He felt ostracized; he felt I had sent him there because I thought him retarded, but in truth I had no say in the matter. One day he called me at work, crying. He had run away from school and crossed a busy highway to reach home two miles away. He told me his teacher was mean but I knew that children sometimes say such things although, having met her, I instinctively felt she was not suited for her work. But we had no options, we were stuck with her.

Then out of the blue, the teacher who had noticed Katy in kindergarten called me. She was now teaching a regular first grade class at the same school and had recognized Scott because he bore a close resemblance to Katy. She remembered the day we had chosen the kittens. Curious as to why he was in this special class, she began to observe him and saw that his teacher did indeed single him out, as though Scott reminded her of something negative that had nothing to do with him at all. She arranged to rescue Scott from his teacher for most of each school day as her teacher's aide, a situation that suited Scott, for he was helpful with younger children. In addition, she arranged private art lessons for him after school. Scott's school life became a little easier and after two years at the special school, he returned to a regular classroom close to home.

Scott always had to learn things in his own way, in his own time. When he was about four, I signed him up for swimming lessons because I believed that every child should learn to swim. I was mortified when he sat at the side of the pool and cried and refused to be coaxed into the water. But the following summer, when we had daily access to our vacationing neighbor's pool, he was diving and swimming the pool length under water in just two weeks. Soon afterwards, he taught a severely dyslexic neighborhood boy to swim and to ride a bicycle.

Born late into the lives of his European parents, both concert pianists, this difficult child obviously confounded them, so they were effusively grateful to Scott.

Despite his difficulties, Scott was affectionate, funny and resourceful. Unlike his sister, who as a toddler, seemed always intent on escaping me in a store, Scott wanted to know my whereabouts at all times. If he lost sight of me, he simply had me summoned over the public-address system.

One day, as I was making my bed, I imagined I heard a duck quacking in the hallway. A moment later Scott's head popped around the door. Guess what I traded for eight coke bottles, Mom? (And thirty-five cents, he told me recently.) Charlie the duck lived in our little reflection pool for a while until we released him at Boat's Beach among the mallards, although Charlie, we later realized, was probably a farm duck. Boat's Beach, incidentally, can't be found on a map. It is actually the bayside beach that headquarters the Harbor Patrol whose mascot was a friendly German Shepherd named Boats. For Katy, Scott and me it was always Boat's Beach.

Scott acquired a tortoise too, which he named Touche, after a cartoon character, which actually was a turtle. Touche had wanderlust; he repeatedly dug his way out of our yard, only to be returned by one neighbor or another until the day he never came back. Both my children loved animals, as do I. When Scott was in his early teens, as we were driving up MacArthur Boulevard in Newport Beach, I swerved to avoid a rabbit that had darted into the road. But the silly creature made a U-turn and went directly beneath the wheels of my Volkswagen. There was a sickening bumpy crunch. Convinced the rabbit was very dead, and lacking the courage to stop to examine the damage, I kept driving. Scott yelled at me to turn around and run over the rabbit again to put him out of his misery.

I had no stomach for running over the poor thing deliberately, dead or alive. Scott called me a murderer and scarcely spoke to me for almost three weeks.

I knew I had to find a job but I felt it important that I stay home with the children that first summer after the divorce. We ate day-old bread from the Langendorf outlet, cottage cheese instead of meat, macaroni and cheese, anything cheap and filling. I placed an advertisement in the local paper to care for other peoples' children at home throughout the summer but became numb and incoherent during my first interview with a mother who hastily left. Fearing I was suffering a stroke, I called my doctor who immediately drove to my house. He told me I was lacking in iron and protein and needed to eat red meat. Norlene and Doris brought us steaks.

When the children returned to school, I went job-hunting. I had been out of the market for eight years; my most recent experience had been in aerospace. I finally found work in a job shop in Anaheim where a kind older man who resembled Santa Claus took a chance on me. My favorite coworkers included a Hell's Angel, a big bearded bear of a man with a baby face who named me Sparkle Plenty, and a strikingly beautiful young Swedish woman who turned out to be a drug addict. The hours were long and erratic, the freeway commute exhausting, the pay inadequate. If I missed work I did not get paid and there were no company benefits; I was thankful that the court had decreed that Donald maintain his company health insurance for the children. Sometimes I drove my Volkswagen to San Bernardino to pick up a government job then returned to the job shop to work an extended shift to meet yet another urgent deadline, straining over a light table, Xacto knife poised to position a microscopic fragment of type. Conditions were deplorable. There were no windows, no air conditioning and the linoleum floors were curled and cracked. No wonder people called them sweatshops. Once during an extreme heat wave, as workmen labored to replace the linoleum, we hauled our drafting tables out onto the sticky asphalt parking lot where, under the blazing sun, we choked on tar and traffic fumes as the ink in our Rapidograph pens dried up.

Since I held a top-secret clearance, I was occasionally sent to nearby Hughes Aircraft to work in-house, in a small windowless room behind locked doors. When workers needed to visit the restroom, an armed guard escorted them one at a time and waited outside. I resented this prison-like environment and had to remind myself that I was lucky to have a job at all.

I went through a series of incompetent baby sitters from a nearby bible college; I could not afford Anne then. One evening I came home to find the baby sitter in the den, sharing marijuana with my children. Every night I sat in commuter traffic and wondered how I could change my life for the better. I found no answers. Returning to school for a master's degree would involve time and money and I had neither; already I spent too little time with my children, so I continued to scratch a living from paycheck to paycheck.

Still, I tried to do the usual things that mothers do for their children. That Halloween, when Katy wanted to be Morticia of the Adams family, I spent hours stuffing octopus tentacles of Morticia's long black dress I'd sewn, with cotton batting that filled every crevice of our family room for days.

Scott was a spaceman that year. In 1969, when he was eleven, he got up in the middle of the night to watch the moon landing with me on our little black and white television.

The Summer of Love

It was 1967, *the summer of love,* a difficult time for a girl almost thirteen. Katy's behavior had begun to change. She and her friends began to look like gypsies in their colorful muumuus and beads; everything became peace, love, hugs and rallies in a tent chapel. When I mentioned this to my father, he said I could send her to Australia to live with him for a year but I knew it was an empty promise. My stepmother would never agree to such a thing, nor would I have expected her to.

Katy became interested in boys I didn't know and felt uneasy about. She became increasingly rebellious and secretive. When I disciplined her, she threatened to *go live with Daddy.* It was an empty threat; Donald wanted nothing to do with his children. I knew Katy called him sometimes but he told her the same thing each time: *I divorced you kids when I divorced your mother,* and hung up.

Like many girls her age, she longed for a horse and when a skinny mare came up for sale cheap at the nearby fairgrounds, I relented: the stables lay between our house and the school, so it seemed an ideal situation. I knew nothing about horses (*what was I thinking?)* but Katy learned quickly. She spent every spare moment before and after school happily tending her charge and under Katy's care, Amber quickly gained weight and blossomed into a fine healthy animal. In fact, Katy was the only person Amber truly tolerated; she tried more than once to wipe me off her back under the stable eaves.

Later that same year, I sold the house, finding it increasingly difficult to maintain. Donald and I had paid less than $19,000 for the house and nine years later, I cleared barely enough for a minimal down payment on a nearby condominium, close to schools and the stables. On uncharacteristic impulse, I invited forty people for homemade lasagna the night before potential buyers were due to sign. It turned into a wildly successful party with an unlikely mix of guests that included friends, neighbors and coworkers, some of whom lingered in the back patio until three a.m. It took a marathon effort on my part to restore the house and yard to order before the agent arrived with his clients at 8 a.m.

Moving day dawned on the heaviest rainstorm in years. A Mexican coworker, married and much younger than I, offered to help me move. I accepted, glad for some help. At the condominium, while Katy and Scott were upstairs, he pushed me against the wall of the small downstairs bathroom and pressed hard against me. Afraid my children would come downstairs, I tried to reason quietly with him. With his arm against my throat he hissed, Don't you feel sorry for me! You better not feel sorry for me! I suddenly realized he was high on drugs; why had I not seen that before? The thought that my thirteen year-old daughter upstairs could be at risk kept me calm. Finally he gave up and left. That night I sat at the dining room table and watched water leak through the cheap chandelier overhead. It was a very low moment at the end of a low day. Back at work on Monday, I avoided him. He did not apologize or refer to the incident at all but it made me determined to escape the job shop grind and its long commute.

I found another job closer to home, at Collins Radio with regular hours and better pay. I was the sole woman in a department of twelve. We sat at large tables equipped with drafting machines and rolls of linen on which we inked schematics with Rapidograph pens, Leroy scribes and templates. It was not unlike North American Aviation but on a smaller scale and in more pleasant surroundings. The people, though, were much the same: engineers and technicians, bright but unimaginative.

I liked the men in my department except one who sat directly behind me. Because he was a bigot, the other men called him Archie Bunker, which he took as a compliment. He did all he could to make my life miserable. He referred to his wife as the gorilla and propositioned me every day for a quickie in a nearby field at noon. He even bragged that he sometimes sat at the bottom of the stairs at South Coast Plaza to look up women's miniskirts. I especially dreaded Mondays when he interrogated me about my weekend, which invariably had been uneventful. Somehow I learned that my male coworkers were paid considerably more than I for performing identical work. In fact, most of them sat over coffee and morning newspapers for the first hour of the day while I bent over my schematic, feeling I needed to prove myself as a woman in a man's world. I tried to talk to my timorous alcoholic boss but got nowhere; I was afraid to push too hard for fear of losing my job. My tormenter overheard and said, Why should you be paid the same as us? You're a woman!

In 1968 America was shaken once again by the horror of assassination, first, Martin Luther King, then Robert Kennedy. These larger than life events made my problems seem trivial.

****

Feeling that Scott needed to be involved in team sports, I signed him up for Little League. I knew nothing of baseball and nor did Scott. His father had never been interested in any sport, either as a participant or a spectator. Not knowing the game, Scott found himself ridiculed by the other boys and even some of their parents who, to my astonishment, took Little League or rather, winning, very seriously. Apparently the coach didn't offer Scott much direction. But when a neighborhood high school boy saw how fast Scott could run, how far and accurately he could throw a ball – away from competition – he took him under his wing and taught him about football. One-on-one, Scott learned to love sports although he continued to be competitive only with himself; his perfectionism made him his own most demanding critic. His mentor later became a professional football player.

I felt Scott should have a good male role model and applied to Big Brothers. They had a long waiting list but when they learned that Scott's father lived ten minutes away and spent his spare time volunteering for the local police department rather than with his children, Scott received priority. Almost immediately, he was matched for a year with a very kind man who took Scott to baseball and football games and included him in his own family life.

Dating Disasters

By now Norlene had divorced; Doris followed within months, both for reasons different from mine. Unlike me, neither of them needed to work so I saw less of them than I would have liked. But on occasional weekends, Norlene and I went to a club where we exhausted ourselves dancing the Twist. I loved to dance but hated the nightclub scene, which only made me feel lonely.

I tried a singles dance group once but recall only women, waiting eagerly by the door for one man to appear. He wore a loud plaid jacket and an unfortunate toupe, but he could dance.

The first man I dated after my divorce was a German doctor, educated in England. It didn't take long for me to realize he was simply a more polished version of my husband and from then on I tried to be more conscious of the danger of repeating old patterns.

For a year after my divorce was final, I went through a series of forgettable men, then retreated, sick of the whole dating scene.

Some liaisons, however, stick in my memory like thorns. One man invited me to a gala formal affair in Pasadena, to be followed by a performance by pianist Arthur Rubinstein. I made an elegant cream crepe dress, appropriate for this exciting occasion, and was chagrined when my date pulled up in his dirty old work truck rather than his car, too high for me to step into in my long sheath, at least not gracefully. The worst was yet to come: when he got out of the truck I stared at him in disbelief. He was dressed in jeans and a tee shirt emblazoned with a huge portrait of Mickey Mouse. His suit wasn't ready at the dry cleaners, he said and he hadn't had time after work to pick up his car.

My immediate impulse was to tell him where to go - without me - but the thought of missing Rubinstein got the better of me. The long drive to Pasadena was strained, my lovely dress soiled. I spent the entire gala affair trying to avoid my escort who was attracting many raised eyebrows, of which he seemed oblivious. Thankfully, the concert hall was dark and the performance brilliant, but the drive home seemed endless. I never spoke to him again.

A young English woman I worked with and liked wanted me to meet a friend of her husband's, feeling sure we would get along well. At dinner at the Madonna Inn, which I find garish, his full set of very bad false teeth rotated wildly around his open mouth as he chewed. He told me about his fifteen year-old daughter, whom he loved and protected. He told me he would be stricken should she ever be raped. Empathetic, I foolishly mentioned my past experience of attempted rape, to which he responded, But that wouldn't matter, you're a grown woman. There was a very long moment of silence as he saw that I, aware of nearby diners, was icily furious. He whispered, I just blew it with you, didn't I? I concurred, we left the Madonna Inn and once again, I endured a very long drive home.

Another man I had dated a few times invited me water skiing with some of his friends on Newport's Back Bay. I had already realized he was extremely competitive with other men; he had an ego that required winning at all times. As I skied on the busy waterway full of speeding boats, he spotted a man on unusual skis. Not to be outdone, he raced across the bay to inquire about them, leaving me to flounder unprotected in the water. I was terrified; I knew what boat propellers could do. Very quickly a Harbor patrol boat was beside me and helping hands hauled me on board. They had witnessed everything and with sirens blaring, pursued my companion.

In front of his friends, they read him the riot act and wrote him a citation, much to my satisfaction. Back in his boat, as he seethed at being caught, I hauled off and punched him as hard as I could. Since he was much taller than I, the punch landed harmlessly on his chest but nevertheless I found it gratifying. I had never hit a man before - or since. That was the end of that relationship although things had not gone well since the afternoon before when we were sunning ourselves on his patio and I had told him I was nine years his senior. He was so startled, he actually fell off his chaise. Apparently I had hit him in the ego, for he had a rule only to date younger women.

There were others, best forgotten, as well as a few good men who were caring single fathers, none of whom I ever loved. I thought it entirely possible that I could die of loneliness but was never tempted to return to my marriage. Yet that year had made me aware, for the first time, of my own feminine powers; I saw that men found me attractive. I began to gain confidence. And without realizing it, I had taken the first tentative steps across the invisible field of fear that had separated me from new possibilities. Through necessity, I had acted in small ways to move forward: I had found a job, I had worked responsibly, I had maintained the house, the yard and the Volkswagen and driven Southern California freeways and cared for my children. I had survived. I suddenly knew that once I crossed that field, I would never truly fear anything or anyone as much as I had in the past.

Fling

Norlene and I decided it was time to celebrate our freedom. In Norlene's Volkswagen we headed north to the Monterey Peninsula, a pace I'd never been, for a long weekend, leaving Katy and Scott once again in Anne's capable hands. It was October – autumn - and I had sewn fashionable wool plaid Bermuda shorts to wear with my heavy sweater and matching yellow knee socks. We arrived to find temperatures in the nineties – unusual for the peninsula at *any* time of year. Our little Carmel inn was not air-conditioned so we spent our days by the bay and our evenings at the cool Doubletreee Inn in Monterey, sipping chilled drinks and fast-dancing. The Los Angeles Lakers were in town. I danced one evening with a sandy-haired basketball player named Rod, so tall that I was eye level with the emblem on his blazer pocket. This discouraged conversation, which suited me nicely, for I had no interest in seeing him again. I only wanted to dance myself furiously into a state of emotional exhaustion.

We left Carmel on Sunday and headed south on the freeway. As we approached Thousand Oaks, we found ourselves in darkness even though it was only three o'clock in the afternoon. An endless string of headlights edged snail-pace as firefighters battled a large brush fire on both sides of the freeway. Even though the heat was stifling, we rolled the car windows up tight against the thick smoke. We were in the far-left southbound lane when suddenly a northbound pickup truck careened across the dirt center divider toward us. Norlene reacted quickly, turning wheels hard right as the truck crossed directly in front of us, so close we could see the young driver's face. Amazingly, he missed other cars as his vehicle hurtled across the freeway and overturned in the far right lane, tossing him unconscious onto the pavement. We managed to pull over. I knelt and touched his hand as big rigs rolled slowly by in the gloom while Norlene stood close by, waving in caution. The young driver's breath was heavy with alcohol.

He slipped in and out of consciousness as firefighters made their way up the embankment toward us. Then, suddenly wide-eyed, he gasped that his little brother had been in the car with him. This sent some firefighters to the overturned vehicle while others went back down the embankment, but they found nothing. He clutched my hand as though his life depended on it and told me that he couldn't feel his legs. I tried to reassure him and he calmed down a little although I think he was in shock; I guessed that his injuries were very serious. A priest appeared, leaned close to the boy and began to administer the last rites. At this, the young man panicked, perhaps realizing for the first time that he might die. I turned on the priest, protesting that comfort and reassurance were what the young man needed at that moment, not a ritualistic chant for the dying. The priest moved away, leaving the young man sobbing and me angry. As medics loaded him into an ambulance, he continued to grip my hand, begging me to stay with him. Of course that was not possible – we were strangers, unrelated. I wanted to follow the ambulance to the hospital, wherever that was, but Norlene was more practical. We could never get through the backed-up traffic and stay close to the ambulance in an unfamiliar area. Besides, she said, we needed to get home to our children. Of course she was right. She asked a medic the name of the hospital. When we called from home, we were told the young man was not at that facility. We had no right to information anyway. We would never know if he had survived or how his life might have been forever changed.

Monticello

In the condominium complex where we now lived, I made friends with a close neighbor, a beautiful and intelligent young woman from the West Indies, married to a handsome landscape architect who ran his own business. They had two little girls whom Katy sometimes babysat.

Jessica called me at work one day, frantic, and told me my condominium was on fire. I was grateful that Katy and Scott were at school. I ran for my car in the parking lot, three coworkers, including my tormentor, hard on my heels. We arrived to see fire trucks and police cars blocking the alley that ran between the rows of attached garages.

A passenger in a speeding car had tossed a Molotov cocktail into my next-door neighbor's open garage, gouging a crater in the concrete floor and melting her car. The flames had ignited my garage roof and laundry room and spread toward my upstairs bedroom but by the time I arrived, the firefighters had them under control. It could have been worse: my neighbor's young children, who usually spent most of their waking hours playing in her garage, were inside eating lunch when the explosion occurred. She had only recently moved in and I had the feeling that the attack was aimed at the previous occupant - a pale, reclusive young woman who wore flowing black and held regular late night meetings to the flicker of candlelight. I often heard strange chanting through the wall that made me think of witchcraft or devil worship. I kept my distance although I rarely saw her outside.

To my knowledge, the crime was never solved. Insurance paid for repairs but not before a splinter struck inquisitive Scott in the eye as he stared up at the sky through a charred hole in the garage roof. Our pediatrician safely removed the splinter and I installed an automatic garage door opener for the illusion of extra security.

Meanwhile, Donald continued to ignore his children. I was standing nearby when Scott called him one day and asked, When will you take me camping, Daddy? Donald said, Put your mother on the phone. To me, he said, Get that little bastard the hell off my back, then hung up. Hit and run; bullies are cowards, Norlene said.

Adoration

Norlene was dating a man whose coworkers met every week for chess and jazz sessions. They thought I would get along well with the odd man out who happened to be their boss. Their obvious respect and affection for him intrigued me since I was used to hearing employees complain about management. He was separated but not divorced from his wife. I had high-minded rules: I had chosen not to date until my own divorce was final and I had resolved never to date a married man. So I was stunned to realize the moment we met that I could not walk away from this man; I had met no one like him before. The attraction was mutual.

When he was in his early twenties, John's genius had caught the attention of Army Intelligence. Fluent in Upper Mandarin, German and Russian, he was quickly recruited by the CIA and after several covert years in the field, became assistant director of Soviet Union affairs in Bavaria, where he lived for seven years. An idealist, he eventually became disenchanted with the CIA's increasing bureaucracy. By the time we met, he had been retired from *The Company* for several years and now ran a division of a major international corporation.

John's parents had been friends with his wife's parents before their children were born just two months apart and had assumed from the start that they would marry. When he returned from WW2 at twenty-six, thinking he should settle down as his friends had, this childhood playmate seemed a sensible choice that would please everybody. He had supposed that romantic love would follow friendship.

On their wedding night, as they gazed on the moonlit Rhine from their honeymoon suite, she said, *Please don't spoil this beautiful scene with sex, John.* The marriage was not consummated; he left and spent most of his wedding night determined to get drunk. The following morning he sought the advice of a diplomat friend of his parents who told him he should do the *honorable thing* and stay in the marriage. His bride believed that sex was a marital duty intended to produce children and eventually they had four. John never blamed her for being asexual; as the only child of a prominent family, she had been strictly molded. Nor did he ever speak unkindly of her. Had he ever complained that his wife didn't understand him, I would have stepped back, for I had heard all that too often before.

Within the context of this unfulfilling marriage, he remained loyal to his responsibilities; he made sure his children were well educated and prepared for their futures. He and his wife had agreed to continue to share their large house until their son, younger than his sisters, left for Harvard. As it was, John was away most of the time and although they did not live as husband and wife, their relationship was not acrimonious.

When he was home, he slept in a bedroom in a separate wing of the house. Still, this caused me some pain and doubt. Doubt, not because I didn't trust him to be honest with me, but because I feared that his sense of duty might never allow us to realize our future.

John was modest: I heard of his exploits mostly from others, including his closest friend and CIA partner, and old newspaper clippings. Both men and women liked him, which I saw as a revealing indication of character. One woman described him as *charismatic,* another as *elegant,* and that was true although in reality, he was slightly pigeon-toed and wore thick glasses as a result of an early childhood illness. It was the substance of the man that shone through, that made me love him more and more.

He played tennis and golf, he sailed, he appreciated nature as I did. We sailed on Mission Bay and hiked through Muir Woods. He said he almost dreaded the beginning of our trips because each day together brought us closer to the day we would have to go our separate ways. He loved jazz - sometimes when we were in a club, he joined the band on clarinet. Although his parents could afford it, he paid for his college education with his own small swing band which he later took into Burma during WWII to entertain the troops. He was also writing a novel based on his CIA years. Sometimes, as we sat by a pool in Palm Springs or Mission Bay, he would look up from his writing and say, *What's another word for...?* We were excited when a major publisher expressed interest in the book.

We spent every possible moment together. Whenever he returned from his European business trips, I met him at the airport and we would spend the night talking, talking, hungry to share everything that had happened since we had last met, then make love as the sun came up. We laughed when a hotel bed collapsed beneath us once and howled hilariously over *Portnoy's Complaint,* as I recalled Lillian's admonition when I was little: *If you play with yourself, you'll go blind.* No man had ever wanted to know me so well or treated me with such tenderness. He introduced me to his friends and invited my friends to dinner one by one and told Doris that he *cherished* me. And that's exactly how I felt*: cherished.* Tenderness, passion, communication, shared values: we had it all. For the first time I had found a man I could trust with my *self.* Furthermore, my children respected and liked him. How could I not love him?

John held a lifetime golden pass to Disneyland which gave my children and their friends unlimited access to everything there as often as they wanted; eleven year-old Scott once took the helm of the Mark Twain. John and I took advantage of this time to steal away for a game of tennis or a quiet meal at the private 33 Club in Disneyland.

I realized one day, as John and I followed Katy and her girlfriends through the entrance, that they all wore something of mine. Often as I was dressing for work I would find that the blouse I had ironed the night before was missing or a favorite sweater was soiled. I found cigarette holes in a silk shirt - I had stopped smoking before Katy was born.

Reasoning with Katy or talking about respect for the privacy of others met with silent defiance and she continued to help herself to my modest wardrobe until I reluctantly installed a lock on my bedroom door. It did little to deter her. She had always been a willful child, seemingly determined to learn the hard way. When one of her friends was sent to juvenile hall, she told me she wanted to have that same experience.

Meanwhile, she was neglecting Amber. I warned her that I would sell the horse if she did not properly care for her. She continued to feed Amber every day but did little else; the novelty had worn off. When I caught her in the aging wood barn loft smoking pot with a boy in the hay, I sold the horse. For a while Katy visited Amber at her new home but soon lost interest.

A detective brought Katy home one afternoon when John was there. He had watched her in a department store as she persuaded some boys she knew to steal jewelry for her although she stole nothing herself. The detective saw her as a sweet girl who had exercised poor judgment. John took her aside and talked quietly to her for a long time. I was sure he had impressed her but he told me no, although she had listened to him politely enough. She stayed silent and gave him that unswerving gaze so familiar to me: direct, with a hint of rebellion, a shadow of a pout. John saw that she would not listen to reason coming from any adult.

Every morning I drove Katy to school only to learn later that she had left the moment I was out of sight. Once I caught her with a boy in a neighbor's bedroom. The boy fled through a window and Katy, misinformed by her peers, said, *Mother, everyone knows you can't get pregnant the first time.* (Was it the first time?)

Whenever I tried to reason with Katy, she retorted, *You don't trust me!* I reminded her that trust has to be earned but she didn't want to hear it.

When drugs began to surface at her school, I joined a group of concerned parents who called a meeting with the school principal, a sanctimonious man who seemed unsuited to his occupation. He denied there was a drug problem at the school, then found himself protesting these assertions in front of a television news camera. Those parents who could afford to, sent their children, including most of Katy's friends, to private schools.

When the day came for Katy to graduate from junior high school, I took the afternoon off from work and drove directly to the ceremony. I watched as a stream of students walked onto the stage to accept their diplomas but Katy did not appear. I found her at home, angry and tearful. The principal had told her she could not appear at the graduation ceremony because her dress was too short, although it was no shorter than the dresses of the other girls. I suspected the principal was punishing Katy because I had been one of the parents who had raised the issue of drugs. I drove straight back to the school and found him in his office. He patronized me with his supercilious smile and refused to give me Katy's diploma. I pointed out that Katy had earned her diploma – despite cutting classes, she had kept up her grades. He remained smugly stubborn until I told him I would go to the school board. I left with diploma in hand and considered what Scott, as Katy's brother, might expect when the time came for him to attend that school.

At fifteen, Katy became involved with a sixteen year-old boy from school. His family was uneducated and newly rich; they indulged their son's every whim. For his sixteenth birthday they bought him a new

Pontiac Firebird that provided far too much freedom and too little accountability.

One day I came home from work and heard my father talking upstairs on my bedroom phone. As usual, he had not let me know he was coming to America. My neighbors told me that he had chased the boy's car, Katy inside, down our alley, shouting and shaking his fist. He told me I had no business working, that I should be at home taking care of my children. There was no point in trying to explain that I had no choice but to work. He said he would help me financially and on the first night of his visit, he offered to pay for our groceries. At the cash register, our basket loaded with Johnny Walker, Bud and Camels, he told me he would repay me once he exchanged his Australian money. I had heard this before but invariably, on the day he was to leave, I had to ask him for reimbursement and invariably, he argued over the amount. He once left me with a phone bill I couldn't afford to pay. It was months before he repaid me as I negotiated with the Phone Company. I found these episodes demeaning and exhausting.

I thought about birth control for Katy but felt that would imply my approval and permission for sexual activity. I talked to her about the possibility and implications of pregnancy, the importance of school, about waiting for marriage and so on...all the things I believed. But Katy was not me and times were different: this was the summer of love. I sought my doctor's counsel and liked his advice: *Put the responsibility on Katy and her boyfriend. Let them decide whether they can control themselves or whether they should use protection.* He examined Katy and performed a pregnancy test.

I talked to them, one at a time and together, and gave them two days to make a decision. They listened politely enough, but two days later they told me they could *not* control themselves. I called my doctor and even though *The Pill* had not been approved for young, single females before 1972, he prescribed it for Katy. I clearly remember that day when Katy and I we were on our way to the pharmacy: we were getting into the car when the phone rang. The doctor simply said, *It's too late.*

I spoke to Katy of abortion although I was concerned about the emotional damage she might suffer as a result. I don't think that anyone *likes* or *wants* abortion and I would not *choos*e it but I had to consider the long-term effects on Katy 's life as a child-parent. I believe abortion should be made safe.

But Katy had romantic notions about babies and the boy's mother encouraged her. As the woman witlessly said, *the kids are in love!* I tried to convince Katy to postpone marriage at least until she graduated from high school. She could place her baby in day care. I had to work full-time; I could not care for an infant, nor did I want to. These ideas were met by Katy's familiar defiant gaze, and in the end, she married the boy. I made her a beautiful white dress and saw her off to a small remote town in Utah I had never heard of, the only place in America where children could be legally married. They flew there in the boy's parents' private four-seat plane and honeymooned in a Las Vegas hotel where Katy's new mother-in-law called after the wedding night and told Katy to be sure her son's socks matched.

Her brief honeymoon over, Katy walked in the door and said, *I don't want to be married and I don't want to have a baby.*

It's a little late, I said, exasperated. But Katy was adamant and the boy, having reconsidered fatherhood at sixteen, agreed to an abortion. He had never been encouraged to think for himself; he would concede to the last person to talk to him, especially if that person were his mother. I had seen this woman throw fits to get her way and she usually succeeded. Now, when she intervened, the boy gave in. Without his permission, the decision for an abortion was out of Katy's hands and the course of her life was forever changed.

We considered adoption but the boy's is mother threatened legal action to adopt the baby herself, an option I felt would be disastrous. I consulted a lawyer and found I had no rights.

Two weeks before her sixteenth birthday, in October 1970, Katy delivered a son. There was some concern at first because the baby was RH negative. The boy's mother was ecstatic, while I saw little cause for celebration over two babies having a baby. Most of all I felt sadness for the loss of that bright future my beautiful daughter's teacher believed had been her destiny. The outcome now seemed sadly predictable. Years later, Katy confessed to me that she had taken LSD during her pregnancy.

When Donald learned that Katy was married, he cut off her support. Although he was legally within his rights, I felt that a caring father might have banked that money for his daughter for later when she surely would need it. There was no wedding present either.
In contrast, my father gave Katy one hundred dollars when he learned she was pregnant.

That Christmas, Katy phoned her father from my place and told him she wanted to visit him with the baby - Donald had not yet seen his first grandchild, although he lived nearby. She had spent hours creating a little seashore sculpture for him, from driftwood she had gathered from the beach and miniature ceramic seagulls. He told her he was busy; *It's not a good time*. She said, *Just for a little while, we won't stay long*. Donald said, *I don't want a screaming kid around.* He finally relented, saying, *Well, for a half-hour. You can just put him in another room.*

Hearing this, I hated that Katy would reduce herself to begging for a little kindness from her own father, who had repeatedly proved incapable of giving it. After all, this was his first and only grandchild.

Katy called me distraught one night from the boy's parents' home. Her husband had fallen through the shower door and she couldn't lift him. He was too drunk to be hurt. While we were on the phone, the parents came home. His mother looked at her inebriated offspring and said, *My baby's a man now, he can drink.* He was diagnosed as an alcoholic at sixteen.

Not long after this incident, several law enforcement agencies closed in on the parents' house and arrested the boy and his father on fraud and conspiracy charges. The boy was later released because he was a juvenile although he managed one of the thirteen gas stations in Orange County that his father owned, businesses that were the target of the investigation. Apparently the father had been holding weekly meetings that instructed employees in ways to cause undetectable damage to customers' cars so that they could not leave the gas station, or would break down nearby. I remember the outrage of the men I worked with when the news broke in two-inch headlines but I never let on that I was connected to this unsavory family.

The father hired a lawyer he could easily afford and managed to delay his trial repeatedly. He finally served six months in federal prison. His employees, however, served several years – or rather, those who lived long enough to testify at their boss' trial. One stipulation of his release was that he could never do business in California again. He opened a successful truck stop just over the border in Nevada. His son joined him and Katy found herself isolated on a farm outside Reno.

Following a Dream

I decide to use my vacation time for my first trip to Europe. John hoped I would visit the house he had lived in during his CIA years. He believed that I could best learn the German language by experience; during his CIA days, he had become fluent in upper Mandarin by living for a year in the home of a professor who allowed no other language to be spoken.

Nevertheless, I studied German for a semester at my local college before I traveled to Bavaria in the spring of 1971. It was adequate enough to help me find lodging and local cafes and to ask for help with train schedules. I flew into Frankfurt, spotless and ablaze with tulips, caught a bus to the train station and traveled to Heidelberg, where I spent a congenial beer-drenched evening in a neighborhood café with eleven exuberant German students, only two of whom spoke any English at all. The following day I explored Heidelberg, lingering at the old castle above the town square - somberly beautiful in the cold rain - then traveled by streetcar to Munich and Garmisch-Partenkirchen. In Garmisch, as I searched for lodging in a misty twilight, I met an American dentist who scoffed at my budget travel guide. He was staying at an American style hotel nearby and suggested I do the same but I declined. It was more money than I was willing to spend and I wanted to absorb Europe through local eyes. As I moved on, I met two delightful elderly women who spoke no English and laughed at my fractured German. They shared their umbrellas and directed me to a nearby small penione where I sank blissfully into a feather bed for two dollars a night - the American dentist paid seven times that! For an additional twenty-five cents, I could enjoy a soft-boiled egg with my pastry and coffee in the small dining room, in agreeable company. A wash bowl in my room provided an adequate sponge bath.

In the morning I opened my shutters to a window box of bright flowers and the musical flow of a mountain stream below. I hadn't expected the view: the breathtaking snowy peaks of the Zugspitze filled my window. The impeccable, pretty street was already busy with bicycles and Mercedes Benz taxis. I took a swaying cable car to the top of the mountain from where, on a clear day, one supposedly could see four countries. Not so this day: my photographs show nothing but the dense white of a blizzard on all sides. I returned from the mountaintop on a cog wheel train and once back in town, spent a leisurely hour in a bakery where I could linger undisturbed over hot coffee as I planned the next day. I was duly impressed with European bakeries: the pastries were so exquisite that at first I thought they had been decorated for some expected royal visitor.

The day I left Garmisch, I ran into the two elderly ladies at the post office and thanked them for their kindness. They seemed disappointed that I could not stay another day to hear the Berlin Philharmonic but tempting as that was, I needed to stick to my tight schedule.

I traveled by train to Lake Starnberg. John had given me clear directions to the house and it was just as he had described, set in a forest by a lake complete with black swans and a Zugspitze backdrop, with a private chapel, tennis court and boat dock. I spoke briefly with a housekeeper who knew little English but didn't seem to mind that I wanted to explore the grounds and the little stone chapel. I saw enough to know I could feel at home here. But then, wherever John was would be home to me. From the beginning, John had intended that Scott and Katy would attend good private schools nearby but now, sadly, that new life was lost to Katy.

I continued on to Innsbruck and Lausanne, then crossed the border by train into Italy and a sunnier landscape. In Florence I stayed in a tiny room with shuttered windows and a sink that allowed what Lillian would have called a spit and a promise. In the shared toilet down the hall, yesterday's news served as toilet paper. I saw less of Florence than I would have liked because I could not leave my little hotel without being harassed by persistent Italian men bent on a handout of one sort or another. I went on to Paris where I joined my cousin Margaret, who was working there with Audrey Hepburn at the time and spoke fluent French. After two weeks of traveling alone, dealing with foreign language and foreign exchange, it was a relief to let someone else make plans in the city she knew well. It was, as the song goes, April in Paris and quite unforgettable. In the Louvre. I saw the original Mona Lisa, and was surprised it was so small. I was eager to share it all with John. Having made the trip on an improbably tight budget, I returned to America with thirteen dollars still in my pocket.

Consequences

I had become friendly with one of John's two grown daughters. She invited me to her wedding and reception but I was reluctant – although her mother had agreed to divorce, no one else would know that until after Suzi's wedding. She was still ignorant of my existence and I felt for everyone's sake, it should stay that way. But because Suzi and I shared a secret known only to her father and her future husband, she wanted me there and so I agreed.

She had had a casual one-night stand with a fellow student and was pregnant. Soon afterwards, she met her future husband and told him the truth. A friend knew a back- street doctor in Los Angeles who would perform an abortion, illegal at the time, for a price. The abortion was unsuccessful.

She carried the damaged fetus for several months – had she gone to a hospital, had she reported the doctor, she would have legally implicated herself. The wedding took place about two weeks before Christmas.

And so it was that I sat in a pew near the back of the church and held my breath as a very pregnant Suzi in a cleverly voluminous gown exchanged her vows. Her mother remained oblivious. The reception was held at John's big house on the golf course. When people asked who I was and how did I know Suzi, I casually replied that I had met her in the bakery next door to my work, which was almost true, since I often ran into her there, but I had really met her earlier through John. I felt uncomfortable in that house, in that situation, the mistress, a role I had never wanted.

When John and I were together just before Christmas, he called his brother and sister-in-law in the northeast and told them about me and our plans to be married as soon as the divorce was final. His wife would continue to live as she was accustomed: John had insisted on that. His family seemed genuinely happy for us. His mother encouraged John to seize this chance for a happier life.

Just before the New Year - and our new life - John and I were savoring a contented evening in the little apartment he had recently rented. There was a knock on the door and when John opened it, he found Suzi and her husband standing there, back from their honeymoon early. She had begun to hemorrhage, the delayed result of the abortion attempt months earlier.

In a driving rainstorm, while I stayed at the apartment, John drove Suzi and her husband to some dingy off-track clinic in Los Angeles where she almost died delivering a stillborn infant. John handed over the necessary cash and his wife remained ignorant of the affair, the pregnancy, the abortion and its consequences, and John's role in the whole sad mess. It was the first in a series of reversals that affected our hopes and dreams.

A national recession that year led to the end of John's corporate overseas trips. Luxury offices in America, with their thick carpeting and well-stocked bars, were caught in the cutbacks. When John pulled off the freeway one night with a suspected heart attack, he knew he would have to change course. He joined a small elite group of genetic pioneers including a New Zealand scientist, a Boston Banker and a former NASA scientist who at thirty-six, was the youngest member of this brilliant team. John invested money and energy and was responsible for fund-raising and marketing; in order to qualify for major corporate backing, they had to maintain consistently successful test results for a year. Several major corporations including Johnson & Johnson had already expressed great interest. Their laboratory was in Petaluma, their subjects cattle. Their goals, years before genetics became a household word, were to prevent birth defects and disease.

They continued to produce excellent results for months at a time then suddenly, inexplicable failure. As results continued to be unpredictable, the group struggled on until one member suffered a fatal heart attack, another a debilitating stroke and a third, a nervous breakdown. Believing in the project, wanting to succeed to honor the others, John moved into a small room in San Francisco, his only luxury a small radio. His wife, still living in their big house on the golf course, was well-off in her own right but John refused to touch her money – his choice, not hers. He felt that it was up to him to support his family (and ultimately mine), as they were accustomed. This was the first time in his life that John had experienced financial adversity; he had always paid his own way and lived well and our time together was always first class. Finally, after several consecutive months of negative test results and diminishing funds, he was forced to abandon the project.

Then the publishing house which had expressed strong interest in John's novel wrote to say that in this time of recession, they had, regretfully, decided not to publish unknown authors. It was a blow to both of us.

Then John's wife learned about me and decided she did not want a divorce after all. When John told her he wanted to proceed, she threatened suicide. Everything seemed to be collapsing around us and for the first time I saw John angry, not at me, but at circumstance. I told him I did not care about a high life style, I would live anywhere with him. Finally, he said what I did not want to hear yet understood: *If we seized our happiness, we would have to step over too many bodies and that would destroy us in the end.*

I knew he was right but I was heartbroken. He found new work in Puerto Rico as his family continued their lives uninterrupted in California. I never heard from him again although I tried unsuccessfully to locate him in Puerto Rico. I couldn't find his daughter - by then she had a new life and a new name I didn't remember. Sometimes I thought I might find it easier had he died, for then I could abandon all hope of seeing him again and stop clinging to the possibility that he might somehow find a way for us. I still dream of him sometimes, just out of reach, and wake with a sense of loss. Whenever I hear that old song, *Time after Time,* I catch my breath, for that was the song John claimed as *ours.* Every year, on his birthday, I wonder if he is still alive but I *know* he is not. I was grief-stricken for years for everything we had lost, including a brighter future for my children.

I believe we would have enjoyed a long, happy marriage but if I met him now, I might find us less compatible for I am not the same person I was then. I think had we married and moved to the house on Lake Starnberg that I would have lived a lovely complacent existence. Now I know too much – one man told me I had become *wise* - and I would never want to suffer the pain of so intense a love again.

Moving On

The same recession that had caught John now affected me. The Nike missile was in its demise; Collins' contract was canceled and I was caught in the layoff that followed.

For a while I worked for Jessica's husband in his small office nearby. Dale was talented, designing landscaping for Newport's expanding industrial and commercial complexes and occasionally for wealthy homeowners. I helped draw up the plans for each project and sometimes supervised workers on the sites. Dale was charming but irresponsible. I frequently found myself making excuses as he missed important business meetings with investors who had flown in early that morning from Texas or elsewhere, because he had been out drinking the night before. The business finally went bankrupt when he was arrested for drunk driving. He had no money to pay my final wages but compensated me with a large architectural drafting table.

Out with his best friend, he had crashed his Porsche into a tree. Jessica told me later she had heard the sirens and knew. Dale almost lost a leg and was left with a permanent limp. His friend suffered severe head injuries and died a few days later, leaving his pregnant wife with problematical twin boys with a rare condition that generated dangerous hyperactivity. They spoke their own language, alien to all others including their parents. They attended a special school close to Dale's s office, a long drive for the wife but easy for Dale. When Jessica asked him to take the twins to school, he declined; I don't think he ever faced his friend's wife. His moral irresponsibility almost broke up their marriage. Just before the accident, Jessica had asked me to search Dale's desk because she suspected he was having an affair. He had never really outlived his USC days and enjoyed annual alumni weekends in Palm Springs. I was uncomfortable with Jessica's request but because she was my friend, I made a hasty check of his desk and found nothing. Nevertheless it was true. Still, she stayed in the marriage. She told me that she saw my struggle as a single parent and did not envy it. They moved away and we lost touch. I heard years later that Jessica had moved to St. Marten. In 2017, we have no way of knowing if she and her family survived hurricane Irma.

Eventually Norlene remarried and our lives took very different paths. She helped raise his four teenagers as well as her own two. It had always been her dream to retire to warmer climes, to sail from island to island. And so she and her new husband pooled their resources and moved to a small place with a yard large enough to build their own boat. Scott and I visited them once aboard their completed fifty-foot concrete vessel in San Onofre harbor. I admired their ingenuity and determination and was struck by the irony of her husband's confession- after the boat was completed - that he had never learned to swim! We think they both died a few years ago in Florida and that Norlene's son may live there still with his own family, although he too may have been in Irma's pat. Scott continues to search for them all online.

A Hopeful New Start

I found another job, working for a young land development company called RBF. On my very first day there, Katy called and told me a police officer had come to the door and said that Scott had had an accident and had been taken to the hospital. I raced down the freeway, afraid of what I might find and wondering if I would still have a job afterwards.

When I found Scott alive and conscious, my overwhelming relief turned to exasperation when I realized he was wearing the brand new Levis he was supposed to change after school; the doctors had cut them open to treat his bloodied knee.

Scott had been racing his bicycle through the undeveloped hills and canyons near our apartment. This was the first of three bicycle accidents Scott had during the course of one year, when Evil Knievel was popular. These produced a badly bruised knee, a broken wrist, countless cuts and bruises. After one incident, I asked him if he had been trying Evil's maneuvers, which I had forbidden. He told me he hadn't but a Polaroid photo I discovered latter proved otherwise. A friend had snapped a jubilant Scott in midair, precariously astride a bicycle high above a stack of old tires he and his friend had somehow managed to drag, unnoticed, to the edge of a nearby golf course.

I called Donald from the hospital. When we divorced, the court decreed that he keep group health and medical insurance policies in full force and effect and shall continue with the designation of (Katy and Scott) as beneficiaries. While I had been paying the children's routine doctor bills myself, this was the first major expense. But now Donald laughed and said, Oh, I dropped that policy as soon as I left the courtroom! He did not ask about Scott. It took me a long time to pay off my son's medical bills. Fortunately I did not lose my job.

When I first began working at RBF, there were only a few employees, housed in a trailer. I liked my new architect boss Woody and my coworkers and I enjoyed the work. I looked forward to each day; I was actually having fun! Often we stayed long hours to meet deadlines but I didn't mind and I needed the money. I drew blueprints that showed the natural habitat meant to be preserved forever – every oak tree, native plant and animal as well as proposed walking trails. It was called Wilderness Glen and it drew enormous favorable publicity. I was proud to be part of this conservation.

RBF was developing a new area called Mission Viejo, where small condominiums were selling for less than $16,000, something I could afford if I sold my condominium in Costa Mesa. Fourteen miles inland, Mission Viejo had a population of twelve hundred people, no traffic lights, no malls. Nowadays it is densely populated and unrecognizable but at the time it seemed a good environment for Scott, away from the growing drug problems in Costa Mesa and Katy's vindictive school principal. I also wanted to remove myself from reminders of John and start fresh somewhere new. I destroyed every card, note, loving memento of John, including my favorite photograph, which I had taken as we sailed on Mission Bay. But as his strong profile fell to the floor, I relented. I taped the image back together and have kept it to this day, along with his mother's old letter and a yellowed newspaper clipping from WW2, about John and his swing band.

While our place was being built, we moved temporarily into a nearby apartment edged by bare brown hills. It was a scorching hot landscape, often threatened by scrub fires. But the complex had a community pool and our apartment was air-conditioned.

During the tome that Scott and I lived in the apartment, my eldest brother and his then wife visited us from Australia. One day we rented a small sailboat in Newport Harbor and were happily crisscrossing the bay near the ferry landing when we found ourselves in the path of John Wayne's large yacht, *The Wild Goose,* as it headed back into the harbor. He had the right of way, we didn't. I have a very clear impression of looking up and seeing Wayne at the bow and realizing he was *bald!* Somehow we avoided *The Wild Goose* and limped back, slightly unnerved, to the dock, and headed for the nearest bar.

The three RBF partners liked to put their employees to the test. They assigned me the task of drawing up plans for the parking areas of a large new Newport Beach apartment complex. It really was a job for an engineer. I had to know city codes and execute final blueprints. I might as well have been asked to learn fluent Russian overnight. I lost a great deal of sleep over it but somehow managed to fumble my way through. When the plans were approved (much to my surprise), the three RBF partners came into the trailer to congratulate me. They toasted me with champagne and heaped me with praise, inviting everyone to join in. I felt a little manipulated. I would have preferred a pay raise but lacked the audacity to say so.

Later that year, Scott and I moved into our new little condominium. A dirt road led to our place through a fragrant orange grove. From our little deck we had a clear view of Wilderness Glen and Saddleback Mountain beyond.

Scott attended the nearby high school but struggled to adjust. Away from the beach and the lifestyle it offered, he had little in common with his classmates. His dyslexia compounded his misery. For the first time, our pediatrician prescribed Ritalin, saying that Scott would know when he no longer needed it. I saw that it calmed him enough to better cope with pressure but he felt it made him dopey, and he quit. He became interested in motorcycles (which I detest) and so I bought him motorcycle magazines to encourage reading and finally, a used Honda dirt bike. I knew he would work hard to learn if he were motivated. But as he continued to struggle, the principal and counselor told me they felt it best that he not be pressured to graduate, that his dyslexia made academics too difficult for him. Learning involved studying, studying involved not only reading but reading comprehension. At that time, and perhaps still, creative thinking was not encouraged and alternative learning outside the system uncommon.

Katy's Troubles

When her child was nearly three years old and her marriage floundering, Katy's husband suggested, Hey, Babe, why don't you go visit your mom for a while? A few days after she arrived with her son, their landlord called. He told Katy he had kicked her husband out because, on the very day that Katy had left, he had moved another woman in. Soon afterwards Katy realized she was pregnant again. When she called the boy and told him, he said, It's not mine, it must be someone else's. The marriage was over.

Once again, I reluctantly reviewed the prospect of abortion. This time, the boy's opinion was irrelevant. Katy did not want another baby. We both knew the boy's family would likely withhold support and I was in no position to help. I found a clinic in Los Angeles and scraped up the necessary cash. As before, I worried about the emotional consequences that Katy might suffer. But we were spared all that: the night before her unhappy appointment, Katy miscarried. She and her little boy stayed on with us. Now there were four of us in my little two-bedroom condominium.

Going Home

Just before my birthday in 1973, my father offered to pay my fare to Australia. It would be my first trip there since I had left in 1946. I left Katy in charge and gave her the keys to my car, a necessity where we lived.

Flying across the ocean, I wondered how I would feel about the place, about the people I had left behind twenty-seven years before. As it turned out, Sydney felt familiar yet different; we both had grown up a little. I had not seen my stepmother since 1963; now I was going to stay in her home. My four brothers were children when they left America in 1950; now the youngest was twenty-three. Meeting them now, I was glad to be their sister. My stepmother had prepared a pleasant room for me and she and my father had organized a small family reunion of various relatives, most of whom had been born since I left Sydney. And, my stepmother said, we invited your Uncle Eric. I had never told anyone of his abuse of me as a child.

That afternoon, as people gathered in the living room, I took a deep breath as I opened my bedroom door to find Eric, now eighty-five, standing there, silent. He clung to me and wept as though I were a long-lost love. I pulled away and moved quickly from the darkened hall. For the rest of the afternoon, I tried to avoid him. I never saw him again. He died in 1980.

Years after that, I told my father of Eric's past advances. His face flushed and he blurted, You are a horrible girl to speak of my eldest brother that way! Yet it was my father who had accused Eric, executor of my grandmother's estate in 1948, of keeping most of the inheritance money and family treasures himself. Who knows if this is true or even what assets survived The Great Depression and my grandfather's death? Later – old, senile and widowed – Eric was said to have kept valuable jewelry under his bed, giving pieces away to nurses who cared for him during his final years.

I often found myself alone and at ease with my stepmother. Our roles had changed, we were equals. She confided that she wanted to play tennis with her sister but my father objected. I asked why. She said that he was suspicious of her relationships outside their home, that once, when she didn't answer the phone in the middle of the day, he came home and accused her of seeing someone else. In reality she was in the garden, tying up tomato vines and had not heard the phone ring. This seemed so like Donald and his attempts to isolate me that I told her she should just go ahead: play tennis, play golf, enjoy lunch in town, do whatever she wanted. Presumptuous of me: I was out of my situation, she never would be.

My eldest brother and his wife of the sailing incident years before, were divorcing. Lorraine, who had met me at the airport alongside my brother, had invited me on a business trip to Canberra where I'd never been. My stepmother, taking sides, felt I was being disloyal but my brother did not object. The divorce was amiable and after all, they both were my friends. I went to Canberra and my stepmother gracefully kept her silence.

There was a happy family reunion and a picnic at Balmoral Beach - did my father arrange this? My brothers were there and numerous cousins, including Ron and Noel of my childhood at Lillianfels. Ron and his family drove over the Blue Mountains from Blayney, the country town that was now their home and Noel and his family came up the coast from Kiama.

Ron had become an architect. At the time I was there, the Sydney Opera House, designed by Danish architect Jorn Utzon and begun in 1959, was near completion. Ron led me on a personal tour through construction dust and workers less than two months before Queen

Elizabeth II formerly opened the breathtaking icon in October of 1973.

Political shortsightedness and controversy had plagued the project from the start until the Minister of Public Works at that time, labeled a fraud and a philistine, stopped payments to Utzon, who, unable to pay his staff, resigned in 1966. He never returned to Sydney to see his masterpiece completed. In June 2007 he became only the second person to have his work recognized as a World Heritage Site while he was still alive. He died in Copenhagen in 2008 at age ninety. The following March, a state memorial and reconciliation concert was held in the Concert Hall of his opera house. Amongst other prestigious awards and recognition, he was posthumously awarded the Nobel Prize.

Back to Reality

I returned to Mission Viejo a month later to find that Katy had gone off to Colorado with a group of people I didn't know, leaving fifteen-year-old Scott in charge of her small son. My car wouldn't start; Katy had neglected to check the radiator water levels. When she finally returned, I told her she had to find somewhere else to live. She moved in with friends and her husband took her little boy to Nevada. I don't know whose decision that was, but I heard the child was shuffled between various family members. When I asked for photos of my grandson, Katy's former mother-in-law sent me a small snapshot that, at first glance, appeared to be an empty, ordinary backyard. On closer examination, I could make out a small figure seated at a redwood picnic table. It could have been anyone's fair-haired child.

That year, Scott and I went with a friend and his two sons to a motor cycle race at the Orange County Fairgrounds. Scott spotted his father, on duty as a security guard. He walked straight up to him and said, Hi Dad! After so many years, Donald did not recognize his son and when Scott re-introduced himself, Donald, in that tight-lipped, cold, flat tone I knew so well, said, Hi hi hi. He often addressed people this way as if to keep them at bay. Their meeting was brief, and Scott shrugged it off. Unlike Katy, he seemed able to deflect his father's blatant rejection.

Meanwhile, RBF grew quickly, too quickly. Woody told me that the RBF partners were moving into a large building in a fashionable new industrial complex in Newport Beach and were bringing in new management. He told me he knew these people and would not work under them and advised me to get out too. But a good job was hard to find and so I stayed.

Several of my former coworkers had left with Woody and I was now the sole woman in a department of several men I liked. But my new boss was an ex-Marine sergeant, one of those men who believes he likes women because he finds them sexually attractive. Craig liked women who knew their place and my place, apparently, was to perform household duties. He expected me to make coffee before the men arrived and make sure it was available all day. He directed me to dust the large-scale tract models that filled the conference room and to be ready to make copies on the Xerox machine upon demand. When our department was not particularly busy, I sought work from others, since staying occupied meant that the day went faster.

When Craig told me to clean up the working area of the often-absent heroin addict whose drafting table sat behind mine, I refused. This unpleasant individual had no concept of order or cleanliness. He was thin, pale and listless, his long hair unkempt and unwashed. His work area was no better; I was constantly staving off the overflow of grime he generated. Once he told me he had hidden in a theater through twelve showings of Clockwork Orange - a particularly violent movie for that time - missing work in the process. Sometimes I had to correct or complete his assignments. I could never understand why a rigid military man like Craig would tolerate this behavior.

Now Craig continued to stand at my desk, insisting I obey him as my male coworkers sat idle. I told him I was working on a deadline from another department. He was furious, fists clenched, face purple. When I stood firm, he stormed back to his office. Moments later his secretary, obviously shaken, came out and said that Craig wanted to see me in his office immediately. I followed her, sick to my stomach, but I knew what was at stake: if I gave in to intimidation now, then the lessons of my past had been wasted. I had to keep walking across that old field of fear or risk losing much of the ground I had gained since my divorce.

In Craig's office, I did not give in. As I left, I heard him shouting at his poor secretary. I went to the women's restroom and threw up. When

I returned to my desk, my coworkers let me know they supported me. Two men even told Craig they thought I was right; they didn't want to clean the addict's desk either. A couple of weeks later I was laid off as part of cutbacks, but I knew the real reason. I summoned up courage to talk to the same three partners who had toasted me months earlier but they simply tried to pacify me. Woody had been right.

Try Try Again

I attended a seminar on resumes and spent time and money to *get it right.* In a time before computers, I typed it on my old typewriter and had it professionally typeset. While I had good references, I had only a few responses that led nowhere except for one. A new advertising agency had opened up in Newport Beach, run by a rather cheerfully inept young man whose doting Jewish parents backed him financially and turned up frequently - I suspect to check on him. I enjoyed the work and I liked my eclectic coworkers.

My job was to produce catalogues for women's clothes, from design to layout to copy writing. I may not have been designing or illustrating fashions, but this was the closest I had come to my dream work. Cherie, my associate, and I interviewed photographers and models then spent hours at the Los Angeles Fashion Mart, selecting clothes and accessories. In a small studio in Hollywood, we set up props and directed the models.

During the shoots, we stayed at the Boneventure and dined at good restaurants. Cherie knew them all – she came from a wealthy family. She was unaffected and spirited and we got along well even though she was much younger than I. We selected the best of the photographer's slides, examined the printer's proofs, waited for the final catalogue and heaved a sigh of relief. Producing such a catalogue now, in the computer age, would be a much simpler process.

I was not surprised when the agency failed. Once again I found myself scrambling for work. I knew a Master's degree might broaden my employment prospects but lack of money and time made that impossible. I was lucky to scrape together my condominium payment each month.

As I continued to search for work, my youngest brother, now twenty-four, arrived unexpectedly from Australia and stayed with me for nine weeks. Now I understood why my father had paid for my plane ticket to Sydney earlier. Scott gave up his room and I lent my brother my car for job interviews; he hoped to find a job as a chemical engineer in Southern California, where he had been born.

He greeted me from my upstairs balcony one evening as I parked the car, with, Don't get mad! - an opening statement that could only predict trouble. He had tossed a cigarette into the kitchen wastebasket, starting a fire that scorched my kitchen cabinets and walls. He had done his best to restore order before I came home and there was no serious harm done. Although I was exasperated, I couldn't help feeling badly for him. As we both continued to search for work, my brother helped me frame little tissue collages I had created in trendy colors to hawk at the Orange County swap meet, where we sat for hours, with little success.

I found another job for little pay in a tiny office with two women who planned to publish a local magazine. I did everything: illustrated the covers as well as all the articles and ads, wrote copy and poems for the children's page and pasted everything together. At a time when women were striving for independence, these two, safely married, were determined to prove themselves. When sales faltered, they abandoned their venture and I was once again out of a job.

Scott and I had lived in Mission Viejo for three years and realized what ocean lovers we really were. I found the inland heat oppressive, the dun-colored hills dispiriting. A favorable article in Newsweek once named Mission Viejo the ideal planned community and I think that is true, thanks to the foresight of the planners. Yet I found it over-structured: where were the creative people, the independent thinkers? We fled to the beach whenever we could. At the edge of that endless expanse of ocean, I felt free.

At the same time, I was finding it increasingly difficult to survive financially; I was facing foreclosure. I thought seriously about moving us all to Australia where I had family, where we wouldn't be so alone. I felt that children were likely to be more accountable if numerous cousins, aunts and uncles were watching. But I could see no way to go and remain financially independent, which was essential to me. Still, I talked to the Australian Consulate in Sydney, who discussed my situation with his counterpart in Melbourne. They both encouraged me and assured me I would have no problem returning to Australia to live, even though I had relinquished my Australian citizenship years earlier.

But when I told Scott what I was considering, he rebelled. He was, after all, a teenager and Australia was another planet. I could not make such a major move without the emotional support of my children, although Ruth thought I should go for the possibility of a better life. She said, If it doesn't work out, you could come back in a year or two. But I knew that without money, there would be no turning back. Also, I knew that Donald could be vindictive and legally prevent our emigration because Scott was underage. Katy's former husband and his mother could do the same if she attempted to leave the country with her little boy. It was too daunting. I gave up.

My father called and told me I was a fool to lose my condominium. He promised to help financially but as the deadline for foreclosure approached, I knew there would be no rescue. I sold the place for less than it was worth to three doctors who knew a good investment when they saw one. I knew it too but without a job or money, I was powerless to act. At least I had avoided foreclosure.

We moved to a pleasant two-bedroom apartment at the beach, in a large complex called Sea Terrace, with a swimming pool, sauna and tennis court. Life was easier.

I made some good friends at Sea Terrace, including Shirley, who lived opposite us, and a Jewish couple from New York. Muriel and Harry managed the complex and were well liked. In the poolroom, Scott was in demand; he was a challenge and he usually won. He became an excellent chess player as well and a force to be reckoned with on the tennis court. I wondered how his dyslexia figured into the intense focus he displayed in these pursuits. He was competitive but as usual, only with himself; he had little patience for the egos he observed on the tennis court. I finally stopped playing with him because his serve was lethal but I was no match for him anyway. I was so bad at chess that he thought I was deliberately trying to lose but I lacked the obsessive concentration that I saw in him. Surfing was his greatest passion and more than once I waited anxiously after dark for him to return from the beach. He would stay in the water for hours and I worried that he was often alone - he preferred to distance himself from the group and the competitive showoffs.

I found a couple of temporary positions, one as a sole employee to the owner of a tiny business in South Laguna, where I created small maps over a light table, right down to every little lane and alley. I hated it, my head hurt, my eyes burned. I wondered what would possess someone to start such a business; there was no market for these maps. Of course the business failed.

Scraps of work amended my small unemployment check. I sold anything I did not need: my Baroque sterling silver and elegant serving dishes, so out of place in my current life, and the ring Donald had given me toward the end of our marriage, which proved of little value. The job market I knew seemed to have dried up. Engineers I had known, seeking security, had become postal workers. I liked that idea and applied to the post office myself and was told there were no openings in my area. I answered an ad for landscape maintenance at the growing university nearby and when I called, was good-humoredly rejected. A woman?! Never mind that I had learned through personal experience a lot about all aspects of landscaping and that I was physically strong and energetic. I applied to Animal Control but someone told me that as a woman, I would be assigned road-kill details. No matter, no one ever offered an interview. However, when I ran an ad in the local paper to clean houses, I received a better response. And so I had work.

To maintain my self-esteem, I enrolled in night classes at the local college: art, writing, literature or yoga classes and even one creative thinking class through the engineering department (for example: How to build a better mouse trap). Life drawing came easily to me and I loved it, as I loved my writing classes, where I learned a great deal about the excessive use of alliteration and flowery phrases. One of my writing teachers co-authored scripts with her husband for a popular television show. She suggested I submit a story I had written for a class assignment to a literary agent she knew in New York. It was a piece of fiction based on a certain family relationship, which I had turned into a murder mystery. My classmates gave it a favorable review but I lacked the confidence then to consider writing professionally and I never felt I could write good fiction; I could write only of what I knew. Besides, my art was my priority. Hatha Yoga kept me balanced; I was lucky to have an excellent teacher. These classes offered me small successes, which I sorely needed.

In an art class I met Joy and we became friends. Joy was skilled in all mediums and on the day we met, the medium was pastel. By the end of the session, I had pastel all over me but Joy remained impeccable in a white suit. Younger than I, married with two sons, she was an attractive green-eyed blonde, down to earth and empathetic. Now she lives with her family on a small ranch in Central California, a haven she has created almost single-handedly from bare dirt.

I also became friendly with a woman in my writing class. Months later we traveled together to Puerto Vallarta for a cheap weekend getaway. Cora was a former nun. She surprised me with her boldness;

she thought nothing of lying to gain free access to banquets or other venues that appeared interesting, while I stood apart, mortified. My mother had tickets but she is dying now and wanted me to take her place. She seemed quite undaunted when her attempts were rejected.

On our final day there, I spent my last nine dollars on a parachute ride over the sea instead of dinner. Cora watched from the beach while I soared happily overhead.

Meanwhile I continued to clean houses. One wealthy woman, a dentist's wife, demanded I scrub all her bathroom showers with straight bleach every week, followed by a critical review. Once, I told her I had won a poetry award, which was true. (Occasionally, when inspiration hits me, I have what I call a poetry attack; I do not consider myself a true poet.) She did not believe me. I could see she was uncomfortable with the possibility that a cleaning woman could be capable of writing a poem; I did not fit into that box. I found her perplexity amusing, looked at my poor rough hands and her big, unimaginative house so lacking in any personal expression, and quit. It felt good.

My favorite housecleaning client, a man in his eighties who lived in a retirement community nearby, had been a top photographer at Disney for thirty-six years. Henry also was an oil painter of fine, unsentimental landscapes, but now he was almost totally blind with macular degeneration. He also was quite deaf. He said something once that has haunted me since: If I had to choose between blindness and deafness, I would rather be blind, for someone who is deaf is shut off from the world.

When Henry realized I was an artist, he lent me all his valuable camera equipment. Powerful long lenses enabled me to shoot interesting faces from a distance: all kinds of characters on the street, on benches, waiting for buses, all unaware. Using these photographs as reference, I pulled together a portfolio of pen, pencil and watercolor sketches for a one-woman show at a small Laguna gallery. One wealthy housecleaning client commissioned watercolor sketches of his children and bought one of my original watercolors of a sailboat. He was interested in a painting I was particularly pleased with, of a group of Black women sitting in a church pew flooded with light. Although wealthy, he pressed me for days to reduce the price until Muriel, who found his persistent bargaining offensive and liked the painting herself, bought it at the price I had asked. Later he told me that someone had stolen my sailboat painting from his unlocked beachfront house. Nothing else was stolen, which seemed peculiar to me, since he had other paintings that were very valuable. I had a terrible feeling that Katy had taken the painting for some misguided reason of her own. Whatever the truth, this incident cast suspicion on me. I never saw the painting again.

I had already suspected Katy of stealing. When she took some potted plants from a model home nearby, I insisted she return them and apologize. I drove her there and waited in the car but I think she left the plants and slipped away undetected. I was learning to be watchful of my wallet and Scott began missing things. When he confronted her, she denied it, but time sadly revealed the truth. I thought of a different Katy at three or four, when, at the beach one day, she found a twenty-dollar bill in the sand. Taught to be honest, she asked several nearby beach goers if they had lost it. Of course several people claimed it and before we realized what was happening, little Katy was quickly relieved of her find.

I received other portrait commissions but soon decided that commissions were not for me. I would hear such comments as, My nose looks too long, or I don't look that old, My hair isn't that gray! Such restrictions inhibited my creativity and diminished the end result. I longed to spend my days painting freely, to explore and develop my ability. I wondered if all my artistic dreams would amount to a few stolen moments here and there. I tried not to think about it. I had to believe life would get better and somehow, through everything,

I managed to remain optimistic at heart.

There were new men in my life during that time. One was from Minnesota, with good mid-western values. He ran his own business and was raising four children alone although he was divorced, not widowed. He was an avid sailor and we spent time with his children on his forty-some foot sailboat. One weekend, headed for Catalina Island just after dark, we all went below for a few minutes, leaving Scott at the tiller. He understood the principles of celestial navigation but was so dreamily transfixed on a guiding star that he sailed past the island, headed for the open sea. No harm done; we all laughed about it. One evening, alone on the boat, far from the shore, my friend and I smoked marijuana. It gave me a sore throat and I was never interested in trying it again; I didn't see the point.

Once, under sail off the Southern California coast, I took the helm while my friend went below. The winds were light, the seas calm, sailing was effortless. Then I heard a strange sound that I couldn't identify; it made me think of an echo inside an oil drum. A moment later I was amazed to see a whale alongside the boat, so close I could almost touch it. Before I could consider the possible outcome of a sailboat/whale encounter, it moved away, leaving me awestruck. My friend had heard it too but by the time he reached the deck, the whale had disappeared. I felt privileged.

I was not in love with this man and we never spoke of marriage. But I did expect honesty from him. So I was disappointed when I found a note his son had left on his kitchen counter saying that a certain woman had called to postpone their dinner date the next night. I happened to be at his home to take care of him because he was sick and to cook dinner for his children. I felt used. We drifted apart but met for lunch years later when I was in Newport for my own art show. He suggested we spend the rest of the day together but I had lost interest. We parted amicably.

Another man, who also sailed, was a music teacher and a depressed alcoholic. His favorite composer was Mahler, who was not my favorite and at the Los Angeles Music Center, I dozed off. I'm sure he was disappointed in me. He had reached an age that none of his family had survived; all had suffered fatal heart attacks. In fact, his sister, who lived next door to him, died one afternoon when he and I were sailing. Convinced he would die within two years, he suggested we marry. He pointed out that I wouldn't have to wait long to inherit a condominium and a yacht. Even if I had loved him, his morbidity would have sent me running.

Then there was the retired Marine commander with a powerboat that never left its slip. Katy and I had been on the beach one day when she spotted him walking his Irish setter at the water's edge. She ran down and told him, My mother would like to see your dog. He asked me to dinner. He was a gourmet cook; he ordered the finest cuts of meat from his personal butcher in Beverly Hills and cooked them to perfection. He offered me a house on the bluff overlooking Dana Point harbor. Our affair was brief: very quickly I realized he was domineering and possessive. He persisted for a while, wanting to know who I was seeing, where I was going. Sometimes I saw his car parked near my condominium; once he came to the door but I wouldn't let him in. Finally he gave up.

Weekends Transformed

My youngest brother had returned to Sydney and married. Now, in the autumn of 1975, he was back in Southern California with his bride. My next-to-youngest brother, also a chemical engineer, came with his bride as well. Both brothers had landed good jobs in Pasadena and their wives easily found work.

Now, every weekend, the four of them escaped the Pasadena heat and drove for almost two hours to sleep on my floor. Saturday and Sunday mornings, we all trekked to the old unspoiled Salt Creek beach, before the Ritz-Carlton claimed it, through a nearby tunnel under Coast Highway. Later we swam in the pool or relaxed in the sauna then enjoyed a cheap, hearty Mexican dinner at the Dana Point marina. Those weekends were happy and sometimes hectic; occasionally young Australian cousins I had never met slept on the floor as well, on their way to somewhere else. Scott recalls it as a good time, and it was, although the picture in my mind is cluttered with sleeping bodies and Scott's lingering passion: dirt-bike parts spread on the white living room carpet.

My brothers were in America when they learned that their mother – my stepmother – was ill. They returned to Australia in the summer of 1977 and she died the following year after a devastating struggle with cancer. I was glad that we had reconciled five years earlier.

Living at Sea Terrace was amiable and for a while, life smoothed out. I joined the San Clemente Art Association and painted plein air as time would allow. I managed to pull a small body of work together to exhibit at the Laguna Beach Winter Art Festival. I continued to clean houses for the wealthy and when Katy was around, she sometimes helped me. But more and more she was gone, often leaving her little boy with Scott and me. I knew Katy was involved with a party crowd.

She made no attempt to return to school or find a job and for a while, lived in a small apartment with friends I knew nothing about. I had lent her my beach bike to find, and commute to, a job, any job. Within days, the bike was stolen, or so Katy said.

Katy formed an alliance with a girl named Marvel who became her closest friend and ally and together they found trouble whenever, wherever they could. They stole the credit cards of a man they met in a bar and fled with my grandson to Kauai where they lived mostly on the beach and out of touch. At some point Katy apparently made a little money babysitting a since-famous surfer. Katy's husband and his family conspired with the Hawaiian police to reclaim the child and took him to Katy's mother-in-law in Reno.

Once again, Katy returned to live with Scott and me. She told me I owed her a living. She said that she would never be poor like me, she would never work as I did. At this stage of her life, she bore a startling resemblance to Farrah Fawcett – not just her tousled blonde hair but her facial features as well. She sought out men with money, willing to indulge her because she was beautiful. I realized she was angry with me, in retrospect, for divorcing her father, not because she missed him but because our standard of living had fallen. She was angry because I had not found a suitable replacement, a kind man who would care. Television sitcoms popular at that time – Father Knows Best, Leave it to Beaver, Ozzie and Harriet, amongst others, only emphasized the contrast between that fictional life and her own.

I told her she could stay, rent-free, as long as she returned to school and worked part time. But she made no attempt to do either and I came home from work each evening to find the sink full of unwashed dishes, empty wine bottles and dirty ash trays. She took over her brother's room while he slept on the living room floor. He caught her once seducing one of his friends. When a man I had recently met came to pick me up for a dinner date, I came out of my bedroom to find my daughter on his lap, her arms around his neck. He did not discourage her advances. I was sickened.

One evening after dinner, when she had lived with us for six months, Katy showered, applied lipstick and slipped into a pretty gauze shift the color of garnets. She went to Scott's room and closed the door. Scott and I exchanged curious glances but shrugged it off; Katy's behavior was often dramatic and incomprehensible. She and Marvel had spent the day in San Diego, one of their favorite playgrounds, and I supposed she was tired or just wanted to be alone.

We were watching an old movie when Katy stumbled from Scott's room toward the bathroom, banging into walls as she went. Thinking she had been drinking, I made strong coffee and with Scott's help, managed to pour some into her. With Katy propped between us, we paced back and forth through the apartment until she seemed sober and finally got her back into bed to sleep it off.

Exhausted, I didn't hear my alarm the following morning. Scott was still asleep by the patio door as made my way dazed to the bathroom, late for work. There was blood splatter everywhere. Katy had wakened during the night, slashed her wrists with a razor she found in the bathroom and returned to bed.

Aware of curious eyes, I half-dragged her along the path to the carport and drove her to the nearest doctor I could find. He took one look at her and told me he would not treat anyone on drugs. Drugs? I should have realized.

Twenty minutes later, in the emergency room at Mission Viejo Hospital, the doctor asked me to wait outside. When he called me back in, two police officers were in the room.

I later learned that Katy and Marvel had stolen hypnotic drugs from a pharmaceutical laboratory in San Diego. The doctors told me that Katy had taken enough to kill a two hundred-pound man. Perhaps the coffee had helped save her. Even though she had lost enough blood to render Scott's mattress unusable, her self-inflicted injuries were not life threatening but the scars she bore the rest of her life served as a constant reminder.

The police told me they were taking Katy to the county medical facility. When they refused to allow me to ride in the ambulance with her, it struck me for the first time that she might be under arrest. I followed in my Volkswagen and arrived to see her vanish behind a heavy security door. When I was finally permitted to see her, I found her crouched on a cot in what appeared to be a padded cell. To my horror, she was wearing a straightjacket. When I protested, they told me they had no choice: she had been physically and verbally abusive to everyone she came in contact with. I tried to reason with her but she would not hear it. Her profane screams followed me down the hall until the cell door silenced them.

Now it had all come down to this: my daughter in a straightjacket in a soundproof cell of a county mental institution. As I drove home on the freeway, I felt as though I were drowning.

The days that followed remain a blur to me but somehow I managed to have Katy transferred to the mental health unit of upscale Hoag Hospital in Newport Beach, where she remained for three weeks. I visited her every day after work and sensed that she had charmed the staff into believing she had no problems except a mean mother. While she was required to attend various creative therapy groups and to meet regularly with a counselor, I thought she was allowed a remarkable level of freedom, including group bicycle rides to the beach, picnics and trips to the movies. I just hoped that her counselor could see beyond her apparent confidence and help her.

During those three weeks I thought long and hard about the past few months that Katy had lived with us. It was painfully apparent that by rescuing her, I had not helped her. Scott said he would leave home if she returned; I myself was at the breaking point. Halfway through her stay at Hoag, I began to prepare her for the day she would be released. I told her that she could not come home again, that the months she had spent with us obviously had not helped her at all. She listened in silent defiance. On the day of her release, she called and declared, You can come and pick me up now!

I took a deep breath and quietly repeated what I had been telling her for weeks: that she could not continue to live with Scott and me. It was the hardest thing I have ever had to do. I was painfully aware that I was taking an enormous risk: she might attempt suicide again. But I also knew that continuing the patterns of the last six months would be disastrous for all of us. Katy was a skillful manipulator – she had successfully made me feel guilty for far too long. I realized that I had been enabling Katy to avoid self-responsibility.

There was silence at the other end and for a moment, I thought she had hung up until a barrage of profanity assaulted my ear. She screamed that I was a f------ b---- then slammed down the receiver. I felt sick. I couldn't stop shaking yet I knew I had done the right thing; it just didn't feel very good. Katy was twenty-two now; time to accept the consequences of her actions.

I stayed home from work for the next three days, fully expecting the police to knock on the door. I imagined Katy lying in a gutter somewhere. I imagined all kinds of things. She finally called and said she had moved in with a friend. No one put up with her for very long and she continued to move from one acquaintance to another.

I don't recall what happened, if anything, to Katy's partner-in-crime. But years later I learned that Marvel had become hopelessly addicted to alcohol and drugs. Katy told me once that she had seen Marvel's baffled parents weep over their daughter's behavior. Her father, a kindly Baptist minister, and his wife had adopted Marvel in their middle years. Katy seemed attracted to negative relationships, her loyalty often misplaced. I had seen her betray those old school friends who cared most. Twenty years on, Scott and I ran into one of those friends who asked, How is the monster? The comment took us both aback.

Rescue

Not long after her suicide attempt, Katy went to a ski resort in Colorado with people I didn't know. In the bar, she met the man who would become her second husband. Jack, seven years older than Katy, had gone there to ski but had broken his leg the first day. It wasn't long before they were living together. They moved from state to state as federal contractors, installing smoke alarms in public buildings.

Katy thrived on the travel and Jack took care of her. They lived in Galveston for a while where Katy took a course that qualified her to work in a medical office. But Katy's old habits, her need for attention from men with the right image almost ended the relationship when she became involved with a doctor. When Jack told her he was moving on without her, she agreed to make an effort. Where else would she go? So they made a pact: if she would stop drinking, stop drugs, be faithful, he would take care of her financially forever; she would never have to work. They were married in Galveston April, 1977.

At that time I had just ended a brief affair with a man from British Guyana who lived at Sea Terrace. Products of very different cultures, we had little in common but I was flattered because he was so enamored. One day, on his knees, he professed his commitment to me then added: Of course you understand that I will have other women. My shocked reaction genuinely surprised him. He protested, But it would mean nothing! As a good male friend so succinctly commented later: If it means nothing, then why do it? The relationship was over. He claimed to be heartbroken, quit a good job and moved to San Francisco, where his family lived. It was not a civil breakup and I fell ill and lost weight. One day, at a tennis tournament at the John Wayne tennis club with Cora, I began to hemorrhage. She drove me home, where I waited for Katy and Jack who were on their way from Galveston, en route to somewhere else, unaware that I was ill.

And so I met Katy's husband for the first time. I suspected that Katy had convinced him I was a terrible person but I could do little about that. He seemed a good solid man who would take care of Katy and for that I was grateful. Perhaps, at last, she was safe. My old friend Ruth said that Jack had probably saved Katy's life.

They drove me to a dismal clinic in Garden Grove, the only place I could turn to because I had no insurance. I was the only Caucasian in the waiting room; no one spoke English. I did not like the doctor (who happened to be White); I think he hated women generally. He was abrasive with the poor Mexican women who waited and rough in his examination of me. He told me I was disgusting, having sex at my age. He said I had a tumor the size of a lemon and scheduled surgery. He sent me to a small rundown hospital nearby where I lay in a bed for hours, ignored. I feared I might not survive surgery under this doctor's knife, or be mutilated.

The next morning, still with no sign of the doctor, I ventured into the hall and told a nurse I wanted to take a shower, which was down the hall; she told me I couldn't but I did anyway. I returned to my room and dressed, found a pay phone and called Katy. Over the nurse's protests, I left and sat on the curb to wait for Jack and Katy to arrive. Later I reported this doctor to the AMA in the hope he would at least be reprimanded, for the sake of all those poor women whose options were limited.

I found a reputable surgeon in Laguna who was not accepting any new patients, let alone welfare patients. But he agreed to examine me. My tumor had grown rapidly into the size of a grapefruit and without an operation, the surgeon told me, I might not survive another six weeks. He scheduled surgery at Community Hospital in Laguna for the following morning but I was to report to the hospital by 6 o'clock that evening. I immediately drove myself to County Welfare where I waited for hours for approval for financial aid. I eventually arrived at the hospital two hours late. The surgeon performed a total hysterectomy after determining the lining of my uterus was pre-cancerous, my fallopian tubes atrophied. He was astonished I had not suffered severe pain, but I had not. The tumor was not malignant but recovery was slow and painful. My ex-lover came to the door one evening, vengeful and unsympathetic and told me he was keeping a watercolor I had given him when our relationship was in its first bloom. I thought the painting was one of the best I had done, of red tile-roofed houses climbing the bush above Sydney Harbor, but I was too depleted to fight for it. He left me huddled on my entry floor.

Finding a Way through the Dark

Just after New Year's, my former son-in-law turned up on my doorstep with my grandson. They had left Nevada in a blinding snowstorm and driven in an open jeep all the way to Southern California. The child was black and blue with bruises, which I documented with my camera. Apparently the current stripper-wife, possibly on drugs, had tried to strangle the boy then held a pillow over his face but he had managed to get away. I suspected he had been sexually molested as well. I don't know when Katy's former mother-in-law had delivered the child into this environment or why. I thought it ironic that Katy's former husband would run to me, after all that had happened.

My former son-in-law returned to Nevada with the boy. As he was leaving, I made him promise never to take the child back into that household or anywhere near the wife. He fervently agreed. Nevertheless he did exactly that. Like Katy's father, he went on to marry several times. The child was passed between the wives and the grandmother until he was nine.

Truth

It was not until the early seventies, when I was in my forties, that I finally learned the truth about my mother's death.

While I was visiting the old family friend who had learned of my existence over my father's Indian curry in 1946, we were recalling, as we often did, some of my father's escapades. She told me that in 1950, when my father and his young family returned home to Sydney, she and her own two small children traveled with them on the same twin engine prop plane. She said that my father ran up and down the aisle shouting that one of the engines was on fire. Such a mischief-maker, my elderly friend said. Fortunately he was not detained when the plane landed in Sydney but then, it was 1950 and life was less complicated.

We were still chuckling over this when my elderly friend, suddenly pensive, said, How terrible that your mother felt she had to have an abortion. The stunned silence that followed told her that I had not known. So many people had protected me from the truth for so many years and now, in a single moment, she had exposed them all. She became very distressed, wishing she could take back her words, but I was grateful. I should have been told the truth long before this, I said. I pressed her for details.

She told me that the circumstances of my mother's death had weighed heavily on my father. He finally unburdened himself to her, a fellow Australian living in America. She went on: It was 1932; the Great Depression was causing hardship for everyone. My mother had been considering divorce. When she found she was pregnant again, she turned to my father's youngest sister, Edna, for help. An attempt at abortion with a coat hanger proved disastrous. My father came home, panicked when he saw what was happening and called his mother. Lillian arrived, summed up the situation and told my father to leave.

What happened next is unclear but by the time my mother reached the hospital the following day, peritonitis was already stealing her life. Who watched over my mother all that time as she lay dying, before she reached the hospital?

A perfect picture appears in my mind, the image I've had forever, the image that never changes. A narrow green windowless room, like the end of a hallway, a door to nowhere just beyond the foot of an iron bed in which my mother lies pallid. Why is she so still? My grandmother sits rigid in a chair next to the bed. My father stands silent nearby. Someone (my father?) lifts me above the hospital bed and for a moment, I hover there, looking down. My grandmother says, Kiss your mother goodbye dear.

But I was not yet three, surely too young to remember. Where was I as Edna took coat hanger in hand?

When I saw Edith, my mother's sister for the last time in 1995, in a convalescent home, nearly totally blind, she asked me if I was claustrophobic. I thought it a curious question but I realized then that in some ways I am: I like space around me, I avoid crowds, I recoil at the thought of being stuck in a cave. Why? I asked her.

She told me that when I was two, my mother locked me in a closet whenever the landlord came to the door. She knew he had come for the rent, which she did not have. If he didn't hear me, he might assume we were not home, and leave. When my father returned home at night, she would ask if he had paid the rent and from across the room he would wave a race track ticket and say, Yes, here's the receipt.

Before Edith died the following year, my cousin Margaret, on my behalf, pressed her mother for anecdotes of Vera. My aunt resisted: after all these years, any mention of her sister was painful. But Margaret persisted, because she knew it was the last chance I would ever have to know my mother.

Edith offered one story of Aunt Mary, spinster sister of Emily, my maternal grandmother. I remember Aunt Mary with her tight white bun, her darting ice-blue eyes, her apple-red cheeks. She always dressed in black from chin to toe, including high button boots. She stood less than five feet tall but she was formidable. On this particular occasion, she had come for dinner to Emily's little terrace house, Halcyon. As Emily carried food from the kitchen, Mary smugly deposited herself in Emily's chair at the head of the table while the others took their places. Vera reminded Mary that it was her mother's place. Mary, who was known to get her way by bullying, refused to budge.

As the others sat in nervous silence, Vera stood over Mary with folded arms, refusing to serve dinner until Mary had surrendered the chair to my grandmother. My mother won out, my grandmother took her rightful place at the head of the table and dinner was served, considerably cooled. When I heard this story, I was proud of my mother's tenacious audacity. She was not yet twenty.

Thanks to Margaret, I hold second-hand memories of my mother - better than no memories at all. Each fragment helps to form the woman who was my mother; each fragment helps to define me. I have learned she spent hours among those same Collaroy sand dunes I was to slide down years later. Within their pale folds, she sometimes made herself invisible, reading or writing poetry. Sometimes she startled her friends by gliding, laughing, into their midst. I am told she was impish and spirited, willing to stand up for whatever she felt was right.

Finally, painful as it was for her, Edith related to Margaret the circumstances of my mother's death – much the same as my father's account to my elderly friend earlier – and why she blamed my father: why had he not defied his mother, Lillian, and stayed with my mother or sought help for her? But my grandmother ruled her family with an iron hand; who would dare defy her?

Because abortion was illegal at that time, I suspect that Lillian was protecting her son and daughter from likely prosecution. Had abortion been legal and safe, I might not have lost my mother before I was three. Religion aside, where is human understanding and empathy?

I don't know why my grandmother and my father denied my mother's family's effort to adopt me. All I know is that, after an inquest, my father left me in my grandmother's charge and sailed for India.

Undercurrents

In 1978, the wealthy absentee owner of Sea terrace abruptly fired Muriel and Harry and brought in a new manager, a big, brassy blonde woman. With her came an unsavory group of men – thugs, really – and our quiet complex changed. One woman was raped, another pushed form a second-story balcony onto a metal gas meter and badly injured. Apartments were broken into and cars were damaged. The big blonde evicted some long-time tenants – one elderly woman came home one day to find her furniture and personal belongings in the parking lot. The police said it was a civil matter. As wild late-night parties and broken glass in and around the pool accelerated, the police ceased to respond to our calls for help. One night as I lay in bed, I heard a gunshot nearby. No one used the recreation room or the pool table anymore.

Muriel asked me if I would help write a letter to the absentee owner, thinking he would appreciate being informed of the problems on his property. We knew he was an older man, married, living well in Newport Beach but suffering from Parkinson's disease.

We did not know that the big brassy blonde was his mistress.

A quiet young schoolteacher couple wanted to help. Together we all composed a letter, which Muriel typed up and we all signed. Then we waited for a response, fully expecting peace to be restored. Instead, we all came home one day to find our doorknobs and locks missing.

We organized a meeting at the local library - we could hardly use the recreation hall. There may have been some mention of it in a local newspaper; when the librarian learned of it, she was upset, although we hadn't realized it would be a problem. Most of our neighbors were there and we all agreed something needed to be done although no one was clear as to what. The police were unresponsive. Surely we must also have called the Housing Authority regarding renter rights, but I honestly don't remember.

So Muriel, the schoolteachers and I went from door to door with a petition in an attempt to have the manager removed. The response dismayed us. Although a few people agreed to sign, most peered out nervously from behind their doors and said they didn't want to get involved. Shortly afterwards a detective came to my door and asked if I would agree to keep an eye out for suspicious activity and report back to him. I was surprised: this was the first time I had seen any real interest from the police. He said they strongly suspected that the manager and her thugs were part of an organized drug ring that operated out of Dana Point harbor. Although I couldn't see how I could help, I agreed because I was disgusted with my neighbors' unwillingness to stand up for their rights.

Shortly afterwards, I came home to an eviction notice on my door. Muriel and Harry and the schoolteacher couple were evicted as well. Shirley had stayed out of the conflict and remained at Sea Terrace for a short while before she moved into her son's condominium a couple of miles away. Muriel's husband decided it was time to fulfill his long-ago newlywed promise to take Muriel to England where she was born. They fell in love with Stratford-Upon-Avon and stayed nineteen years. The schoolteacher couple, disenchanted, slipped quietly away.

All I wanted now was to get away from Southern California. I had never really felt I belonged there. Scott was twenty; it was time for him to be on his own.

With time running out, I had to decide where to go. I happened to see a Sunset Magazine cover, of fishing boats in a beautiful harbor. The place was Monterey, where Norlene and I had once visited. Now I knew where I was going.

I contacted an employment agency in Monterey and landed a job long-distance as advertising manager of an old department store in Pacific Grove. The owner of the agency offered to rent me a room in her Carmel house until I could find my own place.

Shirley and I treated ourselves to a celebratory weekend at the Hotel Del Coronado in San Diego. The weather was scorching, the beach crowded, the sand too hot to walk on. We played tennis in the cool of the mornings but mostly lingered in the grand old lobby and amused ourselves by watching luxury cars pull up one after another, most of them with Beverly Hills license plates. Valets opened doors to perfectly groomed women in fur coats - in this heat! - trailed by children who wore little resemblance to them. We had the impression that plastic surgery was a thriving business in Southern California.

On November 12th, 1978 – the same day I had arrived in San Francisco in 1946 – I left Southern California. Scott helped me put my furniture in storage and moved in with a friend. I packed my Volkswagen with houseplants and a few personal belongings and headed for the Monterey Peninsula.

Carmel-by-the-Sea

I arrived in Carmel around midnight. It was very dark – Carmel has no streetlights or traffic signals – but my host had given me good directions. I made my way down twisting roads erupted by old tree roots and edged by black woods. The stars were brilliant overhead, so unlike Southern California, where city lights erase them.

I found the old Carmel cottage with barn-red siding my host had described. My room was actually a tiny garret above the main house and as I began to climb the steps, I realized a large raccoon was sitting halfway up. I had not had much experience with raccoons but thought better of stepping over him. I returned to my car and waited. I was tired, I had driven for hours and it was late. All I wanted was a bed. When the raccoon finally scurried off, I found an old-fashioned brass key under the doormat and opened the peeling door to the place that would be my temporary home. My bed was a narrow cot, a window seat served as a chair.

As I was falling asleep I heard an owl hooting. The next morning I was astonished to see a large holly bush outside my window turned brilliant gold with hundreds of Monarch butterflies. In the distance, at the mouth of the Carmel Valley, I heard cows lowing and close by, surf crashing. Sunlight flooded in above the café curtains; I could see trees and sky, even a bit of the red tiled roof of the old Carmel Mission. I breathed in the crystal-clear air and hugged myself.

I unpacked my car, set my precious houseplants on the broad old-fashioned windowsills and went downstairs to introduce myself to my host who lived with her adult nephew in the main house. She explained my new job at Holman's and the idiosyncrasies of life in an old house. I quickly learned that the power would fail if two appliances were operated at the same time, and that the hot water heater would provide for only one shower or bath. With no kitchen, I ate mostly fruit and bread but managed to keep milk safe for a day or two by balancing the carton on the sill of a window open to the night air, away from raccoons.

Holman's

A few days later I began my new job as advertising manager of Holman's Department Store in Pacific Grove. Established in 1891, Holman's was the largest department store on the Monterey Peninsula for years. The concrete building which now stands was built in 1924 and the fourth floor, where my office was located, was added in the 1930's.

Now that I had a job, I began to look for my own place to live. I needed more space, to have my furniture out of storage and a kitchen to cook proper meals. There seemed few affordable options but I made a deposit on a converted garage, seduced by the sight of the moon through a large domed skylight. That night in bed, I regretted my hasty decision and was relieved the next day to retrieve my deposit. Through my landlady, I met a large, congenial woman named Josie, who owned a small advertising agency. One day she told me she had found the perfect house for me. The price was too high on my salary so I told her I would not even look at the place. But she said, Let's just drive by, and then it was too late. She was right: it was the perfect house for me, an exquisitely hand-crafted cottage made to look old, with polished wood floors, a fireplace, a deck that overlooked the woodsy Mission Trail, and a spacious downstairs bedroom and bath. I set up my art studio at one end of the bedroom, savoring the natural view through the generous French windows. I was ecstatically happy.

Up to the time when I went to work there, Holman's had been operated by the Holman family. They were loyal to their employees, many of whom had worked there most of their long lives. Walking into Holman's for the first time, I felt I had stepped back into another era, reminiscent of the old department stores of my Australian childhood. Overhead cables shot metal canisters of money pneumatically up to the mezzanine then returned them with change to the customers waiting below.

After years of independence - perhaps trying to keep abreast of the changing times - the family decided to hire an outside manager from Los Angeles, an enterprising Jew with an aggressive approach to management.

My job was intense and varied and I enjoyed the work except there was too much of it for one individual and deadlines were unforgiving. Occasionally a freelancer helped with paste-up or delivery of a completed ad to the Monterey Herald or whatever else was needed to meet a deadline. In the early days, as the new advertising manager, I was courted over lunch by local radio, television and print representatives, all of which took time away from my desk. In between I laid out newspaper and magazine ads, illustrated clothes and furniture, wrote copy and even appeared in television commercials. I met interesting people and made new friends, including a man named Jim, a school teacher who walked into my office one day with a sales representative.

Every morning the new manager phoned me from his adjacent office and, without fail, began by shouting, I told you! Each time, he slammed down the receiver before I had a chance to respond. No matter what I did or did not do, he found fault. One of the Holman daughters who still worked as manager of one department, confided that she was afraid of him. I found this astonishing, since she was not only capable and smart, she was a Holmam! The man was intimidating; it was rumored that he attended weekend seminars on Control and Manipulation of Employees. As far as I was concerned, the man was a bully. From the beginning, we clashed and I wondered what it was about me that attracted such men.

My cramped office faced the south sun. Rotting windows did little to keep out the heat or rain. By now the building was over fifty years old; occasionally a chunk of concrete fell off the exterior onto the pavement below. Now no longer Holman's Department Store, I am surprised it is still standing; it is not listed as historic.

Several of the elderly long-time employees, upset with the new manager, asked me to represent them in an upcoming weekly meeting. I listed their concerns and at the meeting, raised my hand and stood to read them. The manager listened but did not respond directly; in fact, when none of the employees backed me up, he dismissed me and I sat down. It suddenly hit me: I had stuck my neck out once again, as I had at Sea Terrace, for people too timid to stand up for themselves, putting myself in jeopardy.

I continued to work, dreading the daily calls that began with, I told you! But at the end of the day, I found respite in my little piece of heaven on the Mission Trail, where I walked every evening, counting the varieties of wildflowers - nineteen at one count - as I stood still. I prepared dinner in my compact little kitchen as a raccoon observed me from an oak tree branch two feet away. At night I fell asleep to the gentle stream that trickled by my window; in the morning I sipped tea on the sun-warmed deck.

Then in 1979, my father arrived in Carmel, unannounced as usual, and settled in. A few days later I came home from Holman's to find a huge RV parked in front of my house and when I opened my door, was astonished to find Edna and Pete inside. My father had invited them and provided them with directions, since Carmel-by-the-Sea has no street addresses, only post office boxes. (This suits me well: my father has told people I've never met that they could stay with me if they happened to be in California.)

Seventy now, Edna still was devout but she had softened. I saw that she and Pete were comfortable together and I sensed genuine affection. It was a good final chapter, for I never saw her again. A few years after that reunion, I wrote to her to ask if she could tell me more about my grandmother, Lillian, whose background had remained a mystery to me. She wrote back to say that she knew nothing about her mother and wanted nothing to do with the family at all. Besides, she wrote, when you came to Lillianfels, I was dispatched to boarding school.

I had never thought to question this claim until Edna died in 2000. I realized that she was twenty years older than I. She would have been twenty-three when I arrived at Lillianfels, hardly of boarding school age.

I never confronted Edna about her role in my mother's death; there seemed no point now. But I wondered if that event had played any part in Edna's religious conversion. Near the end of her life she asked me to visit her in Modesto – her husband had died by then – but I made my excuses; Modesto was far and I saw no point in revisiting a relationship that never had been close. By then I had begun to learn to let go of negative alliances, even if they were family.

That visit from my father marked the end of his ability to manipulate me. He had always succeeded in making me feel guilty, as his own mother – my grandmother- had. He had been at my house now for three weeks and despite my stress at work, I had resorted to working late every night in order to avoid him.

He chain-smoked filter-free Camels. He drank several cans of beer and several shots of Johnny Walker Black every night then stuck his finger down his throat. That way, he said, he would never be drunk. He slept on the floor above my bed, on a mattress I'd borrowed, and every night he would begin moaning, claiming he was having a heart attack. I didn't believe him. He turned on the evening news one evening as I was preparing dinner across the kitchen counter. When a Black anchorman appeared on the screen, he turned red and spluttered, When did they let <u>those</u> people on? My father had not lived in America for a long time; he had not experienced the social changes of the turbulent sixties.

I played dumb for a moment: What people? Then I asked him his plans

- every day he had been telling me he was going to Newport Mews on business. When do you have to be there? He shouted, If you didn't want me here why did you invite me?

In that moment my old self fell away. Over the Black newsman, in a calm voice I didn't recognize, I said, I did <u>not</u> invite you. I told him he could no longer make me feel guilty. I told him I wanted him gone by the time I got home from work the next night. I couldn't quite believe those words were coming from me, I hadn't rehearsed them in my head. To my relief, he left while I was at work the following day. I felt released; I had stood up for myself at last.

Meanwhile my stress at work had worsened. I could handle my heavy workload but I dreaded the daily calls that were as predictable as sunrise. No longer could I escape the manager's abuse even after my workday ended; I couldn't sleep, every waking moment was consumed with dread of the next day. Even walking on the Mission Trail or along the beach couldn't relieve the tension I felt. My body was a pressure cooker, ready to blow. I feared a stroke. It was not as though I earned a generous salary; my rent, although reasonable by Carmel standards, exceeded half my paycheck.

I had worked at Holman's less than a year when I snapped, on a morning no different from all the others, after a call no different from all the others. When the receiver slammed down in my ear, I walked to the manager's office and without knocking, strode to his desk and told him I was resigning. He said, You can't do that! I returned to my office and wrote a formal letter of resignation, offering the typical two week notice. He kept me on during that time - who else would do the illustrations and meet the deadlines?

Josie, who had discovered my little house, offered me a job at her agency. I was her sole employee, my tasks varied, which I liked. Josie was funny and flamboyant; life was never dull. We spent a great deal of time with clients and other advertising personalities over drinks at Clint Eastwood's Mission Ranch or Sly McFly's on Cannery Row. Josie knew everyone on the Peninsula and introduced me to most and told me stories about the local Italian Mafia that I didn't quite believe. I invited everyone I knew to Sunday brunch in my wonderful little cottage. Life was good.

I have a photograph Josie took of me, unaware, headfirst into her station wagon as I tried to recapture dozens of escaping balloons meant for a television commercial, in which I would play an elf. Only my green pants and kicking high heels are visible.

Josie loved to eat and drink and it showed. She suffered a heart attack and gave up the agency. Through her contacts I quickly found a job doing a little advertising for an exclusive shoe store in the Doubletree Inn, where Norlene and I had danced years before. But mostly I was a salesperson and once slipped shoes onto the feet of Olivia de Havilland, sister to Joan Fontaine. The store was one of many businesses on the Peninsula owned by an Italian family which Josie might have claimed was mafia, an assertion I didn't take too seriously, although their women, dressed in black, made me think of Sicily.

Katy and Jack

Late in 1979, Katy and her husband moved to Monterey. Because they both preferred warmer climates, I suspect that Katy had persuaded Jack to make this move to be closer to me, to family, or rather, Kat's idealistic concept of family. While I hoped that Katy and I might begin a new chapter in our relationship, I was uneasy about her predictable expectations and the letdowns that invariably followed.

Romantic symbols were important to Katy and in November 1979, under an old cypress tree above Carmel Beach, before a local minister known around town for his restored old classic Ford, Katy and Jack repeated their vows. I was their sole witness and afterwards, the three of us lunched at the Pine Inn. I appreciated that practical Jack catered to Katy's romantic notions.

Jack was a hard worker. He started his own iron business in his garage and successfully expanded. Katy continued to stay home. Now settled, they brought Katy's nine year-old son to live with them. Scott sometimes drove from Southern California to visit and thought him a nice little kid.

Scott saw that Katy slept late then spent hours tanning herself on the enclosed patio. When her little boy came home from school, she sent him to a neighborhood store with a note for cigarettes and Coke; Katy had kept her promise to Jack about drinking but she still had other addictions.

Jack seemed content enough. He thrived on work and the company of other like-minded men. I think he tried to be a good father to Katy's son, who sometimes visited Reno to see his own father's family, including the grandmother, who indulged the boy just as she had her own son, with money and material things.

Assumptions

In 1980 my father once again offered to pay my fare to Australia. We'd had little contact since our conflict the year before, but then, my father rarely communicated with me between his surprise visits. I wondered if he regretted that his last stay with me had ended badly. Now he wanted to take me to Melbourne, where my brother Robert and his wife were living at the time. I thought why not? I had no real job, nothing to prevent me from going.

In Melbourne, my brother's wife asked me to take a walk alone with her. She told me that my father had been telling everyone that I was coming to live with him to take care of him. He never spoke to me of this but I should have suspected an ulterior motive for inviting me. It didn't occur to me at the time that my father's mental health might have declined since my stepmother's death two years before; he, of all people, who had traveled so extensively, must have realized I could not have stayed in Australia on a visitor's visa. I think my father assumed that as a daughter, I should be a caregiver, especially since I no longer had a husband. I don't think it ever occurred to him to respect my right to my own life.

That trip marked the last time I saw my Aunt Phyllis, in a rest home, afflicted with Parkinson's disease, in and out of reality. In lucid moments, she seemed to know me but her son Ron, my cousin, told me that she sometimes suffered horrific hallucinations, of murderous men coming through the window with knives. I felt sadness and anger that this woman, who had brought tenderness and kindness into my life as a child at Lillianfels, should suffer so. She died in 1983.

Brother John

In 1981, my second-eldest brother, John, called me out of the blue one evening from San Francisco airport. He said he was flying into Monterey and could I pick him up? When I met him at the airport, he was wearing a Hawaiian shirt and sneakers and had no luggage, only a blue plastic bag containing a change of socks and underwear. He had left Sydney impulsively and was headed for New York. I didn't know until later that he was going through an emotional crisis. New York overwhelmed him and he returned to Carmel and stayed with me. He was cheerful and easy going and I liked having him there.

Jim and I had become friends. Nine years younger than I, in the middle of a divorce that perplexed and dismayed him, he was brilliant and intense and sometimes suffered from depression. He had an odd sense of humor that few understood, while I appreciated his wry wit. From the beginning, neither one of us was interested in a romantic relationship. We paired for social events when required but preferred the outdoors. One day we drove off-road behind Big Sur and found ourselves face- to-face with armed military guards at a gate to Fort Hunter Liggett. Properly advised, we retreated and laughed all the way back to Highway 1. I liked Jim's sense of adventure.

Now John was enjoying Jim too. They were extreme opposites, Jim so intense and John so lackadaisical. But each was a philosopher in his own way. Sometimes their abstract debates sent me to the quiet of my own room.

We spent a lazy summer day together by the Big Sur River, joined by Scott, Jack, Katy and her son, now about eleven. I remember it a little wistfully because it was my largest family gathering in America since Sea Terrace several years earlier and for all I knew, it night be the last. I associate these memories with the smell of pot.

John decided to find a job in California. An experienced art director, he quickly landed a job with an agency in San Francisco. Jim, in the meantime, wanted to distance himself from his former married life. A dedicated teacher, he had no problem finding a job in the Bay area.

Meanwhile I was sputtering along, trying to survive, finding it hard to come up with my rent. I loathed sales work and was not good at it. When the upscale shoe store closed, I thought I might as well try my luck in San Francisco too. I had no reservations about moving to a new area; perhaps I had inherited some of my father's wanderlust. I regretting leaving my lovely little house but I could no longer afford it anyway. So it was that the three of us, and Jim's Scottie, Brodie, moved to Mill Valley together, to a spacious old house half way up the road to Mt. Tamalpais. Shared, the rent was cheap.

Freelancing, I drew storyboards, designed business cards and accepted whatever work I could find. When I drove into the city, I enjoyed the moment the tunnel framed the fog-enshrouded Golden Gate Bridge and the city beyond. There I braved the infamous San Francisco hills in my VW Bug, holding my breath on the up slopes.

I attended an evening art class at the College of Marin where I met Andre, who owned a successful beauty salon and his own art studio. Andre's mother was French, his father English, good, ordinary people. Andre himself was unconventional, uninhibited and ceaselessly enthusiastic. He introduced me to a small group of professional artists, one of whom owned an idyllic studio in Point Reyes where we drove every Tuesday evening and painted live models. When the San Francisco Art Marathon was held at Fort Mason, we spent an inspiring weekend with an extraordinary selection of professional models, moving from one to the other as we pleased, working in any medium we chose, with no instructors to inhibit us. In a grand finale, all the models posed together, thin, fat, naked, some with parasols, ostrich boas or outrageous hats, reminiscent of Toulouse-Lautrec and his French tartes.

Andre had been married six times. He was friendly with all his ex-wives and held annual reunions they all attended. One even flew in from Greece every year, where Andre had often sketched in cafes – quick, clever black and white impressions, which he usually sold to patrons on the spot or left hanging on café whitewashed walls. He invited me to these reunions but I declined. I had gone once to a party with him where everyone lounged naked in a hot tub and snorted coke, typical of Marin County in those days. I felt like a fish out of water. I tried cocaine just once, at Andre's house, but never again; it made my nose runny. But, Andre said, coke takes sex out of this world! To which I replied, I'd rather be here in the moment.

After nine months, John announced that he missed Sydney and left as abruptly as he had appeared. Rather than renting a room to some stranger to help pay the rent, Jim and I decided to leave Mill Valley too. Jim helped move my belongings back to Carmel where my former landlady had offered to rent me the small studio below my old garret. Jim returned to the East Bay where he had secured a good job teaching at a school for intellectually gifted children – a perfect match.

Like many old Carmel cottages, the main house had been built for summer holidays, lacking insulation or proper heating. The garret and studio had been tacked on later, placing further demands on the 110 wiring and inadequate hot water heater. When Andre visited me, he discovered my kitchen floor lay directly on dirt - there was no foundation! About once a week I scrubbed the inside of the north-facing back door with bleach to remove the mold that accumulated after too many foggy days. But the rent was cheap and even with its idiosyncrasies, I was content there.

I found a position as art editor with a publishing firm in Monterey. A quiet, bespectacled young man named Ryan interviewed me. Although he had been born and raised in California, I thought him better suited to the East Coast, perhaps Maine or Massachusetts. A skilled artist and ardent researcher, he produced accurately detailed paintings of old sailing ships. Ryan and I worked well together. I still have a sketch he did of me sitting in the garden of the Robert Louis Stevenson house, wastefully pining over a man of the moment who was not worth a second thought.

For the first time, I worked in an administrative position and wondered why it hadn't occurred to me to do so before. I had always sought work as a technical artist or illustrator, thinking those jobs best suited my skills. Now I hired and supervised freelancers, edited the work, made decisions. Naturally well organized, I enjoyed my job. I liked writing letters but detested the computers we had then. I made a deal with a photo editor who dreaded letter writing but liked the computer. We never told our supervisor who would not have approved but when he retired, our new boss was open to whatever worked best. I was happy working there amongst like-minded coworkers who appreciated good music and good books. My paycheck was modest but adequate; publishing was not known for its high salaries. One English co-worker joked that when he told people he was in publishing, they asked, But where's your <u>other</u> money?

To my surprise, my administrative job freed me to paint. No longer squandering my skills every day on illustrations of shoes and chairs, I enjoyed painting for myself. Inspired, I sometimes squeezed in an hour on a painting before leaving for work. On the weekends that Andre came, we painted outside together. When the publishing company organized a ski weekend, I went along with my art supplies and sat on a little wooden bridge in the middle of a snow-covered golf course while the others skied. Completely alone, I yelled out loud to the wintry silence, I am happy! On borrowed cross-country skis, I relished the solitary white silence of the nearby woods that inspired a watercolor that still hangs on a friend's wall, of flame-colored bushes on white snow against a backdrop of black pines. I sold most of my quick watercolor sketches to coworkers. It wasn't long before I had a small one-woman art show at a local gallery.

My art renewed my creative joy. An editor friend asked me for color advice for the exterior of her old Victorian cottage in Pacific Grove, a challenge I thoroughly enjoyed. I didn't care about compensation. It was all about playing with color.

Down East

In 1982 I spent my vacation at a watercolor workshop in Down East Maine. I had booked a room in an historic old inn, which, although lovely, provided little privacy or independence. As I set out to explore the nearby town the first day, a car pulled alongside and I was surprised to see Jim. He had lived in Maine during his marriage and he knew this area well. We drove into town for dinner and returned shortly after ten o'clock, to find the inn locked. We knocked several times before the manager opened the door. She coolly advised me that curfew was ten sharp.

The next day I told Dan, the workshop instructor, that I wished I were staying at a place less structured. Dan, who had summered in Maine for years, introduced me to a woman named Bea - cheerful, weathered, authentically Maine. When Bea spoke - or listened - she planted her feet firmly on the ground and looked you straight in the eye. Bea owned a cluster of rental cottages near the water and one was available. Dan negotiated a refund for me at the inn and I moved the following day.

The cottage was really a fisherman's shack, set at the edge of an inlet that became a mud flat at low tide, littered with stranded fishing boats, lobster traps, chains, buoys, rusted anchors and screeching gulls. The weathered porch sloped into a narrow kitchen with a pot-belly stove, a small stack of wood, an old kitchen table and four painted chairs. The main room held a worn overstuffed sofa, a rocking chair and a cot. Like the porch, the whole shack tipped, as though blown by the wind. A vertical ship's ladder led to a small loft with a steeply sloping roof that left just enough floor space for a mattress. I told Jim he was welcome to the downstairs cot and he accepted.

That night I listened to a storm sweep in like a freight train until lightning bleached the sky and thunder rumbled the shack. Wind-driven rain lashed at my little attic window and clattered on the roof close above my head. This was the Maine I had imagined! The next morning dawned clear and cool, perfect for outdoor paining. I happily yelled to Jim, stirring downstairs, I love weather!

Now, in late August, most of Maine's summer visitors had left and there were only four of us in the workshop. We painted mostly in Acadia National Park with its abundant natural beauty. Maine satisfied me with its countless little coves, glittering silver beaches, dramatic rock formations, spruce islands, deep woods, paper birches. And the loons - how I loved the loons! I found beauty in things man-made, too: lighthouses, weathered fishing shacks strung with colorful lobster buoys, crates stacked high on wooden piers, old working boats stranded at low tide and, integrated with it all, the hard- scrabble practicality of the fishermen.

On the weekend, Jim showed me his Maine. We viewed the world from Cadillac Mountain, the highest peak on the Atlantic coast north of Brazil, the first place the fingers of the rising sun touch in North America. We explored Camden and places along the way. We drove to the site of Andrew Wyeth's Christina's World: the dark-weathered house and Christina's simple headstone, tucked away beneath the trees at the bottom of the hill in the painting. My camera captured inspiration for later paintings. Between Jim, Dan and a man named Jon, who became my constant painting companion, I saw more than I could ever absorb. Jon had lived in Maine for years, even further to the north, further Down East, in a cabin he had built himself.

I saw that full-time Mainers like Jon lived according to nature's timetable: by this time of year, wood was stacked by every house, seafood frozen, potatoes stored, summer fruits and vegetables canned, boats dry-docked. The seasons set the pace for living and required awareness and responsibility, and responsibility meant survival. It wasn't hard to understand what shaped the Maine character, tough, resourceful and unpretentious. I thought how much Ryan would have liked Maine. Years later I heard that he had moved to Massachusetts, developed a successful marine antique business and had married a local girl.

Dan quickly created watercolors worthy of framing. I, however, never have been a successful plein air painter and so I produced watercolor sketches with careful notes and took photographs to back them up. These would serve me well later for larger paintings in studio. That painting time would be Maine revisited, for I am always in the landscape I'm painting.

At the historic Inn I had feasted on a whole Maine lobster but now I made simple meals on the pot-belly stove. Sometimes Dan or Jon joined Jim and me. By the time the workshop ended, Jim had returned to California. Jon and I exchanged addresses and wrote each other for a while until he met someone he later married. At the post office, Bea gave me a hearty hug and said, Come back.

I made my way to the Farnsworth Museum in Rockport to see its modest collection of Wyeth paintings: N.C., Andrew and Jamie. Jamie was only about twenty when he was commissioned to paint a posthumous portrait of John F. Kennedy. John, my love of so many years ago, gave me a coffee table book of Andrew's work, which I treasured until I reluctantly sold it to help pay the rent. Later I bought myself The Helga Paintings, which I have to this day, although I found the gossip surrounding its publication silly.

To a great number, art is principally an escape from life and they fail lamentably to grasp the fact that the cultivation of life through the arts is a vital need to inspired living...the genuineness of the artist's work depends on the genuineness of the artist's living. In other words, art is not what you do, it is what you are. We cannot in art produce a fraction more than we are. —N.C. Wyeth

As I climbed aboard the bus that would take me to the airport, an early snow began to fall. I wondered if I had what it takes to survive a Maine winter.

Moving Up

Jack was doing well with his iron business. He and Katy bought a house in Monterey, on a pleasant cul-de-sac edged by forest.

Katy decorated her home in a style that bore an uncanny likeness to her grandmother's home: quality dark traditional, not reflective of Katy's early independent creativity. It was as though she needed to recapture something that she had never had, or to fabricate an illusionary existence. Like Anita, Katy was sentimental; she valued symbols, as though things, being tangible, were absolute proof of love given, love received. Perhaps, for each of them, it was a way of surviving reality.

I was aware that Katy tried to hang on to some shred of a relationship with her father by sending him sentimental note cards, which he never answered. Nor did he respond to the messages she left on his answering machine. Katy, desperate for his attention and approval, turned a deaf ear when we told her, It's not your fault. Scott, after being rebuffed several times, somehow managed to distance himself from his father's abandonment. He remembered, at age seven, his father's declaration: When I divorced your mother, I divorced you kids as well. As an adult, Scott found it telling that his father needed to believe he was the one who had filed for divorce. Scott said it reminded him of high school: <u>I</u> broke up with <u>her.</u>

In his twenties, Scott made an effort to establish some sort of relationship with his father. I did not discourage him. He began to take Donald out to breakfast every Sunday morning but Donald, Scott said, only complained about me. After a few months, Scott called me and said, I'm not seeing Dad anymore, he's a full-on jerk!

Long after that, Scott injured his back trying to lift heavy lumber into his truck at Home Depot. He knew he needed to get to Emergency but also knew he could not drive that far. Aware that his father lived nearby, he managed to maneuver his truck there and knocked on Donald's door. Donald opened the door a few inches and said, What do you want? When Scott told him what had happened and asked him to take him to Emergency, his father said Tough, and closed the door. As Scott tried to shift the truck into gear, his father walked to the curb and, with hand on the door handle, begrudgingly said, Okay, I'll drive you. Scott, angry and hurting, told him, Forget it. Donald almost lost his balance as the truck accelerated. It was probably the first time that Scott had called his father's bluff. Somehow he made it to Emergency.

Sometime after that incident, Scott came home from work to find a message from Hoag Hospital, saying his father had been admitted. Apparently Donald, working as a security guard in the parking lot of the fairgrounds, had confronted some young men in a car. An argument ensued and the car ran into Donald and pinned him against another bumper. His injuries were apparently not serious but he was admitted to the hospital for observation.

Scott called the hospital immediately to speak to his father who berated him for not calling sooner. After listening to an abusive barrage of recriminations, Scott hung up. I'm sure it never occurred to Donald that he might be reaping what he had sown. Experience informed me that would prefer to wallow in his self-pity than to give his son credit for anything.

Katy didn't work. Financially she had no need to; Jack had kept his side of their bargain; she wanted for nothing. She tried her hand at some small creative endeavors that seemed clever and promising but nothing much came of them.

When I worked in the publishing house, I sometimes observed my coworkers and tried to imagine Katy there, doing the work they did, exchanging ideas, meeting deadlines, solving problems, getting along.

But I knew she would never fit in. It didn't help that she sometimes burst into the office, indignant about one thing or another, demanding, complaining Mother! She got away with it because she knew I would not contribute to a scene in front of my coworkers. Hit and run, like Donald. One of my coworkers joked, Are you sure they didn't mix up babies at the hospital?

Katy rarely confided in me; I think she wanted to present an ideal image of her life, to show me that she could succeed where I had failed. Perhaps she thought that I would judge her, which wasn't true. In fact, it seemed that nothing about our relationship was true. I had learned a long time ago to not offer advice even when she asked for it because invariably she threw it back at me, distorted. Once she complained that Jack was not romantic enough and I carefully responded that romance was not that important in the long run. Somehow this came back later as you never did like Jack; you didn't want me to marry him. Scott joked that we needed an attorney around to sort out the innuendoes of a conversation with Katy. She kept an inaccurate scoreboard and held grudges, keeping us on guard. Her erratic behavior left me feeling defenseless and sad.

Still, we went through the motions. We took evening yoga classes together at Monterey Peninsula College but she was so competitive and critical of the instructor that I found it hard to relax. She went from one extreme to another, obsessive with exercise and diet one month then inactive the next. Katy couldn't seem to strike a balance anywhere in her life.

She persuaded Jack to pay for breast implants although I don't believe he cared about such things. Knowing I wouldn't approve, she didn't tell me until afterwards. In a way, I understood: childbirth at such a young age had taken a toll on her body and Katy wanted perfection: a perfect body, a perfect marriage, a perfect life. I think she longed for a perfect mother, too - she frequently told me I should have plastic surgery, a little pinch here, a little tuck there. I laughed, but knew she was quite serious. I wished she would develop an inner life that might sustain her. Where was my little Katy who had organized plays in our garage, a leader amongst her playmates, creative and clever?

Caribbean

Life fell into a comfortable routine of work, painting, family and new friendships that have endured the ups and downs of my life. My friends have always been my life support, most notably the women.

In September 1983 I vacationed in Saint Lucia, a mountainous volcanic island in the Windward Island chain. I had seen a documentary on the filming of Doctor Doolittle at Marigot Bay and liked what I saw: a small sheltered turquoise jewel cradled in steep tropical jungle, lacking the usual tourist trappings. It is said that the bay is so secluded that an entire English fleet once hid there, their ships covered with palm fronds, as the French fleet sailed right by.

Our plane arrived late, and from the airport, a bumpy taxi ride through the black jungle got me into Marigot Bay long after midnight. In the middle of the night I awoke to a squall - I hadn't realized Saint Lucia's rainy season stretched from May to December and that I, in my ignorance, had booked at the height of hurricane season. This accounted for the cheap rates! My roof leaked and the next morning I moved to another room. I didn't care that there was no phone, no television, no radio. Once the storm passed, I relished the quiet, stirred only by bird or frog song, the pinging of boat lines in the marina below my verandah and the soft voices of the native employees as they went about their duties.

Saint Lucia had been under British rule until 1979 and the British school system was evident in the educated accents of the native employees but the predominant language is Antillean Creole, called patois, evolved from French, African and Carib. A likeable young man named David operated the hotel launch. He spoke impeccable English and was helpful and informative.

The following morning, with other hotel guests, I took David's launch into Castries, Saint Lucia's most populous city, to shop for food at the open-air market. I was disappointed; the papayas and mangoes were soft or rotten, the bananas brown, the fish swarming with flies. I wondered if Saint Lucians had come to depend on tourism as an enterprise more profitable than crops - I was told that traditional plantations had been abandoned in favor of selling overpriced trinkets to eager tourists. Later I heard that that the government was trying to revitalize the banana industry.

I found a small shop and bought – of all things, in this tropical paradise – tinned fruits and meats. When I returned to the launch, I was startled to see it dwarfed beneath the bow of an enormous cruise ship out of Miami. David and the others were nowhere in sight. As cruise ship passengers drifted back from town with their treasures, I sat in the launch, gaping in astonishment at a scene worthy of a Fellini movie. Aging blondes, wearing wide-brimmed flower-decked hats, tiny shorts and spike heels, tripped by one by one. They seemed foolishly, sadly hopeful. The most normal passengers were an attractive well-dressed couple who seemed very new to one another. She was very young, at least thirty years his junior. As I observed this unfamiliar slice of America, I heard raucous laughter and caught a glimpse of an old native man perched on top of a crate in the shadows of a wharf shed. He was doubled over, howling with amusement at the passing parade, slapping his knees as he rocked back and forth. His laughter was so contagious I began laughing too. He stopped and stared across at me, abruptly serious, and said, I saw you larfin' at me larfin', then began laughing again. It was a shared moment that required no explanation.

I ate most of my meals at the hotel restaurant, the only option then in Marigot Bay. Not a bad option, however – at Doolittle's the food was excellent, the company congenial, the steel band exuberant. I met Americans, Australians and English, some of whom lived on St. Lucia year round. Others, including one couple from Sacramento, ran seasonal boat charters. Others anchored their yachts in the bay by Doolittle's and never ventured beyond. In the restaurant, I met four young English people who had been friends all their lives. Two were brother and sister; they were all in Marigot Bay for a sendoff for the brother, Matthew, a Marine about to be deployed overseas.

An American woman invited me to her lovely home perched high in the jungle overlooking the bay, isolated and accessible only by a long escalator that ran from her private boat dock. I stood among the exotic blooms that draped her white-washed verandah and thought I'd never seen anything so idyllic. Yet, she confided, she was very lonely; her husband was gone much of the time.

Quick squalls continued to move in and out. One morning, at eight-thirty, I wrote in my journal: One of the most terrifying nights of my life! Virtually no sleep, listening to boats whipping about, palms fronds lashing. Even though I had secured and bolted all the louvers, my interior doors slammed open and shut all night. Around two-thirty I heard a launch in the marina – someone securing moorings. Electricity was out, my overhead fan was still. The beam of my flashlight caught mice, frogs, cockroaches, lizards and giant moths as they leaped, scurried and flew across the room from the flapping front louvers and out the back.

The next morning I asked some workers, Was that a hurricane? I caught their quickly exchanged glances and one named Winnie said, Wasn't that somethin' - like 1980. (Had 1980 seen a major hurricane?) A severe tropical disturbance, added her friend Michael. I pressed further and thy admitted that yes, it was a hurricane.

I realized then that resort employees were required to assure guests of their safety. This explained the lack of television, radio and telephone. Ignorance was bliss.

Between squalls, along with the young English friends and one or two others, I saw much of Saint Lucia by launch, having been assured it was safe to travel the open sea, equipped with ship-to-shore radio and life jackets and David at the helm. In Anse Chastanet, on the shady verandah of a charming restaurant called The Hummingbird, we ate excellent Fish Creole, then launched on to a lovely sandy cove to scuba dive in clear warm tropical water, as brightly striped little fish darted around our legs. Very quickly, the air turned the color of sulfur and beach umbrellas went airborne. On the beach, in drenching rain, David introduced us to Walter, an affable taxi driver who, once the storm passed, would take us up to the top of the spiky Pitons to explore the volcano there. Walter looked like a member of a Reggae group with his bleached dreadlocks and a strong face I'd like to paint. According to David, Walter's hair signified his religious beliefs, although he practiced them only by being a vegetarian! As in England, traffic in Saint Lucia travels on the left side of the street but that scarcely mattered since the winding road was so rutted and so frequently blocked by landslides that drivers swerved from side to side to avoid rocks and ditches.

When we had a flat tire, Matthew and I climbed the rest of the way, hustled by clusters of native guides, arguing among themselves. An official guide at the top requested a donation and led us on an eerie walk through the volcano - no signs, no hand rails, just as it was in the 1700's when the mountain was split like a coconut down the middle. At one point the guide instructed us to leap across the volcano's belching black chasm (220 degrees, I was told. Fahrenheit or Celsius? It scarcely mattered). I said, I can't do that. He said, You have to, there's no other way. I leapt with heart in mouth, as a scene from a very bad old movie flashed through my head, when Debra Paget, unconvincingly playing a native princess, sacrificed herself by leaping into a volcano.

I thought I might try to visit Vieux Fort at the south end of the island and stay overnight but Walter told me it was a rough place for a woman alone. I would catch the plane there, but that would be quite safe. Meanwhile, at Marigot Bay, I painted on my verandah then walked, swam, walked, swam, until I could no longer bear being constantly hustled by men fourteen to eighty who chanted, Pretty lady, are you alone, I would like to be your companion, I would like to be your friend, where is your husband? Where you staying, how long you here?

I escaped each day to explore the shoreline beyond the hotel grounds, shooting potential painting subjects until an old man demanded money when I aimed my camera toward his fishing boat at the water's edge.

The four young English friends invited me to join them on a trip to Martinique. We chartered a ninety-foot sailboat and waited aboard for the captain who was late. At 6 a.m. we set out under full sail in a brisk wind and sunshine. Miles from the shore, the sky turned dark and ominous clouds swirled swiftly off the horizon. I remember thinking that the sea looked like India ink. Hurricane.

We had all realized by now that the captain had been drinking. Still, he kept his wits about him and ordered us below and told us to hang on. There was little else we could do and I was glad to be out of the rain and wind. One of the girls said, God, don't look out the porthole. I did and was terrified to see no sky, no horizon, only a roller coaster of dense black water. The girls were seasick and I was trying not to be.

At 8:30 the steering chain disengaged and we were adrift in a heaving Caribbean sea. The captain shouted orders above the wind, Haul in the sail! and the boys went above to help. After an hour and a half of futile attempts to repair the chain, they gave up; the steering had locked then spun loose. Below, I searched the cabin for any sign of a ship-to-shore radio and was relieved when I found one; we could radio for help if necessary. The air turned cold as squall after squall swept across the deck. Finally the captain pulled up a temporary tiller - whatever that was - and in the late afternoon we limped into Martinique, flag shredded. At 6:05 p.m., a tower clock visible from the water struck fourteen times, a telling indication of what awaited us in Martinique.

We slept aboard and in the morning sipped hot tea- our first sustenance since leaving Marigot. The boys rowed the rubber dinghy to the dock where the Port de France authorities would clear our passports. Two hours later they came back, frustrated and angry. They were told to fill in forms, all in French, in triplicate. When they asked for carbon paper, a large-bellied policeman with a kinky bleached crewcut, told them, No carbon. When they asked for pens, the policeman said, No pens, only paper. When the boys protested, a young policeman came forward and offered his pen. When he tried to help the boys translate from French to English, he was ordered to a back room. The boys struggled with the first form then had to copy it twice.

When we finally reached shore, the stench was overwhelming. Shouting vendors sold drinks and food from their decrepit painted buses as they casually urinated into the harbor. Traffic was chaotic, sidewalks push-and-shove, buildings and walls splashed with religious graffiti.

I set out to explore Martinique by myself. I found the open-air market where dark-skinned women, graceful in their summer dresses and turbans, spread their wares, a blaze of color along a canal rank with brown water. As in Castries, the food at the open-air market wasn't fresh. As an adventurous eater, I was disappointed, having hoped for fresh papaya or mango and some spicy morsels unique to Martinique. I bought a few bananas to satisfy my hunger before I ventured further. I took photos of the cemetery, a decaying version of those I'd seen in Paris. The crumbling architecture in the streets beyond made me think of a New Orleans fallen into disrepair. Everything seemed tinged with poverty. On the way back to the dock, I ran into my young English friends who had braved a local bar and learned of a small store nearby.

There we found fresh bread and French cheeses, tinned sausages, marmalade and a pineapple.

Back on the boat, we feasted below, as the radio incoherently crackled the weather forecast. We caught hurricane twice but had no idea where. Matthew, our young English Marine, commented that the sea on the voyage to Martinique was the worst he had ever seen, and he had seen a few.

It would take us over six hours to sail back to Marigot under ideal conditions. I thought, I never want to set foot on a boat again. Fortunately, the return voyage was fairly uneventful but for intermittent squalls. We stayed mostly below and chatted. I mentioned I had seen a cockroach as big as a horse in my room and a fat mouse that scurried across the floor, under my bed, then up and down the shutters and finally onto the verandah. The girls said they had a large centipede in their room. They had no idea it was deadly poisonous until the maid saw it and began screaming hysterically. Everyone bore lumps from sand flea bites on the beach at Doolittles; no one was spared. I thought, I've had enough of the tropics to last me a lifetime. And where were the tropical birds? One of the boys had seen a heron. That was all. No one had seen any cats or dogs either.

When we asked the captain for our passports, he told us we would collect them at Immigration on St. Lucia, across the bay from the hotel. The next day we launched over there only to find a sign on the door: Back tomorrow. The next day we returned and my young English friends retrieved their passports but I was informed there was a problem. I would have to go to the main office in Castries to resolve it. David suggested I talk to the hotel management; they were supposed to handle such matters for their guests. But they claimed to know nothing. I took David's packed launch into Castries and walked to the passport office, where I was passed between four non-English-speaking officials until a sullen woman informed me I would have to pay $25 to get an extension. I protested; I do not need an extension, my departure date is unchanged. She insisted and I again refused. You have to fill in an application for an extension and pay $25. I felt my temper rising. The Chief came out of his office, an intimidating, towering hulk of a man with a big unsmiling black face. He said, Why you refuse to pay? I repeated, I do not need an extension, I will not pay for an extension, I just want my passport back. He said, You fill in application, you pay $25. I said, My correct departure date is clear, I have not changed it. He said, You should have had official in Martinique stamp it. I said, as evenly as I could manage, that I was not going to pay for someone else's stupid mistake. I want my passport! The hostile woman moved closer and asked, What's going on? She refuses to pay, the chief replied. Then he shrugged and said, Give her the passport. I had been in the passport office for almost two hours. I ran all the way back to the launch and was relieved to find it hadn't left without me. Thank goodness for reliable David.

Matthew and I walked to a local store we had heard about, in the jungle beyond the hotel grounds and marina, to buy some food and film. The shop fell silent as we entered; hostile stares told us we were not welcome. No film, the shopkeeper said, and we hurriedly left, knowing we had made a mistake. Later a policeman warned us against going there. It's dangerous to venture away from the hotel grounds, he said, tourists are not welcome. Later David told us that resentment of outsiders had reached a boiling point two years earlier, when a group of natives tied up a white plantation owner and his wife inside their home and set it on fire.

That evening I listened to the distant sound of laughter as some native boys (I was told) exploded coconuts in a fire pit far from the hotel grounds. This seemed right somehow; I was an outsider. Marigot Bay suddenly seemed contrived, an illusion created for tourists at the expense of its rightful inhabitants. After almost three weeks, I was ready to go home. I had found little painting inspiration in St Lucia or

Martinique. Perhaps St. Croix would be better.

There, I stayed at a large resort on the site of an old sugar plantation built in the 1600's. Americans purchased it from the Danes in 1913 and developed it as a hotel resort in 1949. When I was there, the original old pink mansion still sat, crumbling, atop a hill with sweeping views of the sea. Old cottages and more modern condominiums dotted the landscape at various levels. My minimal room, in the basement of an old stone building, was better than I expected for twenty-five dollars. A welcome package included something ominously called Stop Itch. Still, I ate an excellent meal then took a cab into Christensted, hoping for some good painting subjects. Since St. Croix cab drivers seem to keep their radios blaring with hell and damnation religion, I tried to focus on the landscape. I did not find it inspiring: flatter, less tropical than St. Lucia and dotted with parched golf courses, a slightly tawdry version of inland Southern California, geared to American tourists.

Christensted's historical buildings seemed neglected, unlike the well-preserved old adobes at home in Monterey. I swam in the pool until the last morning, when I saw that a mysterious white scum floated on the surface. At the Miami airport, everyone seemed Cuban. Perhaps they were.

When I got off the plane in San Francisco, I said to Jim, I liked Maine better.

Decline

I saw my father again in 1984 when I returned to Sydney for a visit. He had been widowed six years by then and was living in an apartment in the northern suburbs. He picked me up at the airport and drove so erratically that I wondered if I would ever see Carmel again. When he seemed unaware that he had almost hit a bicyclist, I realized his vision had deteriorated. When we reached his apartment, he began to unlock not one, but three padlocks as he related the many possibilities for us to be murdered. Before we were inside, I had recognized the paranoia that had overtaken my grandmother Lillian.

I stayed with him for a month. Whenever one cousin or another invited me out, my father claimed he was having a heart attack, just as Lillian had done with Phyllis. He became angry when I told him I would see Margaret, my maternal cousin; he resented - or feared - any time I might spend with my mother's family; he did not know that I had learned the truth of my mother's death years earlier. Nevertheless, I did see Margaret; ever since his Carmel visit of 1979, my father had lost his ability to control me.

Margaret was living in Double Bay at that time, not far from Lillianfels. As we walked there, she told me the property had been converted into eleven condominiums, very secluded at the top of the same long driveway of my childhood. I saw that the entry gate seemed unchanged too but now it was remote-controlled. Margaret didn't know if the old house had been demolished but thought that she had glimpsed an original chimney once through the trees. We walked up the hill to the street that overlooked the property but still could see nothing. A few years later I saw an estate agency ad that offered one of the condominiums for well over a million Australian dollars. The home my grandfather had built, where I had spent my childhood, was lost to the past.

During that month with my father, my brothers rescued me often but they were so close to the problem I don't think they realized how far my father had deteriorated, whereas, after five years, I could see the difference. Physically, he appeared quite robust but mentally he was slipping away. The sad thing was, at some level I think he knew this and tried to fight it; my father was not one to give up. He must have felt terrible frustration. I remember that Mrs. E had told Mary that she could feel Alzheimer's stealing her mind and I thought how cruel that awareness. At a small family gathering at my youngest brother's house, in the middle of an ordinary conversation, my father suddenly looked at me and politely asked how long I would be visiting, as though I were a stranger he had just met.

He spent hours in front of evangelical television, damp-eyed until he dozed off, head back, mouth agape. If I attempted to change the channel or switch the thing off, he would snap to attention.

My father's decline made me realize this might be the last time I'd see him and I resolved to speak of my mother, to tell him that I had learned the circumstances of her death, that I understood, that he should leave it in the past where it belonged. On the morning I was to leave Sydney, I gathered the courage to speak, hoping to make some peace. We were seated at the kitchen table when I told him that I knew. His reaction startled me: he banged his fist on the table as he pushed back his chair and shouted, You're accusing me of killing your mother! I saw I had made a mistake; I could not reassure him, his remorse was too great. When it was time for me to leave, he drove me into the city to the Wentworth Hotel where I had arranged to catch the airport bus. There was only one other passenger, a young man from New Zealand. I'm sure he will never forget the man who chased the bus and shouted, You're accusing me of murdering your mother! I watched my father's figure become smaller and smaller until he melted away altogether.

When I returned home, I wrote to my father's eye doctor on Macquarie

Street in Sydney for information about his vision. Dr. Taylor wrote back to say he had treated my father many years ago for thyroid eye disease but currently his major problem results from bilateral senile maculopathy. This is of the dry type and is not, in my opinion, amenable to treatment.

I called an ophthalmologist at Stanford University and read Dr. Taylor's diagnosis. He told me that no treatment existed for this condition which is predominately genetic. He said, while the wet type, if detected early, may be managed by laser treatment, the dry type follows a slow progression. I told my brothers that my own ophthalmologist strongly advised annual eye exams.

Note: Ten years later, a retina specialist I trust told me that laser is not recommended for wet ARMD.

I never saw my father again. Shortly after I left, he began an odyssey through a series of rest homes. He died in Sydney in 1988 at the age of eighty-six. My brothers and their wives, living nearby, shouldered the responsibility of my father in his declining years.

Anthony

I met Anthony one day at an art exhibit at the Pacific Grove Art Center. I enjoyed talking to him but I had no interest in seeing him again. He was much younger than I and he was Black. We were not likely to cross paths again.

But he turned up at the publishing company one day and applied for a job as an editorial assistant to a friend of mine. I don't know if he told her he had met me but she hired him. Anthony was intelligent, well-educated and very charming. In college in Atlanta, where he had majored in Economics, he was class valedictorian. He had no Black friends and with Ivy League style, moved well within the White community. He apparently baffled his mother and brothers in Atlanta. His mother was light-skinned and thought Black, while Anthony was dark and thought White. He had only recently moved to the Monterey Peninsula from San Francisco where he had made good money as a television anchorman.

He began to join me on my lunchtime walks and told me about a woman he had been involved with for several years, who still lived in the bay area. She was White and older than he was and he claimed to be completely committed to their relationship. In this way, he kept me off-guard so that I felt comfortable with him. I should have wondered why he had moved away from her and an apparently good job.

One day he told me that he and the woman he had been with for so long were breaking up and that he had feelings for me. I responded by introducing him to a young Black woman who had recently joined my department as a designer. She told me she had already met Anthony but did not elaborate. I could see she was interested in him but Anthony seemed indifferent.

He continued to court me in subtle ways. I found myself attracted to his intellectual intelligence, his appreciation of classical music and good literature, and his ambitions as an aspiring writer. He admired what he called the artist's mystique, and of course, I was an artist and so I was flattered. We seemed to have a lot in common and I appreciated what I saw as his thoughtful calm. Above all, he was nothing like Donald in any way. When the young Black woman realized that Anthony and I were becoming closer, she seemed to think I had betrayed her, although I had tried for months to pair them. Later I learned that he had not discouraged her obvious hopes for a relationship.

Anthony had told me he had been married years earlier to a Black woman. The marriage ended when he came home one day to find his wife in bed with another man. Because of this, he said, commitment, fidelity and trust within a relationship were essential to him. Since I felt the same way, this was very persuasive. He told me that he had a teen–age son he had not attempted to see since the boy was two and that he had no plans to do so. Just as well; my child-rearing years were behind me; I had no interest in becoming a stepparent.

Anthony had a neighbor who had been feeding a big orange Maine coon cat that came out of the woods one day. When the neighbor, a fisherman, was away at sea, Anthony sometimes put food scraps outside for the cat. Although Anthony did not really connect with animals, he was not unkind. This too I found appealing.

When the old place I lived in was sold and scheduled for demolition, Anthony and I decided to share a rustic cottage in the Carmel Highlands. The cat went with us and quickly attached herself to me. Anthony named her Satori, an indication of his preoccupation with Buddhism at that time. I would have called her Pumpkin or Butterscotch.

I told him about John, that I could never love any man as I had loved John. Anthony said he didn't mind. I felt we could build a comfortable relationship and perhaps, having had no serious relationship in all the years since John, I felt I should test myself, prove to myself that I could make it work. Anthony's complete contrast to Donald influenced me greatly and blinded me to different warning signals.

When I told Katy that Anthony and I were going to live together, she responded, Mother, you are doomed! It was such a Victorian era word that I burst out laughing. I knew that Katy didn't approve of Anthony because he was Black. He did not match her image of a nice-looking Caucasian man for me, my age, with gray sideburns and a Mercedes Benz.

I gradually discovered that Anthony had many friends, all women, mostly young, mostly needy. When I expressed concern about these relationships, he said that he had no sexual interest in these women. He said, If you feel insecure, it's your own problem. I thought he must be right: I was older than he, times had changed, friendships with members of the opposite sex outside committed relationships had become acceptable. I tried to talk myself into being more open-minded but when we came home one day to several phone messages from different women, I was upset. He kept his private phone and answering machine in a makeshift office, a closet off the kitchen, but had forgotten to turn down the volume. One of the women actually said, I love you Anthony! I later learned that Anthony and this same young woman had exchanged books on the female/male unconscious, the anima/animus.

He solemnly told me he was committed to me, to our relationship. But I was shaken. A friend referred me to her therapist. I was dumfounded when the therapist said, You know he is manipulating you, don't you? I couldn't believe that; I had been married to the greatest manipulator of all time, I would know a manipulator when I saw one and Anthony was nothing like Donald. But Donald's manipulation was blatant; Anthony's was clever. I didn't see the subtleties; I took people at face value, believing that most said what they meant and meant what they said. I had a lot to learn.

When I returned from the therapist's office, the house was dark and unusually silent, none of the usual strains of Bach or Mozart or Sartre. Anthony was sitting quietly in a rocking chair by the fire, the picture of a tragic romantic figure. He said, Did she tell you to leave me? Of course he knew that a practicing therapist would not tell her patient what to do.

And so I stayed, determined not to fail, even though the therapist had said, Why should you be the one to do all the work in this relationship?

We lived in the Highlands about a year as I continued to work as an art editor. Anthony had quit the publishing company soon after we began our relationship, saying he thought it best we not work at the same place. Sometimes I spent my lunch hours at the Monterey Art Museum and one day walked into a one-man exhibit of watercolors by a San Francisco artist named Mark Adams. I was awestruck. Although I had been painting, I felt my work was ordinary. Mark's deceptively simple paintings of simple subjects inspired me; they were like nothing I had ever seen.

Back at work, I called the Museum and asked if they planned to host a Mark Adams watercolor workshop. I was informed that Mark Adams never does workshops. What about a one-time demonstration? I asked. The answer was No. I didn't give up. Perhaps I had reached the wrong person, so I wrote a letter suggesting this might be a profitable fund-raiser but I never received a reply. I persuaded someone at the Museum to give me Mark's address so I could write him a note of appreciation for his paintings. In the note, I asked when and where he might possibly hold a workshop in the future. To my surprise, he replied and gave me his phone number in San Francisco. I called and asked if he would consider holding a workshop on the Monterey Peninsula or even a demonstration. He said he had never done a workshop but would be willing to try. I told him I had never organized a workshop and Mark said , Let's do it! It took almost a year from the time I had seen his exhibit at the Monterey Art Museum for the workshop to become a reality. I booked a week that suited Mark at the Pacific Grove Art Center, where the idea was greeted with enthusiasm. By the time I reached home that evening, there were thirteen calls on my answering machine from people who somehow had heard the news. The calls kept coming in. Mark wanted to limit the group to twelve, excluding beginners, so we planned two more workshops in Carmel Valley at a later date. I knew I had to work fast. It was 1986, before computers made graphics easy so I designed a flyer the old-fashioned way – cut and paste - wrote the copy and had the type professionally set. On my 1905 Underwood I typed up lists of participants, a waiting list, Mark's list of required materials, press releases and whatever else occurred to me. I kept track of deposits and mailed receipts with directions to the center. Passion for the project made it effortless.

Not having done workshops before, the remarkable Mark Adams seemed a little apprehensive at first; he asked me how I wanted the workshop structured! Any way you want, I replied, laughing. He relaxed and the workshop was a huge success and many participants signed up for the later sessions. Mark Adams was a tall, calm man, quite spiritual, I think, and very private. Gradually I learned more about him. He and his wife Beth had been well known artists in the bay area for years; when they were in their early twenties they were featured in a full-page article in the San Francisco Chronicle. Among their friends and contemporaries were Richard Diebenkorn and Wayne Thiebaud. I had organized the workshop solely for the benefit of leaning from a master; I wanted no compensation beyond actual expenses. But on my wall hang two stunning hand-pulled lithographs, signed For Judith with appreciation, Mark.

Meanwhile, based on his previous experience in Atlanta radio and San

Francisco television, Anthony landed a job as announcer at a local classical radio station.

At the publishing house, we kept the radio tuned to Anthony's program. One day the radio fell silent – dead air. I felt a sinking sensation in my stomach – I suspected that Anthony was playing guru to some emotionally needy young woman he knew. I was right; when I confronted him, he admitted that he was consoling the young woman who had left the I love you Anthony message on his answering machine. He said he had helped her over the phone, not at the studio and I think that was true because I was beginning to realize that physical seduction was not Anthony's priority.

His indulgence almost cost him his job.

Jack and Katy spent Christmas with us in the Highlands cottage and Scott drove up from Southern California. Katy's son, now fifteen, spent the holidays with his father's family in Nevada. Katy immediately began directing us all: we would take a twenty-minute walk at Point Lobos, come home and drink hot cocoa as we trimmed the tree, open gifts and watch It's a wonderful Life, then eat our Christmas dinner at four o'clock. Jack's eyebrows raised slightly and we all turned to look at her then carried on with whatever we had been doing. No one wanted to watch It's a Wonderful Life yet again or perform according to Katy's rigid schedule. Katy moved to the window seat and stared out at the sea. Her obvious slide into disappointment, resentment at our resistance, and finally depression was disheartening. When they all left, Anthony, guru to all distressed young women, said, I never want to spend another Christmas with Katy. He didn't know that Scott had said this before; Christmas with Katy invariably turned dark, with everyone nervous, appeasing, trying to avoid conflict. Of course it never worked. For me, Christmas with Katy was an unhappy reminder of Christmases past with Donald.

Islands

When I started at the publishing company I thought that I would stay no more than three years, just long enough to save a little money to take some time off to paint. By now I had been there more than five years. If I continued to postpone my art, when would I ever get to it? One day as I waited for my laundry to dry at the Carmel laundromat, I opened an old Sunset magazine to a double-page photograph that took my breath away. For a moment, I thought it must be Ireland. But the caption read, Orcas Island, San Juan Islands. I had never heard of these islands but from then on I couldn't get the image of Orcas Island out of my head.

About this time, the publishing company was being swallowed by a huge international organization. I was unconcerned until the day men in black suits came and declared: A computer on every desk!

That was enough for me. I would have a few months to prepare for a move; meanwhile I had vacation time coming. When Anthony asked for the two-week vacation that he believed was due to him, he lost his job. I wondered if the dead-air incident was a factor. Now there was nothing to hold him to the Monterey Peninsula. When the owner of our little cottage remarried and moved to Hawaii, she put the Highlands property up for sale. We would have to move. It all seemed fortuitous.

AAA had no maps or information for the San Juan Islands; they had yet to become a destination and that made them all the more desirable to me. Anthony and I drove to Washington State and took the ferry to Friday Harbor on San Juan Island, the largest and western-most island of the four main San Juans. The beauty of the place and the quiet struck me. Down by the marina, people talked softly as they went about their business; everything seemed as hushed as a place of worship. What better cathedral, with its dark spruce and pine, its collage of islands layered in mist as far as the eye could see, with snow-capped Mt. Baker always in the background, no matter where you stood.

We scanned the local newspaper for rentals but the only one was on Shaw Island, the smallest of the four. There were only one hundred and thirty full-time residents on Shaw and that included three orders of nuns. I wasn't even Catholic, although Anthony was. Besides, where would Anthony work? It all seemed a bit insular. We dismissed Shaw without setting foot on it and searched for properties on San Juan. At that time, property was so cheap that my severance pay might negotiate a small down payment.

We found a house in the woods on an oyster-rich mud flat. When the tide rose, the mud flat became a lovely pond. Anthony was enthusiastic about the house, which was newly owner-built but I wondered about a thick post in the middle of the living room that seemed out of place; I suspected it helped support the second floor. The asking price was low and the owner eager to sell. I agreed to consider the house once a structural engineer had examined it. When his report came back, it confirmed my suspicions and that was the end of it.

I was realizing that Anthony had lived beyond his means in San Francisco and had little to show for his successful career there. Still, he was an Economics graduate; I had faith he would find a good job and manage his money well, having learned the hard way. The possibility of home ownership might be an added incentive. I expected him to be an equal partner in our relationship. Rhetorically, he agreed.

We took the ferry to Orcas Island, subject of the Sunset photograph. Reality exceeded expectation; a drive through the island left me breathless. No wonder Orcas is known as the crown jewel of the San Juans. We returned home, having seen two islands and arranged for delivery of island newspapers. That was in the spring; I hoped we could move north in autumn. Anthony found part time temporary secretarial work here and there but I felt that he was wasting his education and experience. I pushed away creeping disrespect with the thought that things might be better with a new start, away from the needy women who disrupted our lives. I was selfish now, I wanted to move and Anthony was willing to help me. We would make it work.

As summer came to a close, the only available rental was the house on Shaw Island. The rent was cheap, far less than on the Monterey Peninsula. We decided that Shaw could be a start; we could explore further once settled. Anthony went along with my plans. If he couldn't find work in the Islands he would commute to the mainland. I had already arranged freelance work. Shaw had a small post office as well as UPS, so I would have no problem meeting publishing deadlines.

A woman Anthony worked with gave us a farewell party at her big house in the Highlands. In the kitchen, in front of several guests including me, she stuck her tongue down Anthony's throat in a long, overtly sexual kiss. I was not jealous; this woman was not attractive - for some reason she made me think of a great gray frog. But Anthony's reaction, or rather, his non-reaction, did disturb me, for, although he did not respond, nor did he resist. He stood there passively as the others looked on. On the way home I waited for him to speak. When he did, he was not defensive, nor did he apologize. I saw that he would rather be liked than risk a scene by asserting himself in front of others.

Perhaps I should have ended our relationship then and there. Yet I had given notice at work, our little Highlands cottage had been sold, we had rented the house on Shaw, the U-Haul was reserved. It all seemed too much to unravel. Most of all, I wanted to be in the islands and Anthony had never expressed any reluctance about our plans.

At the post office the day we left, the young woman of the earlier I love you Anthony phone message, rushed up to us and threw her arms around Anthony. Then she looked at me for the first time and said, I love you too, I love anyone that loves Anthony! She turned back to him and said, I've' always wanted to have an Anthony of my very own!

Being There

As I drove my car off the ferry at Shaw, I instantly was struck by a thought so lucid it was almost visible, like words written in a bubble floating in the air ahead of me: Ah, I could die here! I was immediately and quite unexpectedly possessed.

My next thought was of Anthony, driving the U-Haul off the ferry behind me. How would the inhabitants of such a small Northwest island react to a Black man, to a mixed couple? Our new landlady was waiting for us. Like the Franciscan nuns who operated the ferry, she welcomed us both without a hint of surprise or disapproval. As it turned out, she had adopted a native child from Tonga, hardly something a racist would do. Later we learned there was another Black/White couple who lived on Shaw part-time, although they kept to themselves.

As we followed our landlady's car to our new home, I wondered why it hadn't rented in all these months. Would it be a derelict old shack with all kinds of problems? Then there it was: a two-story wood house in the woods with decks on all four sides and a big barn for my car and storage. An old double-trunk maple tree sat by the widest deck off the living room. There were no other houses in sight, only the old barn-red wood firehouse, still in use, invisible from the house until we drove to the bottom of our driveway. We walked into a large living room brightened by an entire wall of south-facing windows, with high ceilings, carpet and a wood-burning stove. Before she left, our landlady invited us to drive with her to the World's Fair in Vancouver and we accepted. Once alone, Anthony and I stared at one another in delight; we couldn't believe our luck.

My joy was dampened that first week when Satori disappeared. Coincidentally, the night before, I had dreamed of a cat being carried off screaming in the talons of a bald eagle. It didn't help that Anthony was fascinated by dreams and believed they foretold things to come, while I saw dreams as debris from the day, sometimes lucid, sometimes nonsensical. He thought my dreaming patterns unique but to me they were just drams, although I still remember three in particular, two from my childhood, one after my divorce. I always dream in color.

In the first dream, Peter Pan had invited me to a banquet at the bottom of a pastel sea with a congenial King Neptune. Graceful mermaids served elegant food from pink seashells as colorful sea creatures darted about. When I woke up, I shut my eyes very tight, trying to go back into the dream, because it was so pleasant and because I had not yet tasted the food. Perhaps I had been reading the story of Ondine.

In the second dream, as a teenager, my cousin Bruce and I were standing on a green-covered cot in a red room, as a very green crocodile snapped at us from the floor. I did not find the dream threatening. Anthony was impressed because I had dreamed the identical dream two nights in a row. Perhaps I had been reading Peter Pan.

The third dream was a nightmare. I was in the furniture department of Bullocks Pasadena, where I actually had worked early in my marriage. An electric chair sat on a large raised platform and in the chair was me. I had been sentenced to die for a murder I didn't commit. I tried to convince the gathering sea of blank faces of my innocence but no one listened. As men in black suits approached the platform, I thought how unfair it was for me to die for something I had not done. At the moment the executioner reached for the switch, a very lucid thought struck me like a bolt of lightning: I know how I can get out of this! I will just wake up! And I did. Anthony seemed intrigued by this thinking process within a dream. My unhappy marriage no doubt prompted this one.

We searched for Satori for three days, in the barn and the forest, under the decks, but she was nowhere to be found. Finally Anthony thought he heard her and as we followed her cries, he spotted her perched high in a skinny pine tree on a slope, its lowest branches out of reach. When food couldn't entice Satori down, Anthony hauled an old sink-counter from the barn and piled crates precariously on top in an effort to reach the first branch. He tied a rope around his chest and hauled himself up as I stood below, making promises to God - a fall could be disastrous from that height, near that slope, for man and beast. After several unsuccessful attempts, he managed to grab her. She showed her appreciation by clawing her way down his chest, which fortunately was protected by a heavy sweater. On hearing of our harrowing efforts, a neighbor quoted an old islander he had known: Ain't never seen a cat skeleton in a tree!

Island People

I needn't have been concerned that such a small island might be insular. Some of the most interesting people I have ever known lived on Shaw. There were retired attorneys, college professors, aerospace executives, physicists, doctors and an abundance of creative individuals. There were those whose families had pioneered the island: farmers, builders, woodworkers, fishermen and lumberjacks. I saw no class distinction although it may have existed in subtle ways. Every gathering held at the community center, which had been built by islanders, included one and all. Fathers danced with their tiny daughters, teenage Alex waltzed with eighty-year old Babs. Everything happened there: every holiday celebration as well as workshops and classes, club meetings and school plays, lectures and celebratory memorials to those recently lost. Some of the Franciscan nuns were excellent musicians who sometimes entertained us in the center and sometimes even on the ferry. After the Valdez oil spill, the community center became a hospital for rescued sea birds, a sad and discouraging effort since only twenty-five percent survived and those who did suffered in the process.

A well-known conductor who lived part time in the islands occasionally brought musicians from Seattle for a concert in the community center. Lecturers on various subjects came from the university there, locally known as the U-Dub. Every year, when the killdeer built their nests in the parking lot, everyone knew to park somewhere else, no matter how important the event. I had expected such a small community might indulge in gossip but it seemed quite the opposite. Perhaps because the island was so small, people took care to not talk behind their neighbors' backs.

On Shaw I became part of the caucus process and for the first time felt I had a political voice. In the community center, on different nights, members of each party met to decide their best possible candidate.

That year, Jesse Jackson was running and I was surprised, on this small Northwest island, that he was their Democratic choice. He was not Anthony's.

The Shaw Island library was a small gem designed by Babs and her architect husband who died long before my arrival. Babs herself had studied architecture at the same East Coast university as her husband. That was long ago; Babs was eighty when I met her. The library sat low beneath old cedars as though it had sprung from the earth into its wooded environment. Islanders were veracious readers and whatever the library didn't have could be sent from the mainland. Sometimes, published poets from Seattle held readings. Once, when Anthony and I entertained a visiting poet and his lady over several glasses of wine, Anthony - confident and charming - admitted to an inferiority complex. I couldn't believe my ears; such a thing had never occurred to me. But I wondered then if he counseled needy women because it made him feel superior.

Babs and her husband had found their own property on Wasp Passage by rowing there before ferries served the island. Their secluded sandy cove with its dense backdrop of cedars and pines faced the Canadian islands. They designed and built their home themselves, similar to the library that would come later. They selectively harvested lumber from their wooded lot and gathered bleached driftwood from their beach for the patio and walkways that connected the main house with their guesthouse and separate art studios. In retirement, Babs was a sculptor, her husband an artist. Their home was of modest size and of all the houses I have ever been in, grand or small, Babs' house is still my favorite. Its compatibility with the landscape reflects the philosophy of its creators.

Island women often joked that they wanted to grow up to be Babs. She was small and handsome, independent and spirited. She became a good friend to me and confided once that she had been dominated by her husband, as women of her generation often were, although her husband was not unkind. After he died, she had to discover her own individuality and grew strong in the process. I could relate to this very well although I had a long way to go to catch up to Babs!

At the post office I met a diminutive, soft-spoken elderly couple who invited me to dinner. I wasn't sure I would have anything in common with them but when I walked into their home, on another cove not far from Babs, it was like walking into a small, fine art museum. Beautiful art hung on every wall - huge oil landscapes of Spain, batik hangings, gold-leaf Russian religious icons, life-size oil portraits, and delicate watercolors. I was astonished to learn that Juliet had painted all of these herself. Every piece had a story. I asked her about a life-size oil portrait of a young woman whose dark eyes seemed haunted. Juliet told me that during WW2, she and her husband had smuggled two young Jewish sisters out of occupied Paris; this was one of the sisters. Juliet's husband had built bridges all over the world. They had no children, so wherever they happened to be, Juliet studied art at some of the most prestigious art academies in the world. She painted for the joy of it and didn't care about showing her work in galleries. Once she entered a competition sponsored by the Smithsonian in honor of the Fourth of July, and won. Like Babs, she and her husband had designed and built their own home, unpretentious and beautiful. They had raised a fawn they found half-drowned on their beach and Rudy had the run of the house until he grew up and returned to the woods.

Doris was a weaver. Her spools of yarn formed a brilliant wall of color in her open loft. In exchange for one of my original watercolors, she designed me a handsome garment of creamy linen and silk, which I wore to one of my art openings. Doris, Babs and I rowed together to Yellow Island, a small, idyllic nature preserve across Wasp Passage, where wildflowers not seen elsewhere bloom every spring. Yellow, as the locals call it, was pioneered by a young couple who married over her parents' objections; her family was wealthy, his was not. On Yellow, they created their own Eden and lived a long, idyllic life there until he died. At the end of her life in a rest home on the mainland years later, she told Babs that she had lived the happiest life that anyone could wish for. She and her husband entrusted this special island to the Nature Conservancy. Access to Yellow is limited to protect its delicate environment.

I met Nancy when she came to the island to marry a man who had spent his life there. She was almost twenty years younger than I was and had a lovely teen-age daughter who, like all island high-school students, rode the ferry every day to attend school on the mainland. Nancy and I were both fast walkers and we walked often, talking non-stop, her dogs always in tow. Nancy adored animals and has rescued many, one reason I was drawn to her.

Dina and Hugh lived in a gracious house on Wasp Passage, with a long curved terrace and a separate guesthouse. Hugh was a retired school principal who had learned to sail as a child on the East Coast. He taught Anthony much about boats. Dina, who had been a teacher, sculpted and studied music. She was intensely private and like me, she loved Shaw. We often walked together and I considered her a trustworthy friend. Anthony seemed to appreciate this interesting couple, so I was taken aback when he told me he thought them bourgeois. I had always been grateful that Anthony did not hit and run like Donald but I began to recognize some hypocrisy in his graciousness toward others.

People who chose to live year-round on Shaw were generally independent thinkers, at ease in their own company, in tune with island nature. The tiny post office was a natural meeting place for neighbors to share impromptu conversations, invariably stimulating or informative. The only other businesses on Shaw were the tiny store at the ferry landing, run by the Franciscan nuns, who sometimes came and gathered mushrooms in my little forest yard, and a marine laboratory; one islander who worked there shared in the Nobel Prize for Physics. From Stockholm, he and his wife brought me handmade watercolor paper, so special that I hesitated for years to use it. When their son Alex was home from college during the summers, he worked on the reefnetters and brought me salmon caught that day. I have often sketched and painted the reefnetters of Shaw which, unlike the more modern aluminum versions, are of wood in the traditional style of the Lummi Indians.

There were no B&B's on Shaw, no motels or movie theaters, no cafes or restaurants. Sometimes visitors would say, But what do you do here? The unspoken response was, If you need to ask, you wouldn't understand. A pleasant ferry ride to another island could buy just about anything one might need. Beyond that was the mainland: eighty miles to the south, Seattle; eighty to the north, Vancouver. Shaw seemed like a separate country; Islanders bragged about the things we did not have: freeways, traffic signals, skyscrapers, elevators, big-box stores, malls, fast-food restaurants. The ferry provided time to catch up with neighbors over hot coffee, to read or study or sleep or count eagles atop snags, or whale-watch. I felt a special affinity to the landscape, so different from any I had known, although it reminded me of Maine. Island living suited me. Anthony, on the other hand, commentated that he found it provincial. Nevertheless, he was always gracious, agreeable and charming to our neighbors and I was never afraid that he would insult people as Donald had done.

On Shaw, everything was new to me: river otters, a neighbor driving her herd of cattle along the road below my deck, deer ambling down my driveway (a buck once charged Satori), bats swooping around my head if I walked past dusk. There were no poisonous snakes or spiders on Shaw; raccoons were the wildest animals there. Among the rocks at Broken Point, I discovered a single exquisite avalanche lily that reappeared every year. Lady slippers, tulips, daffodils, iris, wild rhododendrons and sweet-smelling lilac sprung forth unprompted every spring. Fragrant old-fashioned roses cascaded over the postmistress's little Victorian cottage; a small bouquet always graced the post office.

Soon after I arrived on Shaw, I saw a young eagle at the side of the road, trying to lift its heavy prey. Curious, I pulled over and got out of the car. At first I thought it had caught a rabbit but then I realized it had a large black and white cat, already free from its suffering. As I moved closer the eagle hissed at me and flapped its wings, so I stayed still. Never taking its eyes off me or releasing its hold on its prey, it hopped and fluttered until it managed to lift off a few inches before it vanished into the woods. When I told an islander of this, he said, You could get in big trouble for harassing an eagle. No one knew whose cat it was. Some thought it might have been feral and possibly sickly to fall prey to an eagle not much bigger than itself.

Family Ties

Katy asked if her son, now seventeen, could stay with us for a couple of weeks but told me not to let him drive my car. I didn't know then that he had stolen one of Jack's cars and driven it to Southern California, where he turned up unannounced on Scott's doorstep. It was typical of Katy to withhold the whole truth from me. But Scott was happy to see him and let him stay several days until Jack called and enlightened Scott. Jack had to fly to Orange County to retrieve the boy and the car.

I showed my grandson around the islands. We drove to the top of spectacular Mt. Constitution on Orcas where we picnicked by a lake of waterlines. We ate our sandwiches and the boy said, Okay it's nice, let's go. On San Juan Island, we saw a pod of Orca whales very close to the rocks beneath us. He was obviously unimpressed and very bored. I offered to drop him at the ferry landing so that he could explore Friday Harbor as he pleased and catch a movie there but he declined. Hiking was out of the question; when I suggested we walk and explore Shaw, he stared at me in astonishment. WALK?! Nor was he interested in riding my bicycle. Anthony couldn't connect with him on any level and neither could I.

I flew back to California for the two remaining watercolor workshops I had organized. I learned Mark Adams' secrets of the Perfect Wash, so enviable that two other notable artists have since asked me to teach them how it was done. One was Rex Brandt, well-known in Southern California. He and his wife Joan, also an accomplished artist, spent their summers on Shaw and it was at their house that I demonstrated what I had learned from Mark. The other was a versatile Australian artist, a friend of my two older brothers, although we never seemed to find the right moment whenever I was in Sydney. He since has won major awards so I doubt he needs my help. One of my best paintings had thirteen washes in the background, applied one color at a time with a huge round wet brush in constant motion until paint flowed off the paper's tilted edge. Until then, it helped to hold the breath; not all washes were successful.

Anthony found temporary work as a legal secretary in Friday Harbor where he continued to accumulate women friends. The physicist's wife told me she and her husband were walking along a pier in Friday Harbor once when they saw Anthony ahead. He did not see them as he gazed soulfully into some young woman's eyes and said, You have a lovely light. I had heard that before, among library shelves when he didn't know I was nearby, and once to a friend of mine who kicked him under the café table where a group of us had gathered and said, Knock it off Anthony. Sometimes he wrote short stories about these women, thinly disguised: a curve of the neck, pale skin and red hair, the muse, the feminine mystique. If I stubbed my left toe, he said I was unconsciously hurting my feminine side (or was it my masculine side?). I tried to understand but felt annoyed. As a self-pronounced Buddhist, he claimed no attachment to material things but seemed content with mine. Having known others who quietly practiced Buddhism, I sometimes felt that Anthony wore his beliefs like a hat, to be pulled from the closet and donned when useful.

Avoidance of attachment, it turned out, included intimate relationships. Anthony was a rather passive lover; his perfunctory kisses made me think of goldfish. A passing hug met with a stiff response, so I became self-conscious about touching him at all. When I first met him I asked him if he was moody in the morning, something I had dreaded with Donald. He told me he was not but he was, although not in a surly way. When I occasionally persuaded him to walk with me in this beautiful place, he asked me to not talk because he was thinking. This was very different from the Anthony who had chosen to walk with me every day and talked non-stop when he was pursuing me. He seemed unaware of the natural world around him; he was in his head most of the time. Erich Fromm might have considered him intellectualistic. (From Man for Himself, positive versus negative aspects of human nature and character, marketing orientation.)

We acquired a 1978 twenty-six foot sailboat for a song in Friday Harbor and hoisted it to sand and paint the keel. Having an aversion to pretentious boat names, I wanted to call it The Rudder Duck, and call the dinghy Just Ducky, but we never got around to naming it anything at all. Anthony didn't know how to sail and I was certainly rusty, but Hugh guided us through. At anchor in Blind Bay we dropped crab traps from the boat with occasional success. When we worked on the boat together, I watched fascinated as ospreys hovered motionless then dove swift as arrows for their prey. Such skillful hunters, they never missed.

When we sat down to work out a budget, Anthony suggested we postpone certain expenses until the following month. I pointed out that they would only accumulate that way and lead to overwhelming debt. He had admitted he had indulged himself freely when he made good money in San Francisco. He still indulged himself, but now it was at thrift stores. Still, to me, it was all relative. What we needed was less spending and more income and I felt it was up to Anthony. I was already freelancing steadily and whenever I could, I painted. A fine little gallery called Waterworks, founded just a year before in Friday Harbor, accepted my watercolors and I began to develop a following. I won a competition for a logo design for the 1988 Friday Harbor Dixieland Jazz Festival.

When he ran out of work in the islands, Anthony found a job in Seattle, as a secretary at the university. Since he didn't own a car, he would need mine to commute. A thoughtful island friend offered me her second car, an old yellow VW bug, fun to drive. Anthony found that his Master's degree meant little in Seattle; his paycheck didn't amount to much but at least it was regular. He continued to collect young women and told me of one he took to poetry readings. Not for the first time, he said, If that bothers you, it's your problem, since you are responsible for your own emotions. Logical to a point, I suppose, but I thought he might claim some responsibility for his own impulses and how they might affect our relationship. I wondered if each of Anthony's young women believed herself to be the sole subject of his affection. I could not help but think of John and the trust we shared, without jealousy or doubt.

Only once did Anthony display jealousy over me. One weekend I worked with other islanders to clean up the grounds of the community center and when I returned home, Anthony accused me of going there to be with a certain man. I think, because this man was attractive and successful (and quite happily married) that Anthony felt threatened. I was surprised then amused. I thought, Now you know how it feels.

One weekend he came home and parked my car outside the barn, saying he would put it inside later. We were still standing on the deck when the car rolled backwards down the slope and into the woods where it wedged against a tree. Anthony had forgotten to set the hand brake. My second-hand Mazda, in perfect condition when I bought it, was becoming derelict. It never seemed to occur to Anthony, who had sole use of my car all week, to check water and oil levels or tire pressure, or to avoid damaging the bumper repeatedly on those concrete blocks at the head of marked parking spaces or even to wash my car occasionally. I had reason to suspect he had been sleeping in it. We decided to sail the boat to Lake Union so that Anthony could live aboard.

In preparation for the ninety-mile journey from Shaw to Lake Union, we took a Power Squadron course in Friday Harbor. Anthony even learned how to cut his own gaskets for the OMC sail-drive. Still, I had reservations about a ninety-mile maiden voyage; while I had sailed in Southern California, in calmer waters, someone else had always been in charge.

We took the boat to Friday Harbor where a mechanic ran a safety check. It took five hours to sail back to Shaw. At 10 p.m. at the nuns' dock, I secured the stern line as Anthony attended to the bowline. In the dark, I didn't realize for a moment that that the bow was drifting away from the dock as Anthony, oblivious that he was tilting in slow motion toward the water, continued to hold the line. Without a word I lunged and grabbed his belt. Still clutching the line, he regained his footing but I ended up in the cold dark bay. In my heavy Peruvian wool sweater I sank like a stone but scrambled out laughing as I came up for air. Bowline finally secured, we drove home as I shivered in my drenched sweater, which had sagged to my ankles. I couldn't stop laughing.

All the way home Anthony, who was not a good swimmer, kept saying, You tried to save me, you love me! He seemed to find it romantic but I thought it absurd. I hoped that the nuns, whose quarters overlooked the dock, had missed our comedy of errors.

The next morning we set sail for Seattle. Contrary to a favorable weather report, we encountered rain and whitecaps off Willow Island just as the engine sputtered. Across the channel, a ferry slid by and sent a generous wake rolling our way. As Anthony tried to restart the engine, I fended off the rocky shore with a whisker pole. The wake subsided, the engine revived and we made our way uneventfully down Swinomish Channel. Off Strawberry Pint, the engine died completely and as Anthony tried to get it going again, we drifted – in the wrong direction – for two hours. Finally we hoisted the sails although neither one of us felt confident about our sailing skills. By dark we made it to Poinell Point and dropped anchor in a rocky little cove. In Power Squadron, Anthony had excelled at charting and enjoyed it, whereas I did not. Thanks to his precise calculations, we missed the rocks.

The following morning we sailed into Oak Harbor where we found a gem of a mechanic named George who couldn't understand how we had made it so far on only one cylinder, especially with a battery that was improperly connected. We actually had a backup battery but the failing engine had, George said, killed it dead. In addition, there was an alternator where there should have been a starter generator (or vice-versa). We were grateful for George, who managed to get things running, as well as a personable high school boy who offered to tow us to a quiet mooring for the night. Cripped up, are you? he quipped. Yes indeed.

However, with three hours of daylight left, we continued to Langley where we safely anchored in a quiet little cove. We stayed aboard, having discovered the rubber dinghy had sprung a slow leak. Anthony changed the spark plugs and added gas to the tank and the next morning we made for Edmonds. Off Edmonds, the engine failed again and we drifted toward a sandy beach. We quickly realized the water was very shallow and that the tide was coming in. Anthony's efforts to re-start the engine failed and as we tried frantically to raise the sails the wind died and we drifted helplessly toward the beach. As a small crowd gathered, a man on the beach waved his arms and shouted instructions, which we couldn't hear. Just then I heard the awful sound of the keel scraping bottom and raced below to winch it up while Anthony raised the rudder and bailed gas and water out of the bilge. Finally we broke loose and Anthony emerged triumphant, the engine humming.

The next time the engine died, we were in the shipping lanes with huge Japanese tankers and cargo ships close enough to read the words stamped on their crates. Up went our sails and for a little while we progressed slowly until the wind died completely.

Becalmed. We were sitting ducks in the middle of Puget Sound. Anthony went below and changed the spark plugs again but the engine was dead. He tried to make some contact on the CB but heard only strange exchanges about picking up clothes from the cleaners and what

I had for lunch. Finally the captain of an unseen ferry came on and promised to drive directly to the harbormaster as soon as he docked. Another voice said he would contact the Coast Guard Auxiliary and a few moments later a powerboat pulled alongside with a couple aboard who were members of the CGA. They said they were pleasure cruising – imagine pleasure cruising – when they heard the call. They offered a tool to loosen a troublesome spark plug (we had a set of tools but not the right one, apparently) and were gone before we could thank them. I hope they knew how grateful we were.

We limped into another marina where we patched the rubber dinghy and found a mechanic who checked the engine and said we could probably make Lake Union before dark. Thank goodness for Northwest daylight that lingers past ten during summer months. As we headed for our first experience through the locks, I read instructions from the Power Squadron manual with mounting anxiety but it was easier than we expected and soon we were on Lake Union, headed for our slip. By now it was dark.

Within sight of the slip, the engine died again. Amid partying powerboats and loud radios, Anthony changed the spark plugs one last time and we finally pulled into our slip. We were exhausted and hungry and I never wanted to sail again except for delightful afternoon spins off Shaw Island under bare-faced blue skies. Still, I had to give Anthony some credit: he had plotted the charts perfectly, handled the boat well under sail and remained outwardly calm. We were still speaking.

Jumping without a Net

When our landlady told us she intended to sell the house, I was determined to buy it. I loved Shaw Island, the landscape was in my bones and I liked its people. I had bought a tiny plot to hold my ashes someday, under a huge cedar in the Shaw cemetery, for twenty-five dollars. I was on Shaw to stay.

Anthony worked out the finances, too complicated for me. The down payment and the monthly payment were manageable. The only thing that made me nervous was a future balloon payment but I was confident that between the two of us, we could save for that. There were no rentals available on Shaw. Leaving this house would mean leaving the island. I couldn't bear the thought. No matter what, I would make it work.

I asked Mark Adams if he would be interested in teaching a workshop on Shaw. He told me he and his wife had old friends in Seattle - nuclear medicine researchers at the U-Dub - so the idea appealed to them. Babs offered Mark her idyllic little guest cottage at the water's edge. I have slept there, lulled by the slap of waves on rock beneath the floor and the mournful echo of loons and I can say I felt privileged. Mark completely entranced Babs; the workshop was successful. Anthony and I offered our house to Mark and Beth to entertain their friends but they insisted we stay and join them. We spent a memorable evening in the company of brilliant and diverse minds.

At the little red schoolhouse, a poet from an outer island and I helped students create a book of their own poetry and ink sketches. I attended art and psychology workshops in Friday Harbor and met people I liked. I continued to show my paintings at the gallery there; I entered a poetry contest at the county fair and won. My island life fulfilled me and I enjoyed its physical demands as well, like stacking wood for the winter and gathering kindling in my barn boots. I ate blackberries plucked from roadside vines as I walked and picked apples from Leon's orchard and vegetables from Jack's garden. It was not unusual to find heaps of fresh-picked squash on the bench outside the post office, free for the taking. The Benedictine nuns ran a productive large farm across the island. They delivered just-laid eggs and milk fresh from their cows that morning and cream so thick it didn't budge from an upturned jar. The Benedictines kept to themselves and discouraged cameras. One day as I walked past their field on the way to Hoffman's Cove to shoot painting subjects, I saw Mother Miriam skillfully wielding a tractor among her geese and Highland cattle, black habit flying behind her. It was such a rare and lovely sight that I found it hard to resist the urge to photograph her. Mother Miriam was beautiful; island men privately called her Mother Movie Star, and she was very kind. Anthony, schooled by nuns, found her captivating.

Anthony was in Seattle when the first arctic freeze hit; they called it the hundred year storm. There were no snow ploughs on the island; Shaw rarely saw measurable snow. But that year, below-freezing temperatures iced the rocks and turned the beach at Blind Bay white as boats tore from their moorings and began to sink. Neighbor helped neighbor, boat by boat. Hurricane-force winds roared across Mary Lou's new pond and felled every single pine tree in the woods just beyond. All power was out. Ferries stopped running; planes couldn't take off from Wayne's airstrip, medi-copters couldn't land on the Nichols' farm. Anyone with a serious medical emergency was out of luck although a couple of capable retired island doctors could have dealt with most emergencies. Chicken coops, sheds and trucks were crushed by falling trees but the only house to be damaged was mine.

In the middle of the night I heard the crash on the corrugated tin roof. A jagged branch pierced the exterior cedar siding and poked into my closet. I gathered my comforter and retreated to the other end of the house with Satori. What else could I do in the dead of night? On a tiny island, you don't call 911. I was not afraid; in fact, I felt quite nonchalant.

In the morning, I saw that toppled trees had completely blocked my driveway. I heard chain saws and from my deck I saw men I knew clearing trees off the road below, although the road itself was nowhere to be seen. They shouted up to me to stay inside, power lines are down everywhere.

The only source of heat in the house at any time was the wood-burning pot-bellied stove in the living room. That turned out to be a blessing because I could cook on it; I always kept my freezer stocked with my own curries, stews, soups and chili; everything would stay safely frozen in this weather. The toilet froze too but I was lucky to have one of the few outhouses on the island. An Australian had built the house as though he still lived in the outback, outhouse and all but apparently he was ignorant of arctic storms and their certainty of frozen pipes. He had built on a raised foundation and had not insulated the exposed pipes. Nor was the pump-house insulated, rendering my well useless.

By noon, the men who had been on the road earlier arrived with their chain saws and cleared my driveway. Later two of them – Doug and Al, always helpful - arrived with big blue tarps and built a plastic room around my wood burning stove. In weather like this, my large living room with its high ceilings and generous windows was almost as cold as the outdoors. I dragged my mattress down the stairs to my blue room and there Satori and I spent most of our time. I wore almost every warm item of clothing I owned and added more when I ventured to the outhouse. It took time to carefully pick my way through the fallen branches and downed wires. One side of the outhouse was open to the woods and I had often seen deer foraging nearby but not in this weather. I hoped they had found safe shelter somewhere.

I ate hot meals and slept and read by the light of my hurricane lamp. Five-gallon containers of water appeared mysteriously on my deck and sometimes milk and cheese. In Maine I had wondered if I would have what it takes to survive a winter like this and now I was finding out, although I knew that it was only temporary. Still, I felt quite pleased with myself although I had no desire to be tested further. When the worst of the storm had passed, I cautiously ventured out, camera in hand. The island looked like a war zone, roads and fields and woods unrecognizable. Huge old trees, their root systems taller than most houses, lay felled by the ferocious winds. Ice glazed branches, icicles graced eaves. Once the wind and the buzz and whine of power tools ceased, the silence was absolute. I could imagine that Satori and I were the only living things in an ice-white world frozen in time.

I knew that Anthony would be quite safe, stranded in Seattle. We had no way to communicate in a time before cell phones and WiFi but I didn't care. Before damage from the first storm had been cleared, another storm hit. I survived three weeks altogether in my blue room, without power or running water and was never fearful or lonely. Neighbors checked on neighbors; everyone was safe. I thought how much America could learn from this little community.

I had to admit I felt lighter when Anthony left each Monday for Seattle and apprehensive as the weekend approached. It was as though I reclaimed myself away from him. I was certainly happier and more relaxed.

Ten months after our maiden voyage to Lake Union, Anthony lost his job at the university. He decided to return to the islands, which meant bringing the boat back to Shaw. Anthony seemed to have a convenient memory: This time, he said, it will be fun.

On a sunny morning in May we left Lake Union. Anthony had found a capable and cheerful mechanic named Doug who was willing to work on sail-drive and had the engine running more smoothly than it ever had. With a Johnson outboard as backup, we headed north. We had hoped to make Oak Harbor by nightfall but with the currents against us, we decided to put in at Everett instead. For the first time, Anthony misread the charts and we approached the harbor from the wrong direction, interpreting the water depth inaccurately in the process. We found ourselves close to a sand-spit and a logging operation and for the second time in less than a year, felt the keel touch bottom. But this time, Anthony reached the keel winch quickly and we were out of a bad spot almost before we got into it. Soon we were on our way to safe harbor at Everett.

The next morning we made the short run to the other side of the Marina for fuel. For some reason, Anthony poured oil into the engine first instead of mixing it in a separate container as he usually did. That was a mistake that cost us two extra days in Everett while Anthony tried in vain to revive the engine before he reluctantly called Doug who was willing to drive from Seattle after work. It was good to see that big, smiling face. Doug not only revived the engine but also explained the process along the way. He was dismayed when he learned that Anthony had attempted to start the engine without sparkplugs. Doug said that if the wires or connectors had been within three inches of the gas line, we would have had a BOMB!

By the time Doug left, thunder and lightning were splitting the black sky. This was not the weather report we'd heard. Since the Power Squadron manual referred to lightning and sailboats as disastrous, we delayed our departure until the following day. In foul weather gear, we left in a steady rain under a fuzzy gray blanket of a sky.

Off Langley, deadheads and logs littered the increasingly rough sea. I stood watch with binoculars for a while then went below for hot coffee to warm us against the chill. As I handed Anthony his mug, I saw a log, longer than our boat, directly off the starboard bow. Before I could speak, the log hit the hull at a sixty- degree angle, went under the boat and bumped noisily against the keel, giving us a rough ride as it went.

I thought we would sink then and there, but when Anthony checked the forward bilge, he found no sign of damage and we were not taking on water.

We sailed on under gold-edged white clouds piled on a sky that had turned mauve, yellow, blue, pink, gray, aqua and black - an artist's sky. The sea was fairly calm now, the winds light. We pulled into Oak Harbor accompanied by the roar of military jets overhead. We planned to leave the following morning but were awakened during the night by howling winds. Even in the shelter of the marina, gusts slapped our boat about. At dawn I found a pay phone and called the weather service. A recorded message said, Winds 5-10 knots, 90 percent chance of rain, 51 degrees. Reasonable enough.

Optimistic, we prepared to leave at six o'clock but unexpected wind gusts made it difficult to even maneuver the boat out of the slip. As we set out, the tide was up, making the narrow channel less formidable, but there were white caps on the darkest mid-channel water. The engine began to sputter and gasp but we hoped it was only a sound effect created by wind and choppy swell.

Halfway up the channel the wind gusted so hard that the rubber dinghy on the bow rose up like a bloated yellow whale and stood on end, secured for a moment by a single stay. As Anthony tried to hold the boat steady, I ventured forward to lash the dinghy down, hanging onto the mast for dear life with one hand. When I couldn't reach it, Anthony went forward and secured the raft as I took the tiller. We were both wearing life vests but that didn't mean much in these cold waters.

The wind bounced us speedily toward a big concrete bunker in the middle of the channel. Neither tiller nor engine seemed to make any difference to our direction. Reacting quickly, Anthony turned sharply to starboard and missed the bunker by a narrow margin.

We returned to our slip - not an easy task, given the wind, even though the slip was double-width. We sat there, beaten, listening to the sharp slap of water on hull. One thing was certain: the weather report was wrong.

Finally the wind settled down and we made for Shaw. I don't recall much after that, except steady gray drizzle and miserable cold exhaustion, and relief when our island emerged from the mist. The seas had calmed by the time we reached Shaw late in the day. I have never been so grateful to be back on land, home.

Parenting

Anthony suddenly decided he wanted to visit his family in Atlanta. He had not seen his mother or brothers for years. When he called me from there, he told me he had met the teenage son he had not seen since the boy was two. Excitedly, he said that the boy reminded him of himself. He said that they got along well and that he wanted to bring him back to live with us on Shaw. Young Anthony was a Black inner-city boy, raised by aunts and uncles and sometimes a mother who had converted to Islam. How could he adjust to a small island, to me, to the father he did not know, to a life so alien to his experience? Had Anthony considered how difficult it would be for all of us? Anthony thought we could just move to Seattle.

He was asking far too much of me. I felt he was caught up in the idea of playing father. Besides, Anthony's income was unreliable; he was unreliable. How would he pay for his son's basic needs, let alone his education? Anthony already owed me money – there were times I had to pay his share of the house payment or risk losing the house as well as my good credit. I began to think that he chose women who would foot the bills, never suspecting they would have to. By the time he returned to Shaw, he had calmed down. Young Anthony would complete his school year in Atlanta.

Brandy

Katy called to say she wanted to talk to me about her beloved Irish setter, Brandy, just diagnosed with cancer. Would I help her decide whether or not the dog should have surgery? She would come for two or three days including one day in Victoria, which is impossible because the journey from California to the islands alone takes a full day. She agreed to forgo Victoria and I asked why not stay for a week? She said that Jack couldn't get along without her. Actually, Jack gets along very well on his own, but Katy had become increasingly restless away from her own comfort zone. I met her plane in Seattle and we drove back to Anacortes to catch the ferry. Because she chain-smoked nervously all the way, I kept the sunroof and windows open.

At home, we talked about Brandy. I was careful not to tell her what to do but said that I would want to consider what was best for the dog. I would ask the vet to be very frank with me: what was Brandy's prognosis, with or without surgery? How painful would recovery be, for how long? I wouldn't want my dog to suffer, I said. Sometimes the kindest thing is to let go.

Katy stayed one full day and left the following, as she had planned. But not before she had walked briskly through my house, telling me what pieces of furniture she wanted when I died. I chose not to react but her attitude saddened me.

Anthony and I drove her back to the airport. We had time to kill before her flight so we stopped at a mall somewhere south of Seattle. Anthony wanted to go off by himself, so we agreed to meet at a chosen spot at a time that allowed for freeway traffic. Katy and I became increasingly nervous as we waited and waited until Anthony strolled toward us, appearing oblivious of the time. We continued on to the airport as Katy seethed in silence. I was exasperated. What was Anthony thinking?

He lost his way and continued to drive around aimlessly. I tried to remain calm because I did not want to fan the flame that might cause Katy to explode. I finally told Anthony he had to stop at the next gas station for directions. By the time we arrived at the terminal, Katy had lost her seat and was placed on stand-by. She walked away, obviously furious, and waited by the loading gate. The plane finished boarding and finally her name was called.

The next day, I plucked dozens of cigarette butts from the slots between my deck boards. I had forbidden Katy to smoke inside the house so she wrapped up in a blanket and sat on the deck, smoking non-stop late into the night. I worried that she always seemed so agitated but I knew there was little that I, of all people, could do. With Katy, as with Donald, I never seemed to get anything right.

Katy called and said, You were no help! Brandy had the surgery and lived several more months. Katy had always loved her pets fiercely and I have no doubt she dedicated herself to Brandy's care but I don't think it was an easy time for either of them.

Finale

I had become increasingly impatient when women, young and old, exclaimed to me, Oh Anthony is so charming! And he was, although not all women fell for it. I noticed when he spoke to a woman he had just met that his voice became low and sultry, always accompanied by that soulful eye contact. The frequent response was, Oh you have such a beautiful voice!

I was beyond jealousy, I had lost respect for Anthony and with it, love. The manipulation the therapist had observed years before was all too clear to me now. Later I read a line from a Wallace Stegner novel that struck me like a thunderbolt because it so aptly described Anthony: Charm is no substitute for character. And who was it said, Never trust the words of a charming man, good or bad? Some lessons come late!

Finally one day he said, This relationship is depressing. I was relieved. We had been together about six years. I had not, after all, had the courage to initiate a breakup. He said, At least this relationship lasted longer than my last one, as though he had proven something to himself. I, on the other hand, had been guilty of staying too long and not for the first time. We were wrong for one another and I should have admitted that much sooner.

Now, with Anthony's declaration, I felt released. He left for temp work he had found in Friday Harbor and all day I felt I was flying. But that evening he returned and declared that he had changed his mind, that he loved me, he was committed to me. He said we should get married right away, that we could go to Vancouver that week for a license and a ring then on to Victoria to be married. I was suddenly drained; I didn't want to revisit this issue again before bed, so I said nothing. I spent a restless might, dreading confrontation in the morning, but Anthony made it easier when he asked me if I could pay for the license and put a wedding ring on my credit card. So, that was the end of that.

It was not until we were finally parting that it hit me: emotional infidelity was a form of unfaithfulness, even more devastating than sexual infidelity because it was a betrayal of the very essence of the partner. Anthony indulged in serial emotional intimacies that did not require commitment. Emotional seduction to Anthony was like sexual seduction to other men.

This was a revelation to me; I had never heard of emotional infidelity before. Now recognized as an addiction, I have come to understand it so lucidly that I am now quite immune to charm. I want to ask the charmer, What do you <u>really</u> want?

When I expressed this realization to him, Anthony seemed dumfounded. He exclaimed, You're right! He went on to say that he had just remembered that he had been unfaithful to his wife long before she had committed adultery. Whether this was convenient memory or successful self-deception no longer mattered to me.

Still, I learned a lot about myself in those years. Only recently I came across the forgotten journal I had kept from November 1987 through December 1989 as I tried to analyze and sustain the relationship. The final entry at the end of December was a letter of support I wrote to Anthony, encouraging him to write. He had always claimed that writing was the most important thing in his life yet he seemed to do everything to avoid it, inferring that I was to blame. That was Anthony in all things: rhetoric versus action, never taking responsibility for his failures. In the spring of the following year, we parted.

Reading that old journal, I realized how much time and energy, how much angst, I had invested and how much I had suffered in the process. I had forgotten just how many women there were: I can't recall even half of them. I had forgotten that Anthony did not like my women friends – they saw through his charm. I had forgotten the extremes of his manipulation, catapulting me one way, then the other. Shortly before we ended things, he said, I want us to be closer. In my journal I wrote that I replied, It's not possible, it's too late, and how completely calm I felt. At the end, he made a simple statement: I give you nothing - no sarcasm, no rancor, just a simple truth.

Twenty years later, at dinner with publishing friends, one said, He was an extremely intelligent guy. That was very true; it was one reason I was attracted to him in the first place. But, we all agreed, he misused it.

He took the boat, I took the house. I was naïve in that settlement; he had sought the advice of an attorney he knew who probably had no idea that Anthony owed me several thousand dollars for his share of house payments I'd had to pay or risk losing the house. In a store in Friday Harbor one day, I felt someone standing very close and turned to see him. I said, Oh hi, and was pleased I felt nothing but flat indifference. With his charming smile he said, I was afraid you'd be mad at me. I shrugged, said goodbye and left the store. I heard that he had invited his son to stay with him on the boat that summer and I hoped that might be a positive step for both of them.

Having no neighbors within earshot, I turned up CBC radio and danced around the house with Satori. I felt relieved and joyful. Free again!

I wrote to Wallace Stegner to say that I found his writing insightful and was pleased to receive an appreciative reply. Later Mark Adams told me that he and Wallace Stegner were good friends. Such a small world! How lucky I was to have connected with these two outstanding men who so positively influenced my life.

That New Year the Benedictine nuns invited me to lunch on their beautiful farm, along with my next door neighbors, Leon and Berit.

Years before, Leon, an attorney in San Francisco, had bought their property on impulse while his wife and fourteen year-old daughter were shopping during their vacation in Friday Harbor. I loved to watch Leon in his orchard, patiently pressing apples the old-fashioned way while, for some reason, his big black dog excitedly circled the operation non-stop.

I don't know why the nuns invited us three in particular; none of us were Catholic. It was a special day, sitting at a long table with all the nuns and their priest, enjoying pleasant conversation and excellent food fresh from their farm. They asked me if I would like to see their chapel, actually a large cave, lit only by candlelight, with its own chapel cat to keep the mice away. There are many secret caves on Shaw; one neighbor brought me a lovely pink rock he had excavated. I treasured the rock and used it as a handsome doormat weight until it was stolen in Southern California.

Soon afterwards, the Catholic Church dispatched Mother Miriam to an isolated third-century abbey in rural Italy, one other nun from New York her only companion. A team of British archeologists was there too, digging for an even older abbey believed to be beneath the first. I wondered if Mother Miriam had been transferred because she was too well liked on Shaw. Whatever the reason, she was greatly missed. She gave me her address, exquisitely penned in the tiniest script I have ever seen, and for a while we corresponded. She invited me to the abbey to paint, and said I could bring a friend. I thought immediately of Joy but neither of us was in a position to abandon our responsibilities.

The balloon payment on the house was looming. While I was still freelancing for publishing and selling paintings at the Friday Harbor gallery, it wouldn't be enough; I needed to increase my income. The Marine Lab on Shaw hired me to work from midnight to seven in the morning, making microscopic tags for salmon on huge computers taller than me. I worked alone and didn't mind it, feeling quite safe on my little island. My body did not adjust easily to working graveyard but I stayed until the project was completed.

I was happy living alone but I had to be practical. Reluctantly, I advertised for a lodger. Shaw was not a rental market; most people owned their homes and job opportunities were almost non-existent. I received only one reply to my ads and at first it sounded hopeful: a Sacramento man was planning to retire to the islands and from there spend much of his time cruising. He would keep his boat in Friday Harbor but didn't want to live aboard full time. The idea of an absentee tenant appealed to me until he said that he expected me to cook three meals a day for him when he was on land. Suddenly he sounded like Donald, of a generation often set in its ideas of a woman's place. I imagined him to be a retired military man, with a crew cut, just like Donald. I was relieved when he did not call again.

Later another man wanted to rent the house for a week. I was hesitant but desperate and when Babs offered me her little guesthouse for the week, I agreed. He arrived with two women, his sisters, he said, but I doubt it. When I returned to the house at the end of the week, I found all my glassware and dishes had been moved to different cupboards.

Shortly afterwards, some long-time islanders held a meeting and decided to prohibit short-term rentals. They were right, Shaw was not a place for weekend partying. Then a large young family with a rambunctiously friendly dog turned up on the island, having seen my ad. They reminded me a little of gypsies and I had the feeling they were poor.

When a wealthy old woman, who divided her time between Shaw and Seattle, offered me her guest studio overlooking Blind Bay in exchange for chores, I accepted. The young family moved into my house, I moved into the old lady's guest studio with my art supplies, a few necessary belongings and Satori. I tended the old lady's large garden and pulled weeds along her steep garden steps - labor I enjoyed - but she was critical and demanding. I had been in the guesthouse for only a week or two when she announced she was expecting weekend guests and I would have to find another place to sleep.

Finally, stress–induced TMJ brought me down with excruciating pain. I lay on the bed in a fetal position, clutching my head, sobbing and wishing to die, until the retired doctors next door came and shot me with morphine.

Once again Babs offered me her guesthouse for the weekend and there I was able to be quiet and consider my next step. I returned to the old lady's house on Monday, hating that I was at the mercy of her whims. Not long afterwards the young family, struggling to pay their rent, gave me notice. I moved back to my home, sadly aware that my days there were numbered. I had managed to hang onto to it for more than a year but it wasn't easy. I was able to get a small loan from the island bank in Friday Harbor but it was only a temporary fix. One day Babs drove down my driveway and handed me an envelope, which she told me not to open until she shad gone. Inside I found one thousand dollars and a note which read I give you this money on the condition that you tell no one or ever speak to me of it again or try to return it. Instead, when you can, do the same thing for someone else in need in the future.

This loving, generous gesture reduced me to tears and I cried out all the stress that had made me miserable for too long. I resolved to pay the money back somehow and wrote a persuasive response in my head that Babs might accept.

Scott and his girlfriend flew from Seattle to the island on a seaplane. Scott made small repairs to the house and stained the cedar siding with a color I had matched to tree trunks on my property.

Little Lies

When I told Al I was selling the house, he said he knew of some property on the island that few knew about and might be for sale. He knew the elderly owner who had moved from Shaw to Seattle years earlier. Al brought me plot maps from Friday Harbor that showed the land divided into three lots – one large plus two small, adjacent to one another. Al told me he thought the owner preferred to sell all the property as one parcel but he might be amenable to selling the two smaller ones at the same time. I became excited; with the sale of my house, perhaps I could buy a small piece of Shaw Island to return to someday. On a rainy day, wearing our barn boots, Al and I plodded through woods rich with ferns and old trees, staking boundaries, measuring, speculating on best home sites - not too far from power hookups, not requiring excessively long driveways. With his divining rod, Al probed for possible well locations.

A couple I knew in Monterey had decided to move to the island – perhaps due in part to my enthusiasm. I had worked with the woman in publishing and considered her a friend. They found a short-term rental on Shaw while they looked for land they could build on. I told them about the land Al knew of and said that I was interested in purchasing the smallest lot – something I could afford once I sold my house. They were very interested and agreed to meet Al and me later that week to retrace the steps that he and I had taken.

When they kept postponing our walkabout, I was baffled. When I ran into them at the ferry landing, they said they had some important business to take care of first. I was eager to start the process rolling in order to make my plans.

It all became very clear one day when they knocked on my door, trailed by another couple - friends, they said - who were visiting from

Monterey. They announced that the four of them had just bought the two small adjacent parcels, including the one I wanted. Shocked, I didn't react immediately but phoned them later and asked why they hadn't talked to me first. After all, they knew that I was selling my house and that I wanted the lot. They didn't seem to think they had done anything wrong. But it was very evident to me now that their delays were intended to put me off until their friends could travel from California to the island. They had a reason: their friends had money to build right away which meant driveway and well could be shared, reducing their costs. Since I couldn't consider building for some time, I was of no use in their plan.

I saw this as unethical, or at least, deceitful. They might never have known the land was for sale but for Al and me. As Katy so succinctly stated, All they had to do was call you first. I would have been disappointed but I would have understood.

I sold my house to a pleasant Baltimore woman who had summered on Shaw for years and wanted to retire there. After I moved off the island, she occasionally sent me little notes expressing her appreciation of the house and once included a dried crab apple from my young tree that had been a gift from Al.

From the sale of the house, I repaid Babs. I wrote the note that had been in my head, saying that I would like her to use that money to repeat her lovely gesture for someone else in need. Whenever possible, I would do the same.

Reluctantly I sold back my tiny plot in the cemetery for the same twenty-five dollars I had paid for it. Fair enough - the small cemetery was meant for Shaw Island residents only and space was limited. Selling the plot broke my last fragile connection with my life on Shaw.

Some years later, I heard that the former Monterey friendship had soured and both couples had left the island. I remembered the husband's objections in a community meeting early on, to the lack of commercial development on Shaw - he did not want to have to travel off-island to a hardware store. Well, everyone reminded him, you knew that before you moved here. Outsiders who wanted to change everything that Shaw islanders valued were not popular.

Lopez

I had been on Lopez Island only once before and as I drove from the ferry, I saw a sign at the side of the road that said, Loose dogs will be shot on sight! Perhaps a single farmer had posted this sign after losing some sheep, perhaps the sign was official. Whatever the case, I found it a bit unnerving.

Nevertheless, Lopez was the closest island to the mainland and had a small federally funded apartment complex in the village. This was fortunate: a little-known Federal law mandates that government-sponsored housing must allow seniors small pets and I had no intention of giving up Satori. I moved into an affordable one-bedroom unit very different from my haven on Shaw. But at least I was still in the Islands.

Whenever a ferry arrived at Lopez, traffic streamed by my apartment, making it unsafe for Satori to be outdoors. I watched as she became increasingly depressed, shut in for the first time in her life. Sometimes I set her loose in a nearby field, following closely until I decided it was too risky; she might run off.

I settled into my life on Lopez but occasionally returned to Shaw to housesit for Dina and Hugh, sometimes weeks at a time. I took my art supplies and continued to work. From Dina and Hugh's terrace, I saw eagles so close I could hear the whoosh of their enormous wings as they lifted from a nearby snag and soared across the sound. I marveled at the perfect white-on-black patterned feathers of loons as they glided in the cove shallows. When their soulful cries carried across the water, I stopped whatever I was doing and listened. One night, contentedly alone on my birthday, I watched spectacular lightning bolts dart from island to island all the way to Canada. These things gave me deep pleasure.

At Dina's, I continued to keep Satori indoors, away from eagles and aggressive raccoons. One day as I sat on the terrace languidly sipping tea, I caught a movement out of the corner of my eye and turned to see a raccoon charging along the terrace toward me. I dashed for the screen door but it jammed off its tracks. I squeezed through its narrow opening, dropping my teacup in the process. Inside, I slammed the glass door shut then locked it when I saw the raccoon deftly maneuvering the latch. Later Dina told me she had recently barricaded herself with her cat in a bathroom because an aggressive raccoon had opened the same sliding glass door in pursuit of her pet. She described the raccoon as thin and unhealthy looking, much like the one I had seen. Now the raccoon continued to appear, sometimes at the deck door, sometimes on the front porch. I called my physicist friend who came armed with a rifle. He thought that the raccoon's aggressive behavior suggested it was rabid. I went to the opposite end of the house and covered my ears while he disposed of the creature.

Scott, about to be married, decided to drop his father's surname, which held few happy associations. He had called Donald to tell him he was engaged and Donald had only bitter words for him, about women is general.

Scott and his fiancée decided to be married in Friday Harbor and since I was staying at Dina and Hugh's at the time, they had the private guesthouse to themselves. Doris held a celebratory reception on her waterfront deck with several of my friends and neighbors as the setting sun glowed over the Canadian Islands.

In early 1993 I had a one-woman show in Newport Beach. I flew there for the opening and wore the special outfit that Doris had created for me. Scott and his wife helped with everything, from hanging paintings to playing gracious hosts. The show included a watercolor I called Island Hopping, depicting glimpses of islands through portholes on the car deck of the Nisqually, one of my favorite smaller ferries. I sent a slide to the Northwest Watercolor Society for consideration by a jury for their annual exhibit. It was accepted, so I had to ship the original painting from Newport quickly in order to meet the deadline. When it arrived, I was horrified to see that the painting was damaged beyond repair by its shattered glass.

After a restless night I resolved to paint an exact replica from scratch. It was a monumental challenge; it would be compared closely by a jury to the slide I had submitted – no substitutes. With little time to spare, I set to work and was satisfied with the result - the second painting was better than the first. I framed it and on the day of judgment, carried it off to the mainland where it was compared to the slide. The painting was accepted and although I won no prizes, the Seattle Chronicle wrote a favorable review.

In July of 1993 I returned to Sydney for the launching of a book that recorded family history unknown to me, written by a cousin I had never met. (I have written of this occasion in Part 1 of this story.) While there, I took a series of photographs at the Mosman Rowing Club in Sydney that inspired me to paint the watercolor I feel is my best although the painting bears no resemblance to the actual scene. Scott named it Easy Rowing. I made limited edition prints but the original hangs on my own wall. Mark Adams bought one of my signed prints as well as an original watercolor I painted later, of the Carmel Mission against a green sky.

I stayed connected to Shaw. In the winter of 1993, I helped form a writing group of twelve interesting and diverse Shaw islanders, including Babs, Leon, Berit, the physicist, a woman lawyer, Al, who was a former vice officer, and a carpenter whose family pioneered Shaw. Together we put together a book of our writings called Reflections, (Mostly True Stories and Occasional Poems, by Shaw Islanders.) I designed and illustrated the cover and drew all the interior ink sketches.

In January 1994, I flew to Southern California to meet Katy and Jack, who had driven there from Monterey in Jack's vintage Lincoln. Katy had decided to see a Newport Beach plastic surgeon known for breast reconstruction and augmentation. Among his clients, Katy said, was Cher. Katy's original breast implants had deteriorated and shifted. She claimed that another surgeon in Santa Cruz had only made matters worse and that that procedure had caused fibromyalgia. I honestly didn't know if Katy was exaggerating or what the facts really were. Scott and his wife stayed with Katy through her surgery and recovery. The surgeon removed Katy's implants, restored her breasts to their natural state as well as to Katy's apparent satisfaction.

I had agreed to drive the Lincoln back to Monterey with Katy comfortable on a mattress in the back; Jack would fly back to deal with work obligations. Ah, the best laid plans: on January seventeenth, the Northridge earthquake hit and made the roads heading north from Orange County impassable. I was relieved that I didn't have to drive the big Lincoln.

Katy and Jack stayed in Newport until the roads reopened and I flew home to Lopez. Later I heard that the surgeon, facing several lawsuits, flew off one day in his private plane. I never heard the outcome of the story.

Walking with my daughter-in-law toward her car one day, I heard what I thought was an unfamiliar birdcall. It wasn't a bird at all, but an electronic device to unlock her car as we approached it, one of many unnatural sounds invented since I had left Southern California. In the islands, I never heard alarms of any kind, not even police sirens. No one had cell phones; when one company came to Shaw to convince islanders of the need for cell service, they left empty-handed on the next ferry. Islanders had survived very nicely for decades without electronic gadgets. That may have changed since I left Shaw.

Back in Washington, at a mall in Mt. Vernon, I heard what turned out to be a car alarm. Curious, I followed it to a car with – guess what – California plates. It made me think of a bumper sticker I had seen in the ferry line on Orcas Island once: Please don't Californicate Washington. I understood; I had not grown up with this level of noise pollution that newer generations seem to find acceptable. In fact, I think the people who invent such devices – including leaf blowers - should be strung up by their thumbs. As for car alarms: no one seems to pay any attention to them anymore.

In March of 1994, before Reflections went to press, I legally changed my name back to my birth name. In part, I was prompted by my new awareness of family history but now, with my children grown, I also wanted to separate myself from any connection with Donald's name, as Scott had. Afterwards, I felt I had reclaimed a piece of myself.

Free Willy

In May of 1994 I read in the local newspaper that extras were being hired for a movie called Free Willy 2, based on an actual killer whale named Keiko, to be filmed at Camp Nor'wester on the south end of Lopez. I thought, Why not? Extras earned just five dollars an hour but feasted like royalty. I was cast as a newspaper reporter although I did not have a speaking part. I would up on the cutting room floor but I didn't mind; the experience was fascinating and I met two people who remained special friends until they died. Tony and Barbara were about fifteen years older than I was. They had retired from San Francisco to Lopez to be near their son, a master stained glass artist. In San Francisco, they owned a graphics business and were fine artists as well; in fact, Tony's paintings had shown with those of Mark Adams. They were ardent gardeners and their garden was not only beautiful, it also supplied most of their fruits, vegetables and herbs. Barbara could tell you the name of every island wildflower and has exquisitely illustrated most of them. She and Tony were well informed and we have shared many lively conversations.

In the movie, Barbara and Tony played campers and in our first scene together on the beach we introduced ourselves; Barbara recognized my name from my paintings. Tony bent to pick up a small rock and handed it to me. I still have it, a comical little fellow with two barnacles like crossed eyes. Extras do a lot of waiting around, so we had time to talk between takes. My sweet friend Barbara did not end up on the cutting room floor.

A gourmet Hollywood caterer fed us so grandly that I wondered if I could ever adjust to my own cooking again. A wardrobe person checked our clothes, accessories and hair styles to be sure that they were identical to those of days or weeks before, when shooting of today's scene may actually have begun - scenes are not always filmed chronologically.

Working on Willy shattered all my illusions about movies and turned me into an appreciative skeptic. Rainy nights became moonlit, shooting that began on a scene one week in dense fog picked up two weeks later in brilliant sunshine but on the screen, the weather is seamless. When I watch a movie now, I find myself analyzing the techniques behind it and I am always aware that the camera crew is there, just out of sight.

The mechanical Willy stand-ins were so convincingly real that I almost felt empathy for them. I hadn't realized how many technicians it took to create a movie. The large Hollywood crew was efficient and pleasant, as were the two teenage main characters. A third actor, slightly younger, was less cooperative and was often mollified by his attending psychologist. I heard he was the director's son.

In the village market one afternoon, I had a brief conversation with the girl who played the lead role. I asked her if she lived in Hollywood and she said, Heavens no, I wouldn't live there for anything; I live in the Midwest. I found her refreshingly unimpressionable for one so young in that business.

When shooting ran late the day of a reception for my one-woman show in Friday Harbor, several members of the crew sped me there in their launch. They stayed on for the party and launched me back to Lopez afterwards.

Grief and Sadness

On November 7th, 1994, the same month that our Shaw writing group published Reflections, Babs died as courageously as she had lived. We dedicated the book to her.

Then, on Katy's fortieth birthday November 16th, my brother Bruce called me from Sydney, terribly distraught. His wife Gilly, beloved by the whole family, had died suddenly of a brain aneurysm. She was only fifty years old. Nine days later, her little boy turned just seven. It was a shockingly sad time for my family.

I returned to Sydney for a month in May of 1995 to help Bruce and his son however I could. Bruce threw himself into work. Little James kept asking, When will my Dad be home? He delayed bedtime by hauling out a heap of books, all of which he read fluently as he listened for his father's car. I felt painfully inadequate. I was happy when my brother quit the familiar rat race of advertising and committed himself to his passion – painting. Gilly's uncanny financial foresight only a couple of months before she died gave him the gift of time. He became a stay-at-home father and painted and was successful at both.

I returned to Lopez and a pleasantly uneventful life for a while. I walked, I saw friends, I painted, I gardened. I took the ferry to the mainland and drove to Seattle or Bellingham. On Whidby Island I photographed its prolific resident Canadian geese – Shaw islanders called them honkers - for painting reference. I now had paintings in three more galleries including one in Seattle but Waterworks in Friday Harbor represented me best by far. Sometimes I painted with a group of Lopez artists at a friend's studio in the middle of the island. In Friday Harbor I attended watercolor and acrylic workshops under a talented friend named Sam who has since written children's books. I was never bored.

In the summer of 1995, while staying at Dina's house on Shaw, Doris, an animal lover with cats and dogs of her own, told me bluntly that I should have Satori put to sleep. She said, The poor thing is miserable and depressed, something I had seen ever since I had moved her to Lopez. On Shaw she had been free to roam my property, although she never ventured beyond the firehouse fence, where she would perch and observe her world for a while then stroll back down the driveway to the house. At night I had called her in and she slept on my bed, away from nocturnal raccoons. But when I moved to Lopez, Satori became a prisoner.

I did nothing about Doris' suggestion until one night, at the end of summer, as I sat with Satori on my lap, she suddenly leapt up and began to claw frantically at my robe, her eyes wild. I had never seen her like this and when she didn't respond to my voice, I rolled away from her. I didn't dare touch her.

The next morning I made an appointment with my vet on Orcas for the following day. Always, in a car or on a ferry, Satori screamed non-stop in terror and lost all bodily control, no matter how much I tried to sooth her. This had happened when Anthony and I had driven the U-Haul from Monterey to the islands. We had stopped at every rest stop and led her, safely leashed, on the grass, to no avail. She had refused to drink water and was dehydrated and panting. I was afraid she would die.

Now I decided I would set her loose in Dina's cove. I watched her from the window and kept my eye out for eagles. She explored the beach, clawing logs and sniffing driftwood, obviously happy to be free. I went out and stood on the terrace for a while longer then called her in. When she finally came up from the beach, I saw that she dragged her hind legs behind her and I knew then that something was terribly wrong.

When the vet examined her, she told me that Satori had all the symptoms of a brain tumor. Pressure on her brain had apparently caused her sudden frenzy and the paralysis in her hind legs.

I held her until the vet's sedative sent her into the deep sleep from which she would never awake. Because she had come out of the woods, we had never known Satori's exact age but the vet estimated she was now about fifteen. I left her empty carrier with the vet and returned to Shaw, telling myself that I had done the right thing.

Dark October

On the third of October 1995, I was driving off the ferry onto Lopez when my radio announced a verdict in O.J. Simpson's murder trial. The radio crackled and I lost transmission for a crucial moment and thought the announcer had said convicted. I was still cheering when, a moment later, I heard acquitted. I was outraged.

On the seventeenth of October, I ferried to the mainland for my first eye exam in two years, with a new young ophthalmologist I liked named Linda. I carried my father's records with me and asked her to add them to my file. After she examined me, she told me that I had begun to develop my father's condition, age-related macular degeneration. I was taken aback, I had not expected this diagnosis. I was in good health and I took care of myself. But ARMD is genetic and there is no cure. I had the dry type, which is gradually progressive, while the wet type may be more sudden and cause bleeding in the central vision. Without prompt treatment, in the form of certain injections, it can cause devastating vision loss. Having the dry type of ARMD, however, does not preclude developing the wet type.

Distracted, I returned to Lopez. On the ferry I ran into a casual neighbor and told her what I had just learned. Her reaction, intended to be sympathetic, hit me like ice water. She exclaimed, Oh how tragic, you are an artist! I resolved then and there to tell no one but close friends and family. Sympathy was not helpful and I certainly did not want pity. I knew I could deal better without negative input, no matter how well intended.

Back on Lopez, I headed for the library and spent the afternoon studying a pile of medical books. I resolved that I did not want to be ninety-five and blind, regretting that I had not done everything I possibly could to help myself. If, at ninety-five, I had done everything I could, I might be more accepting of vision loss. My research confirmed that my regular diet supplied all essential nutrients. I added specific eye vitamins, since research indicates that these may slow the progression of dry ARMD and help prevent the wet form.

I watched my ninety year-old neighbor lose pieces of her life bit by bit from ARMD: her farm where she had lived most of her life, her pets, her love of gardening, driving, her independence. One day she said to me, All I can do now is sit and watch the walls disappear. I never forgot that. On the other hand, I remember Henry's comment years ago: If I had to choose between blindness and deafness, I would rather be blind, for someone who is deaf is cut off from the world.

Resolved to do all I could to help myself, I saw a Seattle retina specialist who suggested light laser treatment. I wrote to John Hopkins University for more information and learned that laser treatment would not help dry ARMD and Linda, my ophthalmologist, agreed. My best allies would be eye vitamins, a healthy diet and good sunglasses.

When I told Scott of my diagnosis, he said, I'll be your eyes, Mom. Katy, after a long pause, said, What are you telling me? You're going blind? Not long afterwards she called and said, Mother, you are living in fantasy land. If you think Jack and I are going to take care of you, you can forget it. Before I could respond, she hung up.

I realized that I could not remember a single call when Katy had begun with, Hi Mom, how are you? In fact, Katy often slammed down the receiver if she didn't like something that Scott or I said. Like Donald, she was touchy, oversensitive to anything she perceived as criticism. With Katy, I had to tread lightly, which meant our conversations were never true.

Not long after my vision diagnosis, in thin October sunshine, I sat on a cold metal chair in the hilltop Lopez cemetery. Tender strains of island-made music - cello, flute, violin, keyboard and angelic trumpet - drifted from the little white church that was packed with mourners. Two weeks earlier I had cheerfully marked my calendar for two events on this same day: a gala reception in Friday Harbor for an artist I admired and the launching of a classic wood boat built by a Shaw islander. But I couldn't be on two islands at once; I would have to choose. Then I learned that a long-time Shaw islander had died after a long illness and was to be honored at a memorial service that same day. I knew I needed to be there. But that was before I knew about Diana.

Diana

A flutter of butterflies
Silken wings in many colors
Delicate paintings that come to life
A momentous vision, a lifelong memory.
By Diana.

I first met Diana in the laundry room of our apartment complex. She had already filled both washers so I walked back to my apartment and continued to paint for a while. The laundry room was meant to be shared but when I went back, Diana had started two more loads. I left again, annoyed at interrupted painting time. When I returned to the laundry room again, Diana was there with yet another pile that looked like horse blankets. Not more!? I said, exasperated but trying not to sound that way. I asked her name and she whispered Diana. Struck by her apparent timidity, I softened and said, What a lovely name!

For the first time, I really looked at her. She was a child, perhaps twelve, and she was beautiful: slender, fair complexioned with long, dark, silky hair. Her large hazel eyes met mine fleetingly then darted away. She seemed painfully shy, shoulders rounded, head lowered. I wondered where her mother was and why she wasn't helping her young daughter. I withdrew, not wanting to make her more uncomfortable.

I didn't know then what I learned later, from the words that floated from a faceless minister inside the church where Diana now lay in eternal sleep. I learned that Diana was a child of nature and an idealist. She loved all living creatures and mourned their passing at the hand of man. She wrote the poem above on a journey to Mount St. Helen's in the spring, wildflowers at her feet. She was exceptionally intelligent and a veracious reader – she read long before she was old enough for school. She loved to write. She was a formidable volleyball player and she could outrun anybody. She was a self-taught card shark. She carved wood. She enjoyed the far-side humor of Gary Larson; she got the joke.

Recently, Diana had been home-schooled, her main focus on Native American culture. Like those early tribes, she believed that nature must be protected, that one must thank nature for its bounty and give something in return. Later I learned she had been seeing a counselor. She did not believe she was beautiful or clever. Her parents were separated but she spent time with her father. She was the older of two children and it is said that she loved her sister dearly.

For her service, her father wrote:

Diana, our rose, stunningly beautiful
With thorns to guard her heart.

On the night of October twenty-third, Diana rode her bicycle to a gazebo near the beach and hanged herself. She would have been thirteen the following February.

I was not brave enough to view her as she lay in the church and too heartbroken – that is the only word for it – to see her casket lowered into her grave. It was enough to look through my own veil of tears upon the naked, inconsolable grief of her parents as they passed by me. Diana's death shattered Lopez. On an island, whatever touches one touches all. Counselors came to help people understand what was impossible to understand. Barbara, Tony and I found solace in one another.

Revenge

One evening I was surprised by a call from my grandson, surprised because he rarely made any effort to be in touch with Scott or me. He said he had just called Scott to tell him, and now me, that he was gay, something Scott and I had believed for a long time. Now twenty-five, he said that he had told his mother and Jack when he was sixteen and that Katy had said, Don't you dare tell Nanny or Scott! Hadn't Katy realized that this admonition was paramount to telling her son she was ashamed of him? Why did she care so much about what Scott or I thought? Now, hearing Katy's angry voice in the background, I knew that my grandson's call was his way of getting back at her. He was calling me on her phone, which I knew was near her favorite chair in which she spent a great deal of time watching QVC, credit cards and cigarettes at hand.

I don't know how my grandson expected Scott or me to react to his admission but both of us were nonchalant and even talked openly to him about homosexuality. He was who he was and nothing would ever change that.

After another upsetting call from Katy on a day I had intended to paint for an upcoming exhibit, I spent five hours pouring out my feelings on paper but still couldn't pull myself out of a deeply sad sense of failure. When I talked to Dina, she suggested I see a psychologist who had helped her, the same psychologist whose workshops we both had attended in Friday Harbor a year or two before. Jack C. was a practical, likeable man with a direct approach. He said, Why do you feel you should accept such abuse? To which I protested, But she's my daughter!

He said, That makes no difference. You do not accept abuse from anyone! Your daughter is manipulating you by making you feel guilty because you are her mother. You have to let go of negative relationships, no matter who is involved. I had four more sessions with Jack C. and came away feeling resolved and better able to cope with Katy's hit and run calls.

Changes

When Nancy's marriage ended, she left Shaw. We have stayed in touch over the years although distance separates us. I visited her on the Olympic Peninsula once and helped with preparations for her daughter's wedding on an old ferry on Lake Union. We picked beautiful hydrangeas from her friends' gardens - varieties I had never seen before - and wildflowers and ferns from the roadside. Knee-deep in clippings in the basement of the bride's newly acquired home, we made the prettiest wedding bouquets I've ever seen.

We spent one lovely afternoon in a green Olympic Peninsula meadow, listening to live classical music. Another day we wandered through the beautiful gardens and woods of the Bloedel estate, a magnificent one hundred and fifty-acre reserve on Bainbridge Island. Nancy and I always have a lot to talk about including Nancy's perceptions of Shaw society, quite different from mine and probably less idealistic.

In the late spring of 1996, I reluctantly decided to leave the islands. I knew my driving days were coming to an end, and to live on an island, one must have a car in order to leave it. Scott, having ended his unhappy marriage, suggested we share an apartment until I could find my own place. I admit I had reservations about returning to the dun-brown landscape of Southern California; my heart wasn't in it.

I sold my car and gave away items I didn't need to Barbara and Tony, who knew islanders in need. They helped me pack and, thoughtful as always, brought a picnic lunch.

Scott flew in on a seaplane and rented a U-Haul truck, which meant ferrying to Orcas Island and back, at the mercy of ferry schedules – such is the way of island living. We loaded the truck then spent our last hours on Lopez hiking in fields overlooking the sea until the sun dropped below the horizon. I told myself that leaving Lopez would be less traumatic than leaving Shaw; I did not feel the same deep connection. But I knew I would miss this landscape and the sublime quiet of the islands themselves. I would greatly miss Tony and Barbara and I would miss island humor, like the wag who posted a huge sign at the south end of Lopez, clearly visible from passing ferries. It read, Spandex-free zone! Once, on Shaw, a colorful character I knew climbed unseen to the top of the ferry landing in the dead of night and hung a sign, Private Island! Unnoticed for a day or two, the sign discouraged a few tourists from setting foot on Shaw.

Running Backwards

Scott and I headed toward the shadows of my old life in Southern California. I had left there for Carmel in 1978, almost eighteen years earlier. On a hot July day we stopped in Monterey to see Katy and Jack.

Katy had changed her style. I saw immediately that she had had a nose job; apparently she was still striving for perfection, although she was not imperfect. She had let her fine long hair grow out to her natural color, no longer childhood flaxen but quite dark, as mine had become after Scott's birth. Katy had never given in to short hair trends; now she wore her hair pulled straight back to the nape of her neck. She wore no makeup but lip-glass and her modest but elegant long gray dress made her seem almost pious. With her pale skin and green eyes, I thought she looked beautiful. When I told her so, she said that she was trying to look less attractive because she was tired of men coming on to her.

When I asked her if she had made friends in Monterey she became defensive. Oh, everyone on the peninsula is on dope, she said. I suspected that Katy rarely left the house - the shopping channel was on constantly while we were there, her comfortable big chair pulled close. In that beautiful forest setting, she kept the blinds shut tight. She showed me an expensive emerald ring she had bought from QVC, although Katy never wore jewelry, and told me how much she had saved. I joked, Think how much more you could have saved if you hadn't bought it at all! I caught Jack's complicit grin. He took Scott and me into a storage area adjacent to the garage, filled with commercial racks hung tight with clothes, many with price tags still attached. Katy had run out of closet space in the house. She seemed addicted to shopping and Jack apparently indulged her. She had four good black wool coats and gave me one, which I appreciated.

After the long drive in the U-haul, Scott and I wanted to walk. Katy said she didn't feel well, Jack had work to do, so Scott and I set off alone for the Mission Trail. Even though the weather was too hot for my liking, it was good to be in that silent natural beauty. By the time we returned to the house, despite protective clothing, my legs were swollen with poison oak. A pharmacist wrote a prescription and told me that for some people, airborne spores might cause a breakout without actual contact. The prescription reduced the swelling enough that I could wear shoes. We had made dinner reservations for six, including my grandson and his partner, at Clint Eastwood's Mission Ranch with its incomparable pastoral setting overlooking Point Lobos. (Years later I would meet the interesting woman who, with her Australian Shepherd, tends the Ranch's resident flock of sheep.)

Scott and I arrived on time but Jack was already there, having a drink at the bar. Katy stood nearby, looking angry. I thought, What now? I did not ask. The old agitation I had seen when she visited me on Shaw was still there; she still smoked nervously non-stop.

I sat between Katy and my grandson. Katy was brisk and edgy; my grandson sniped at her under his breath. Jack, seated at the head of the long table, stayed on neutral ground, talking to Scott about work or cars. True to her pre-marital promise to Jack, Katy did not drink but I worried about her addiction to cigarettes. I had smoked moderately once, before we all knew better. I quit once for six years before just one cigarette during a moment of stress hooked me again for eleven more months. I finally quit altogether, determined that a habit I found so offensive would not run my life. My mantra became Never have the first puff. I knew quitting wasn't easy.

But Katy did not smoke in moderation. She rationalized that if she didn't inhale, smoking could not harm her. In reality, she constantly breathed the thick blue air in her closed house. Jack smoked heavily too but quit years later after a serious health scare.

As Scott and I were leaving to continue south, Katy asked, How come you're not staying here? I heard what she didn't say: Why are you choosing Scott over me? Although I loved the Monterey Peninsula, I had no job, no place to live there. Even if Katy had offered me a temporary home, I knew better. I could never forget her words a year earlier: If you think Jack and I are going to take care of you, you can forget it.

After eighteen years away, I was taken aback by Southern California. The persistent thin haze I remembered still veiled the air but the population seemed to have exploded, the maze of freeways had become an endless tangle. (My fifteen year-old niece, visiting from Sydney, once said, Southern California is just one big strip of concrete!) When Scott and I went to Little Corona beach, which had never been particularly crowded when Scott and Katy were little, the grassy picnic area near the sand was packed tight, every table taken, every patch of grass spread with blankets. Instead of the young fair-haired families in swimsuits I remembered, everyone there seemed to be covered in long dark clothes - Cambodian, Scott told me. He added that a large area of Fountain Valley was now known as Little Vietnam, with a population larger than Saigon.

Newport and Balboa, on the other hand, had remained conservative White. While high-rise buildings now dominated the low hills near Corona de Mar, Balboa Peninsula- where I had once summered, where we had lived when Katy was a toddler and when Scott was born - had changed the least. It was still a pleasant residential neighborhood with broad tree-lined streets, protected from over-development by its natural boundaries of ocean and bay, but it had become unaffordable for most.

Balboa Island, too, is hemmed in by bay waters but many of its charming old cottages had been replaced by more ostentatious houses. In fact, the island represents some of the most expensive real estate in the country even though the lots are small. A popular tourist destination, its only access, other than the ferry across the bay to the peninsula, is narrow Marine Avenue where anyone sitting at Starbucks knows when you are coming and going. It is always crowded, no matter what time of year, so different from the days when Norlene and I savored the post-Labor Day quiet, when all children were back in school and the summer crowds had left. The feeling of the place has gone for me too: I still love the small boats – the clinking of sailboat lines, the slap of water against hulls, the sight of seemingly disembodied masts drifting by over rooftops. But now it seems more of an address to impress than home for people who truly appreciate the beach and its simple pleasures. Now Balboa Island holds aggressive competitions on Halloween and Christmas for the best-decorated waterfront house. It's a serious business. People hire professionals to adorn their rooftops and patios with animated displays and flashing lights. The residents enjoy cocktails on their patios as throngs crush by to see who has outdone whom. A small group of trumpeters – a lovely thing in the midst of this madness – plays traditional Christmas music as noisy party boats threaten to drown them out. I suspect that those who choose to live in bay front houses on Balboa Island must be exhibitionists at heart, since the houses sit right on the concrete walkway that encircles the island. When my eldest brother was visiting, he was astonished by people sitting at their dinner tables, draperies wide open. He asked, Doesn't anyone value privacy?

Much of the open land that I remembered had been swallowed by development. A tide of look-alike houses, condominiums and strip malls had swept inland toward the mountains. The stables by the sea in Corona Del Mar had gone but happily, that property had become a state park. More recently, a little further south, the old, rotting beach cottages at Crystal Cove - site of a trailer park for years - have been restored to their original simple charm. Tucked below the bluff, out of sight of Coast Highway, Crystal Cove is now a resort, an idyllic location to escape the madding crowds.

We rented an upstairs two-bedroom apartment in the Westcliff area of Newport, where Norlene had once owned a house. Unlike her quiet street, our complex was close to a busy commercial area where the crash-bang of delivery and garbage trucks began early in the morning. One night I was awakened by a police helicopter hovering outside my window, its brilliant lights sweeping the ground for someone up to no good. After the quiet of the islands, I found this disheartening. When we first moved in I asked the landlord about the black oily substance that coated my stove and the walkways outside. It's only jet oil, he said and explained that planes dumped excess fuel as they climbed sharply from nearby John Wayne airport. I thought of the bird sanctuary nearby. The roar of jets close overhead began at seven o'clock in the morning and continued about every ten minutes. I realized that this same flight pattern went directly over all that expensive real estate on Balboa Island where millions of people would give anything to live.

Westcliff was up the hill from Coast Highway, away from the beach, so I walked the well-groomed neighborhoods that appeared deserted but for gardeners, until I began to suffer leg pain from hard concrete sidewalks. A short dirt trail along the high bluff overlooking the nearby Back Bay made for a pleasant escape. Old eucalyptus trees still stood along the path – just about the only trees left to their natural shape in that neighborhood. Later the trail was extended but high-end houses also went in and dominated the landscape.

My discontent made Scott unhappy too. He had been born in Newport and although there were many things he did not like about it – he saw that people were often judged by what they drove or where they lived- he appreciated the best of it - surfing, kayaking, bicycling, walking on the quieter Balboa Peninsula or Lido Isle. But I was isolated all week without a car and an inadequate bus system. To get anywhere in Southern California, you have to drive.

My escapes came mostly through Ruth because Ruth loved to drive. As old friends, we could talk endlessly. But Ruth loved to shop, I didn't, and walking or any physical exercise didn't interest her. Funny about old friendships: we form them when we are young and incomplete; we don't realize how little we may really have in common. What holds us together is time, loyalty and a loving familiarity; we don't have to explain ourselves to old friends and after all, they are part of what we have become.

When Cora, of the Puerto Vallarta escapade, came to Orange County for a workshop, we met for lunch. Years before, she had moved to New Mexico and had created a wonderful little house – much of it from bits of the surrounding landscape – in the red rock canyons above Albuquerque, where she could hear wolf howls echoing off the canyon walls. She lived there with her menagerie of pets in contented isolation until illness forced her to move into town, where, as a former nun, she became involved with the church there. I remember that I was feeling very stressed and unhappy at the time and that she said she would pray for me. Our lives were very different. We were very different

Christmas in Monterey

My brother called and told me he dreaded another Christmas in Sydney without Gilly, so I suggested he and his little boy join Scott and me in Newport Beach. When I told Katy they were coming, she begged me to spend the holidays at her house in Monterey. She said she would love to have a little boy around, would take care of him while my brother, Scott and I went hiking. She would buy everything for a traditional Christmas dinner, she said. Everything would be wonderful! Her familiar expectations made me uneasy and Scott was downright opposed. But in the end we relented and, with my brother and eight year-old nephew, drove up the lovely rain-green coast to the Monterey Peninsula.

Katy, wearing a graceful red dress, greeted us in the driveway. I saw immediately that she had cheek implants. Later she confessed that she had a chin implant as well. It made me felt hopelessly sad. But she was very excited to see my brother's little boy and had bought such an extravagant number of toys for him that we couldn't fit them into the car; carrying them on the plane back to Sydney would be out of the question. Everything would have to be shipped. What was Katy thinking?

She had turned her house into a Christmas wonderland for a small boy. Old-fashioned ornaments adorned the big tree, holiday decorations covered the formal dining room table, not yet set for dinner. While the others stayed in the living room and talked, I prepared food in the kitchen, which I had promised to do because Katy had told me she hadn't been feeling well. She kept darting into the kitchen, saying things like, You and Scott need family therapy, you're f.....g screwed up, he needs to see a shrink, why doesn't he just do this or that....

I did not respond to these hit and run attacks - the kitchen was within

easy earshot of the living room and I wanted no conflict for the sake of my brother and his son. Of course Katy knew that and took advantage of it. I did not tell Scott for years and by then Katy was gone.
We balanced Christmas dinner on our laps as QVC mimed back at us. Later, as we were leaving, Katy said she wasn't well enough to care for James at all. My good friend Sue called her own sitter who regularly cared for a small group of children in her home. With James in good hands, my brother, Scott and I hiked to the crest of Garland Park as I kept an eye out for mountain lions. It was an exhausting climb but I think it was a positive distraction for my brother, away from parental responsibility for a while.

I wanted to find my own place but knew I did not want to stay in Newport. Scott needed his own place too, closer to the island where daily networking had always brought him work. We both were finding it difficult to share a small space - we were on entirely different clocks and I had lived by myself for too long to be a good roommate.

During the time I lived at Westcliff, Ruth drove me twice to the Monterey Peninsula. On the first trip I carried several framed paintings to show to a few galleries; some suggested I contact them again once I had moved back. I applied at the Carmel Foundation for senior housing although their waiting list was discouragingly long. I was lucky to qualify at all after being away from Carmel for so long.

From our little motel in peaceful Pacific Grove I called Katy several times but she never returned my calls. Ruth and I stopped by the hair-cutting shop that Jack had set up for my grandson but it was closed, even though it was early afternoon. We tried again later and found him in. The shop was tiny but delightful, thanks to Katy's creative touch. My grandson told me he worked when he felt like it. He said he liked to party and was restless in his relationship. With the subject of AIDS at the forefront by then, I expressed concern about the risks my grandson might be taking but he shrugged it off. When I told him

I had tried to reach his mother, he said, Oh, Mom's a b...h. I thought to myself, We have become the classic dysfunctional family. It was apparent that my grandson was immature and irresponsible and I wasn't surprised when the shop closed. Jack had tried to help Katy's son but the boy's early conditioning with his own father's family had set his course. He told me, flippantly, that he wasn't as honest and ethical as his partner. Although he claimed he couldn't stand his own father, he bragged that he could visit him in Nevada and get money out of him and his grandmother whenever he wanted. I didn't like my grandson very much.

Back in Newport, I checked the Carmel newspaper regularly. After five months I found an ad for a room in Carmel, in exchange for helping an elderly Jewish woman. Ruth was happy to drive to Carmel again and we went to the woman's house. She decided I would do but I suspect I got the job by proxy: I think she was influenced by the fact that Ruth was Jewish too. Ruth had done this sort of elder care many times over the years and was good at it. She was more patient than I was.

And so once again Scott helped me move back to Carmel. He and a good friend decided to share an apartment on Little Balboa Island, an ideal situation for them both since they were rarely there at the same time. I put everything into storage and moved into the spare bedroom of the old woman's home. It had a small private bathroom and it suited me well enough. My room faced the quiet street and had its own private entrance but I soon discovered that the warped door was jammed irreversibly shut. Her son was a local realtor – I mentioned the door to him but he never had it repaired or replaced.

It wasn't long before I saw that the old woman made life so difficult for her family that they rarely visited. She confessed to me that she complained all the time about everything they did for her and everywhere they took her, including her favorite restaurant. I asked her why she did this and she said, I don't know.

I found I had little privacy because whenever I wasn't actually asleep, she wanted me to sit with her - she could not seem to bear her own company. A Friendly Visitor came now and then, allowing me a small respite. She showed me dozens of photographs and I encouraged her to make a scrapbook for her grandchildren, then organized everything for the project. She was very enthusiastic at first but soon tired of it. I offered to push her around the neighborhood in an old wheelchair but even though she was small, I found it almost impossible to control the thing on Carmel's uneven roads and hills. I had visions of her flying down a hill and me being arrested for elder abuse.

When she complained that her family wouldn't clean out her garage, I offered to. I had a selfish motive: I did her laundry and the washer and dryer, in the garage, were almost inaccessible. Besides, I enjoy organizing spaces. Her married sons stored their things – including motorcycle parts, tires, half-empty cans of used motor oil or paint, greasy rags – in her garage. She agreed to rent a dumpster for a few days and I suggested we work together. I parked her in a chair with a cup of tea and had her handle every item before it went into one of several piles: Goodwill, family, the dumpster, or to-be-decided-later. I threw away the oil and rags. I organized and labeled shelves for each son's items for them to sort at leisure. When the old woman became weary, we stopped working for the day. I swept the garage and cleaned and organized the laundry area and felt a sense of accomplishment. But after the dumpster was hauled away, she accused me of throwing out things she wanted to keep. I think complaining was her sole pleasure in life.

When I awoke one night and smelled something burning, I ran down the hall to the kitchen to find a pan aflame on the stove that she had left on before she went back to bed. She told me afterwards that she got up in the middle of every night and cooked! In the event of a fire there would be little hope of getting her out of her bedroom, down the hall, past the kitchen, through the living room and out the front door.

Even my own escape was blocked by my jammed door and there was no phone in my room to call the fire department. After nine weeks, as I became increasingly discouraged, the Carmel Foundation called to say a studio apartment had become available if I wanted it.

Haseltine

Haseltine had been built in the 1930's as a stopping place for travelers but had been converted into twelve low-income senior apartments by the Carmel Foundation. My upstairs studio had its old-age idiosyncrasies: neighbors were close, the walls thin. An old iron radiator, ticking quietly, provided heat. I loved that thing – it warmed my sweats and socks for my walk to the beach a few blocks away. It was all very charming, very Carmel. Most of all, it was a place of my own and the rent was reasonable.

Although I didn't have my own outdoor area – there was a common courtyard where people sometimes gathered – I was able to hang chimes and a hummingbird feeder by my little porch. I cascaded dozens of potted geraniums down my stairs where cheeky scrub jays stored their peanuts. Sometimes I sat very still on the top step, a peanut in my open palm until I felt the fleeting whisper-light touch of tiny bird claws. Peanut gone!

I sketched and painted the view through my windows that faced an invisible bay beyond dark pines. Sometimes at night I could hear the surf crashing. As I sketched, I became increasingly aware that my vision had worsened. Still, I could see the colors of nature clearly, and nature was my lifeblood. But detail work – my pen and ink sketches, my life drawings, my precise stylized realism watercolors for which I'd been known, were no longer possible. A designer friend, Lisa, suggested I try some abstract art for textbook covers. Abstract? It had never interested me much. She persisted from Thanksgiving to Easter and I finally said I would try.

One never knows how the creative spirit may come alive in unexpected ways. I found abstract techniques remarkably liberating. The images seemed to create themselves, not just with paint but with textures too.

I found myself scrutinizing everything for materials to incorporate into my work – bark, pebbles, sand, needlework templates, things in hardware stores, even gauze a nurse gave me, which I used on a series of math book covers. My friend Joy told me of an inspiring book called Arteffects, written, it so happened, by a fellow Australian.

My vision now ruled out the quest for a gallery but I set up a booth at the Carmel Art Festival and sold some originals I'd kept as well as some limited edition prints. I sold several paintings to the owner of the four inns where I worked part-time and gave others to friends. Book covers paid very well, so I quit the inns altogether. Sunday afternoons I worked at the Foundation, preparing and serving Sunday afternoon tea for members. I found myself fending off a few persistent men, which I found annoying rather than flattering. One man always wore his old service jacket and talked endlessly about WW2 and his gun collection and ranted about the state of the world. When he told me several times that he had seen me here or there, I suspected he was stalking me and I became watchful, especially when I left work in winter dark. He would turn up at the Foundation well before opening time and become angry when I wouldn't let him in. When tea was over, I moved quickly to secure all the doors and windows of three buildings as he went from door to door trying to gain entry. I heard later that he died of Alzheimer's.

A man I had met at a friend's wedding years earlier heard I was back in town. I had dated him briefly but now I couldn't even recall what he looked like. I arranged to meet him at the park and recognized him right away for his preference for brunch dates, in the kinds of restaurants Donald liked. We dated occasionally for a few months only because I had not been involved with anyone since Anthony - it was as though I wanted to wash the taste of that relationship out of my psyche. We had little in common – he thought I should own a gun, listened ardently to Rush Limbaugh and drove his Cadillac around and around parking lots until a spot next to our destination became available; even though he looked fit, he did everything to avoid walking. When he told me he would drop me if his old girlfriend came back to him, I thought, What on earth am I doing? Once again, I had spent too much time waiting by the phone and too little time living my life. Afterwards, in a sudden flash of recall, I remembered why I hadn't remembered him before. I had found him boring!

When their landlady in Stratford-Upon-Avon died, my old friends Muriel and Harry, from Sea Terrace days, lost their apartment there. After nineteen years they thought it might be time to return to America - their two sons lived in Vermont and Oregon and there was a grandchild now. They stayed that first week with Muriel's sister in Beverly Hills and were anxious to find a place of their own – the sister had made it clear they were not welcome. Within that week, their lives turned upside down. All their possessions were somehow lost en route by ship from England, then Harry broke a hip when he tripped over the leash of Muriel's sister's hyperactive poodle. They were shocked at medical complexities and costs in California – worse, they sad, than in England.

Muriel said she would like to live near me in Carmel and decided to make an exploratory visit by train. An editor friend who was going out of town for a conference offered her pleasant cottage where Muriel could relax. She lent me her car, as she often had while she was out of town. Muriel and I checked newspaper ads then drove around Carmel, Carmel Valley and Monterey with little success - prices were higher than Muriel had expected. I suggested we explore Pacific Grove, which might be a little less expensive but Muriel said she was too exhausted. I had noticed she was frequently short of breath but then, Muriel smoked. Disheartened, she returned the following day to Beverly Hills and a handicapped husband. My heart ached for her.

When Muriel called me at the end of the following week, she told me she had just been diagnosed with advanced lung cancer. She learned of a senior apartment complex in Santa Barbara, close to stores and medical care. It was not what cosmopolitan Muriel would have chosen but choice was irrelevant now.

Muriel told me that she wanted no chemotherapy or radiation; she did not want to prolong the inevitable. I told her that I would support any decision she made. But her sons pressured her until she relented. I suspect she didn't want them to remember her as a quitter. She told me that Harry was in complete denial of her illness and her sons, out of state, did not come to help her. You'll be fine, Mom. Muriel had always been an independent and decisive woman but now that she needed real support, she had little. This upset Scott, who had known the younger son well at Sea terrace. He drove up from Southern California, picked me up in Carmel and took me back down to Santa Barbara to spend a little time with Muriel. She told me I was the only one she could really talk to; I did not brush off her fears with, You're going to be fine.

She survived almost another year but told me it was the worst year of her life, that if she could do it over again, she would never let anyone pressure her into undergoing chemotherapy or radiation. I never forgot that. When she went into Hospice, she said that she received more love and understanding there than from her own family. Again she said, You're the only one I could really talk to. When I called the next day, I was told she had fallen into a coma. She died shortly afterwards, at just seventy-three.

On a happier note, Nancy took the train from Seattle to visit me for a few days. She didn't mind sleeping on a borrowed futon on my floor at Haseltine or exploring the Peninsula by bus and she shared my penchant for fast walking. I wished she could have stayed longer. But the Foundation has its rules; guest visits are limited.

My cousin Bryan visited me there too, with his German wife Ana and their two children. Bryan's father was my cousin Noel, with whom I had grown up at Lillianfels but I met Bryan for the first time when he came to Shaw Island and stayed with Anthony and me. I enjoyed this interesting, well-traveled family. They lived in Cambodia for a while but Australia is their home. I will always remember how kind and patient their nineteen year-old son was to his little sister.

The Ultimate Party

Scott and I flew to Sydney in mid-December1999. It was Scott's first trip to Australia and his first experience with a large family. On Christmas Eve, on a perfect Sydney summer evening, we all gathered for a picnic supper on the lawn of the historic Vaucluse House in the Eastern Suburbs, where I had grown up. There, amongst the flowers, we sipped wine and ate as we listened to live Christmas music, sang carols then strolled through the surrounding woods. It was a lovely way to spend Christmas Eve.

Then, thanks to my youngest brother's wife, who somehow had managed to find tickets, we celebrated New Year's 2000 on the terrace of the Sydney Opera House, agape at the spectacular fireworks that exploded over the bridge and turned the harbor into a watery rainbow. Music filled the night, people danced, as Circus OZ performers shimmied down the sails of the Opera House like tiny spiders on invisible webs. Unforgettable!

Scott and I walked one day to the Waverly cemetery to find my mother's grave, which I had never seen. My father had sent me photographs fairly late in his life, of the new engraved rose granite headstone he'd had installed long after my mother's death. Because it was a holiday, no one was in the office to direct us, and we searched unsuccessfully for hours.

Once home, I researched online only to find that we had been in the wrong cemetery, something my half-brothers would not have known. When I was in Sydney again in 2003, my eldest brother took me to the right cemetery at Botany Bay. On a gray blustery day, we walked up and down rows for hours. As I was about to give up, my brother called out that he had found it. The beautiful rose granite was there but had caved in and broken but I could still read the inscription. I saw that all the graves in this section were in disrepair; so many years had passed that there were no family members left to tend them. It was a bleak setting there on the bluff above Botany Bay but I was glad I had finally seen where my young mother had been laid to rest. It was too long ago, too far away for tears but it was a gentle closure. My brother took photographs and I was very thankful that he had been willing to bring me here and to help me search.

Spring Break

Shortly after I moved into Haseltine, I enrolled in a creative thinking class at the Foundation. There I met my friend Ella, a fellow Australian from Sydney, who had come to America the same year as I had.

In March of 2001, Ella and I set out to hike along the dramatic bluffs above Garrapata Beach, south of Carmel. We planned to spend the day, thinking we might also explore the inland hills. I no sooner stepped onto the trail before my foot slipped on gravel and twisted sideways into a deep rut. Ella said, Can you stand on it? I knew I couldn't. We had no cell phone. There was no one in sight but a young man with long hair, standing with his mongrel dog behind his old painted van that looked as though it had just driven out of the sixties. The young man picked me up and carried me to Ella's car and buckled me in. Ella drove me to the hospital where X-rays revealed a complex break, diagonal and horizontal. A doctor recommended that I wait until a very good orthopedic surgeon cam to work at seven-thirty that night. I had checked in at one o'clock. I spent a dreamy afternoon in a wheelchair by the fountain, quite content in a painless drugged haze.

When the surgeon arrived, he asked me what I wanted to have happen. I replied, I'm a walker, I want to be 110 percent. Dr. Clevenger said, Okay and delivered what he promised, with the help of a metal plate in my ankle, which has never inhibited my lifestyle in any way. He even purchased one of my limited edition prints of Easy Rowing.

For several months, I never left my upstairs apartment except for doctor appointments and then my friend Lisa's husband carried me bodily down my old steps to a borrowed wheelchair. At first, a physical therapist came several times a week then less as I progressed. The doorways at old Haseltine were too narrow for the wheelchair so I went from wheelchair to walker to crutches – whatever would get me there. In the kitchen my swivel art chair scooted me from refrigerator to stove to cupboards; a picker the therapist had given me reached high shelves. Lisa stacked big boxes under my art table so I could prop up my cast while I continued to work on book cover art. Sue brought me a cordless telephone and watered my geraniums. I discovered that a wheelchair makes for a very comfortable computer char but once healed, I had to relinquish that. Stranded upstairs for months, I resolved to make the best of it and when I wasn't painting abstracts, I cleaned out files, worked on my computer and read – magnifiers still allowed me that pleasure. I was quite content.

I healed well and began to resume my independent routine. The woman in charge of Foundation senior housing at that time decided to hold a small exhibit of tenants' arts and crafts. I submitted a sketch of a large, nude woman I had done in a life-drawing class. A neighbor asked if I would sell it to her – it reminded her of a friend. I had never tried to sell any of my life drawings: I had done so many, I mostly gave them away. I sold the sketch to her for thirty-five dollars and as she carried it off, I felt someone standing close behind me. The woman who managed the housing said, You know you have to give thirty-five percent of that to the Foundation, don't you?

From that point on, she requested records of all my income upon demand. Much as I dreaded paperwork and tax time - mostly because of the time-consuming business of adding up hundreds of tiny amounts that freelance artists accumulate, for stamps, copies, mailing and so on - I had resigned myself to the required annual report. I kept careful records and paid self-employment tax. I resented this woman's watchfulness that took time and focus away from my real work. In excellent health, I began to develop stress-related irritable bowel syndrome, which became steadily worse. I was losing the sense of peace I had felt at Haseltine.

Ankle healed, I resumed my long walks. One day as I returned through the courtyard, my elderly neighbor, a pleasant Scandinavian woman who was out and about town every day, asked me to help her with her door key. I tried the key but I could not unlock the door either. As we were standing there, the manager who made my life difficult came up the path behind me and said, Tell Erika she doesn't live here anymore!

Dumfounded, I said, What? No, I won't do that! I turned my back on her and went up the stairs to my own apartment, shaken. Now, there may have been a good reason for moving Erika out – perhaps she had been perceived as unable to care for herself, although I saw no sign of that. What was so wicked to me was the way the manager went about it, with absolutely no compassion or tact. Apparently it was not the only such incident: shortly afterwards I heard that she told a woman whose only son had died of cancer, that she had mourned long enough and to get over it.

My IBS worsened. I felt at the mercy of this manager. It was not the first time that I had observed a misplaced sense of power in middle management. The unspeakable horrors of 9/11 only underscored the worst in human nature, trivial or not. Scott, who had fond childhood memories of the mountains, told me of a senior complex in Big Bear and said he would visit often if I decided to move there. Every year, in early autumn, I have a hunger for the mountains and its clear starry skies but I have never actually lived so far from the sea. Impulsively, I applied and was accepted in February 2002.

Once I left Haseltine, all signs of IBS disappeared. Had circumstances been different there, I might have stayed forever, content.

A full seven years later, during a rare conversation with a neighbor who valued her privacy, she confided that she had been harassed by this same manager for several months and finally had to hire a lawyer. Apparently, as a result, the manager lost her job. When I heard this – so many years after my own experience - I felt vindicated.

Mountains

The Big Bear senior complex was large and fairly new; it sat at the edge of the National Forest and was within walking distance of the village. My one-bedroom apartment was pleasant and I enjoyed the luxury of my own washer and dryer. The managers were agreeable, helpful and respectful of tenant privacy.

I had called Katy to tell her I was moving to Big Bear. For the most part, she had avoided me ever since I had returned to Carmel and rarely returned my calls, letters or cards. It was almost a relief, to be away from her unpredictable moods and inevitable hit-and-run attacks. During that time, Scott and I maintained occasional contact with my grandson's partner at his place of work until he left his job there. We gathered that my grandson's relationship with his mother was toxic.

Katy did not return my call.

However, shortly after I arrived in Big Bear, Katy did call. It was as though she felt a certain safety in the miles between us. She told me, then, something I had not suspected: that she and Jack had been divorced for three years, an arrangement that for some reason I didn't understand was financially beneficial to them both. He had bought a condominium for her in Monterey, as well as a late-model Volvo and he supported her financially. He checked on her every few days and sometimes dropped cash through the sunroof of her Volvo because, she said, she needed it. One time, Katy claimed, her old partner in crime, Marvel, had come to visit her at the condominium and stolen all her money. Occasionally, when she felt lonely or depressed, she begged Jack to let her stay at the house although Jack made it clear the bedroom was off limits to her. I think he still felt responsible for her.

Katy told me that she had met a woman veterinarian she liked who offered her part-time work. I enthusiastically encouraged her - this seemed the perfect job situation for Katy, who had great empathy for animals, and it was part time, close to home. It would get her out of her closed house and social isolation. But when I asked her about it later, she scoffed, Oh that woman was a bitch.

Then she thought she might apply for a job at an historic inn overlooking the bay in Pacific Grove. I encouraged her there too but suspected she was romanticizing the job as she described which old-fashioned dresses and little slippers she would wear. I had worked in several inns and knew that such work sometimes meant dealing with demanding guests or overflowing toilets. And invariably, new employees were assigned the worst shifts, even split shifts. I said none of these things which might discourage her but she never applied anyway.

Now Katy told me that, before Donald and I were divorced, he had often come into her bedroom after a night shift at the police department, climbed into bed with her and fondled her. I was horrified. Scott was furious and wanted to confront him. But I do not know if it was true although in retrospect, I can see, given Donald's psychotic personality, that he might be capable of such behavior. On the other hand – also in retrospect - it is possible that Katy might have imagined it.

My grandson also called me in Big Bear. He told me that he and his partner wanted to move away from Katy and were interested in Whidbey Island. Since I had lived in the islands and loved it there, he thought I would encourage him but I told him that Whidbey Island was very different from Shaw. It was larger, geographically connected to the mainland and had a strong military presence which, for a homosexual couple, might be difficult. Nevertheless, they packed all their belongings into a U-Haul truck and drove to Whidbey, spent less than a day there, turned around and drove back to California where, inexplicably, they bought a small condominium downstairs from Katy's, a move that set the scene for disaster.

Hoping to pick up some freelance work, I invested time and money in an updated resume and portfolio and sent it to an agent in Newport Beach who had been highly recommended by a businesswoman I knew there. The agent never responded and when I finally reached her, she admitted she had lost my entire portfolio. I didn't try again. Determined to continue walking, I found that in order to reach the road that looped up to the edge of the National Forest, I had to cross a field of slippery ice. It was, after all, winter in the mountains then but I was a winter novice. Having experienced one broken bone incident, I was extra careful but each step was so tentative, I could not walk freely at the brisk pace I was used to. Even without ice, I couldn't go far go far unless I wanted to venture into the forest itself – out of the question, alone, unarmed. The houses that backed onto the forest all seemed to have vicious dogs that were clearly not socialized.

One warm day, I was walking the loop at the edge of the forest when I saw a very large dog picking its way through the woods, down the hill toward the road. I kept a wary eye on it as I continued to walk. As it drew closer, I realized with a shock that it was not a dog, but a mountain lion. It had not yet seen me. I laugh now at my almost comical reaction. I stopped dead, stared at my feet and whispered Oh boy oh boy oh boy. What are the rules? Bear-assume a fetal position, mountain lion- what? Run? No, that wasn't it. Stare it down? Ah, wave madly, make myself look big, wave my jacket. Oops, no jacket. Oh boy oh boy oh boy. I looked up and at that moment the mountain lion saw me. To my surprise and relief, it turned and ran back up the hill into the forest. I never walked that way again. The lake was out of the question too – with a bear population of twenty-five hundred, warnings were posted everywhere. The village was my only recourse.

Once, in Yosemite, I came face to face with a bear. I was walking along a dirt path with Lisa's husband Steve, his little girl, my friend Sue and her little boy. The children were about five at the time. We had all been swimming at a waterfall pond a mile or two from camp. The children skipped ahead of Steve and me as Sue trailed behind. As we came around a curve, a large black bear blocked the path directly ahead of us. We stopped dead and Steve quietly told the frightened children to walk backwards very slowly. The bear was standing on his hind legs, looking directly at us as my eyes fixed on his enormous curved claws, clearly visible. We all retreated in slow motion. I, for one, held my breath. Sue, further back around the curve, had not seen the bear; afterwards she said all she remembers were four white faces! We took a different path back to camp and reported our encounter. Luckily for us, this particular bear was apparently kept well fed behind the camp kitchen. My memory insists that the bear was holding a big chunk of watermelon but I might have imagined that.

Big Bear village seemed full of toothless mountain men and smoking teenagers; religious retreats and conference grounds seemed abundant. I had looked forward to summer thunderstorms like those I had experienced growing up in Sydney. I expected a thunderstorm to bring refreshing rain but instead it brought a brief smattering of jumbo raindrops that created suffocating humidity as steamy as I had once felt in Fiji. When lightning strikes that summer set off fires in the forest close to the complex, I began to regret my impulsive decision to move to the mountains.

My new ophthalmologist was capable but limited in the help she could offer. She told me that in the event I might need a specialist for my worsening vision, I would have to drive down the mountain to San Bernardino. Without a car, this was impossible. Even with a car, my limited vision would make such a drive hazardous.

As forest fires continued to threaten the mountain communities and talk of evacuations increased, I knew it was time for me to leave Big Bear.

Before I left, Scott and I explored real estate in Cedar Glen, a nearby community that we liked, where prices were reasonable by California standards - Scott dreamed of building a small getaway cabin there someday, a place he could work without all the restrictions of a city.

The following year, in October 2003, Cedar Glen was totally devastated by fire. When Scott and I went there later, nothing remained but scorched chimneys and foundations. Most of the old cedars we loved had perished.

The Little Island

I lived in Big Bear almost six months then Scott, with great forbearance, moved me once again with all my belongings. His roommate and friend, who had other options, moved out and I moved in.

Scott's apartment was on Little Balboa Island, across a small bridge over a narrow canal. With no shops or cafes, tourists have little incentive to explore it and so it is a far more peaceful environment than the main island. The apartment was upstairs, part of a main house owned for years by a pleasantly eccentric woman who liked Scott. Her house was more red barn than house, a crumbling warren of odd little rooms. A life-size plastic cow filled the front garden – a great attraction and source of amusement for locals and tourists alike. You never knew from day to day what the cow might be wearing.

I had no sooner moved in than the woman retired and talked of moving to a rural area closer to family. She hoped to keep the island place and rent it to several people she knew, including Scott and me. We would move into the main house, Scott's friend and former roommate would have one studio off the patio, another friend and his wife could have yet another section. We had it all worked out but in the end she sold the house for an irresistible sum to an out of town builder who wanted a summer place and planned a major renovation. He raised our rent then deposited us into a dank apartment on the main island while he had the property fumigated. He asked us to store any outdoor things that we owned – my wind chimes, large pots and planters, door mats, my precious Shaw Island cave pink rock – in the garage, which he locked without giving us a key. When we returned, all our things, including the Shaw Island rock, had been stolen, apparently by workers who had access to the garage. Men came one day and cut down the only big tree on the property, a tree we valued for the bird life within it and the privacy it provided us. Then he evicted us. The timing could not have been worse; it was mid-summer, when rents were at their highest, even if anything was available.

A woman we knew told us of an available studio on Marine Avenue. Her son lived there and wanted out of his lease although he didn't say why. In fact, he never said a word while his overbearing mother expounded the advantages of the place, to which I was blind. The idea of sharing a hot upstairs studio with Scott over a bookstore on Marine Avenue on Balboa Island sounded like a nightmare to me. But we were out of options.

The only access to the studio was a flight of steps against the front windows of the bookstore. A gaggle of chatty women ran the store and I was privy to it all - there were no secrets, no privacy. Repetitive generic music rose up through the floor and windows from ten in the morning to ten at night. Headphones and the classical radio station helped mute the annoyance while I worked on my computer. Every morning after the first jet roar at seven shattered my sleep, I chased cockroaches off the kitchen counter while Scott slumbered on, oblivious. A tangle of heavy cables and humming wires stretched from the street to the alley between our tiny aluminum bathroom window and the next building that I could almost touch. There was absolutely nothing to please the eye or the soul. All night a flashing neon sign next door (Frozen Bananas?) blinked at regular intervals into our bare, floor-to-ceiling-high window that faced west. During the day, temperatures in the apartment sometimes soared into the 100's.

I read in the newspaper that The Museum Store in Fashion Island was closing and needed workers for a month to clear inventory. A pleasant young woman hired me, although I suspect my age concerned her. I caught the bus on Coast Highway and didn't mind walking the rest of the distance coming and going. It was a month of unrelenting hard work and I sought out quiet, flowery spots for my half-hour yogurt break. But the most difficult part came at the beginning when the manager was teaching me the computer checkout system. The screen was blank; I could see nothing on it at all! I knew then that my vision had deteriorated more than I had been willing to acknowledge.

I performed a variety of tasks, which I didn't mind - stockroom, inventory, sweeping, dusting, vacuuming, wrapping, mailing, telephoning and so on. When I had to work at a computer screen, I was allotted one that didn't face any glare but I still found it difficult. I hung essential magnifiers around my neck so as not to misplace them. I was grateful when the month ended and the crush of demanding shoppers had gone, although I appreciated being around all those elegant replicas of museum pieces. In all of Fashion Island, I thought The Museum Store superior but I resisted purchasing anything; I needed nothing and I was happy to have a little money. Scott, meantime, stayed busy painting bay-front homes and private boat docks. His reputation for excellence kept him busy, although his dyslexic perfectionism diminished his profit.

I often walked around both islands for exercise but once again, found the concrete pathways hard on my legs. My doctor said, Then walk on soft trails. I replied, I have to walk forty-five minutes on concrete to reach a soft trail!

One day I walked by a bay front house where a big dog I liked lived. As I played with the dog through the gate, his owner came out to the patio and as we were talking, two other women stopped and joined us. I found myself in the middle of an intense conversation about facelifts – all three women had had them. One, wearing a big hat that shaded her face, was out for the first time since her surgery and the others advised her at length. Having nothing to contribute to the conversation I moved on, feeling as though I had landed on another planet that I didn't like very much.

Late one night, as Scott and I walked around the island, we bumped into a woman he knew. He didn't recognize her at first because she seemed to be wrapped in headscarves. Then she explained in detail her most recent facelift procedure, how they cut here, here and here and laid her whole face on her chest and.... I must admit it was fascinating. She too was walking late to avoid people. Later another woman at Starbucks said, I thought she looked better before.

Balboa Island allows little privacy. A cup of coffee at Starbucks yields more information about others than you'd ever want to know and alliances seem to switch from day to day. A great deal of banter goes on but little real conversation. I found it claustrophobic, a strange insular little world unto itself. An Australian friend who lived there for a while often said, This place is so beige! By that she meant bland, uptight, conservative, unoriginal. She was anything but. I thought of Shaw, so very different. No two islands are alike.

I resolved to find my way back to Carmel eventually. I called Sue who put me in touch with her good friend who ran the social services office in Monterey County at that time, and started the ball rolling. Scott and I had agreed we did not want to renew our lease for the studio over the bookstore when it came due.

While I lived on the island, I contacted my old friend Shirley from Sea Terrace. She had moved into a pleasant condominium, owned by her son, shortly after I had left Sea Terrace for Carmel. One day she drove her big immaculate white Cadillac to the island to pick me up. As we left the island, she started to make a right hand turn from the left lane onto Coast Highway – not only illegal, but dangerous. Then, as we entered Fashion Island, she ran over several orange cones in a construction zone. I turned my head to see the astonished reactions of scattering road workers. Shirley, I said, do you know what you just did? She was oblivious. I resolved I would never get into her car again. Scott recalls that I suggested that she take Vitamin B6 and B12, which might help mental agility. Shirley was agreeable but when she asked her doctor, he was dismissive.

Not long afterwards, her son and his wife moved her into a private rest home owned by the son's business associate. I did not care for the son – he was alcoholic and had made advances not only to me, but Katy too. Once, on a trip to the Monterey Peninsula with his wife and mother, he invited me to join them for dinner at a good restaurant, where he laid his hand on my thigh while the other two women were in the restroom. I never told Shirley.

Ruth took me to visit Shirley at the rest home. She was miserable there - she shared a room with an Alzheimer's patient who screamed all night; the staff spoke no English. It was clear that Shirley needed some help but I couldn't believe she needed to be in this environment at this time. She knew and liked an educated young woman from South America who had helped her occasionally in her condominium. I felt, as long as this young woman was there, Shirley could manage. Driving, however, would be out of the question.

I told Ruth what I was considering and Ruth agreed. We drove to the rest home and I told the owner I was taking Shirley home and would explain everything to her son. As he protested, Ruth went to Shirley's room and gathered up her belongings. Over the owner's objections, we left and drove Shirley home. The cat litter bins overflowed, their food bowls were empty but the cats had survived.

I called the son and persuaded him to give his mother a little more time at home. He re-hired the young South American woman and for almost a year, Shirley lived contentedly amongst her cats and her plants. She returned to the rest home – necessary by then – and died quietly in her sleep shortly afterwards. Her son wrote me a note and called me an angel. No, just an old friend.

I look back and think how presumptuous it was of me to do what I did and to make Ruth complicit. But I don't regret it and nor, apparently, did Ruth. We could imagine ourselves in the same position someday, hoping for an angel.

Foreshadowing the Future

Because Katy had told me that her health had worsened, although not in a very specific way, Scott and I drove to Monterey that Christmas to be with her at Jack's house. We had not seen her for about five years, mostly because I had been living in Southern California, but also because too many visits had turned into conflict. Scott suggested we take our big box of family photographs to share with Katy - neutral territory that we might all navigate without conflict. It was a smart idea; like her grandmother, Anita, Katy was sentimental. Old sepia photographs of my grandmother's era as well as my own childhood, were there, even an unfinished baby book in which my mother had recorded my very early years before she died. Even my forgotten childhood poems were there. Donald had long ago given Scott all the slides he had taken during our marriage and Scott had carefully organized them chronologically.

Even though it was early afternoon, Katy was still wearing her robe – forest green, I recall, beautiful with her green eyes and pale skin. She seemed uncharacteristically vulnerable; she said, Oh thank you guys for coming. She became tearful when I read my poems, written at age nine, all about animals and nature, although I find them sweetly funny all these years later. Then, as we looked through Donald's color slides, which had recorded much of her and Scott's childhood, she became distraught. Why doesn't he love me? I've sent him cards and notes, I've called, but he never answers.

We all chimed in at once: It's not your fault! It's his problem. Scott added, He is not capable of loving. But there was no convincing Katy. I hadn't completely realized before just how lastingly devastating an unloving father can be to a young girl, even though it was Katy, at age eleven, who had said, Mother, we are better off with him gone.

Later I found Katy in the kitchen, sitting on the floor against a wall, crying. I knelt down and touched her and asked, What's wrong?

Oh Mom, I love him so much, she sobbed. Then she spilled out the story of a man she had fallen in love with. She went on to tell me that she and Jack were at a juice bar on Alvarado Street in Monterey one day and as Jack waited for their order, a man approached Katy, slipped her a business card, left and climbed into a Mercedes parked outside. The name on the card-which I never saw-was a well-known actor.

Katy told me that they had begun a relationship shortly afterwards. She told me how, when she was sick, he treated her very gently, tenderly pushing her hair from her face, how he brought her special meals and flowers. He had built a big house in Monterey where he kept dogs and horses that she could enjoy whenever she wanted. When he was away working on a film, he called her every day; she had even met his mother. She went on in great detail, sobbing all the while because, for some reason I didn't understand, they couldn't live together yet. The details of her story were so specific that I almost wondered if there might be some truth in them. Clearly, she was emotionally fragile. (In late 2017, this actor revealed he was gay.)

When she calmed down, I asked her if she had shared her problems with her doctor. She said he had referred her to several other doctors and they had all agreed she should go to the behavioral clinic in Monterey. She told me she could not afford to do that, her insurance wouldn't cover the cost - she would have to go three times a week. She could lose her condominium, she claimed. She said she did see one therapist she liked once, a woman who, however, couldn't possibly understand because she was young and inexperienced.

Scott and I went with her later that week to her primary doctor. When we picked her up we saw her condominium for the first time. In the living room, Scott spotted his treasured Peanuts books from his childhood as well as the Koala bear my father had given him as a child. My father had given Katy one as well but when she lost hers, she simply took her brother's and forever denied that she had. The beautiful book my father had sent me from Paris when I was little was there too, but I had given that to Katy and was pleased to see she apparently treasured it.

I saw that Katy was trembling slightly as she described her symptoms to the nurse. Her drugs weren't working, her fibromyalgia was worse. It was clear to Scott and to me that the nurse did not believe that Katy was physically ill. I was in doubt as well – her symptoms had always been elusive but then, I was not a doctor. Certainly Katy had convinced herself that she was seriously ill.

From the doctor's office, we went to Del Monte Center for coffee. Sitting outside Starbucks, she suddenly launched into a verbal attack on Scott. I tried to diffuse the situation but she went on, disregarding the curious stares around us, flinging collective grievances, knowing we would not contribute to a scene. Scott pushed back his chair and walked away. Katy, who had never really worked her entire life, told Scott what he should be doing with his life. Scott, despite his lifelong struggle with dyslexia, had developed multiple skills on his own, worked hard and was responsible for himself.

I felt sick at heart that my forty-eight year-old daughter could be so blindly judgmental, because it was a trait I hated in Donald: that he could never look at himself, would accuse others of behavior of which he himself was guilty – projection? Transference? It didn't help that Katy seemed to have inherited her father's misery gene, and along with it, an inability to laugh at herself.

I found Scott and we drove Katy home.

Once evening later that week as I sat between my grandson and Scott in Jack's car outside Safeway, waiting for Katy, Jack suddenly said, I have created a monster. I understood. Katy had been particularly strident and ill- tempered all afternoon and as usual, we had all attempted to mollify her, to keep the peace, even though we knew better. I understood that Jack was referring to the pact he and Katy had made years earlier, before they married. If she promised to be faithful, to stop drinking, to stay away from drugs, he would take care of her; she would never have to work. Unwittingly, they had made a pact with the devil. Never having had to take care of herself, Katy never discovered her own strengths or potential. Dissatisfied with her life, she blamed others for her own discontent.

Not long afterwards Katy acquired a cat - a white Himalayan with a flat nose - that Katy called her comic book cat. Jazz-Purr had been found with the body of his elderly owner. He was mild-natured and never meowed. He would sleep on Kat's bed but resisted being held. I wondered if he had been traumatized by his previous owner's death. Katy adored him. She told me how he sat, not cat-like at all, but like a little old man, upright against a wall, paws folded on his lap. I was pleased for her and for the cat because it had been rescued in time. Perhaps Jazz-Purr might brighten Katy's life, give her something to care for.

Back on Balboa Island, I pursued possibilities for my return to Carmel. Meanwhile, in January, I wrote a passionate letter to George W. Bush, condemning his intention to invade Iraq. I knew the letter would never reach him but I found satisfaction in expressing my frustration. In March he did invade Iraq and everything I predicted happened. Anyone with a functioning brain could have foreseen that.

On a Sunday around the middle of March 2003, Katy called me, extremely agitated. She claimed that her son and his partner, from their downstairs condominium, had a clear view of everything she did and threatened to report her to the police. I could not visualize any possibility of a clear view into Katy's condominium nor what they might report her for. She told me that my grandson had said, We hate you and we're going to get your condominium. I asked her if she had told Jack of this and she said he was going to install stronger locks on her doors and windows the following weekend. I then asked her if she and Jack had updated their wills and was shocked when she told me that their lawyer didn't even know that they were divorced. I told her to take care of it right away but she said Jack was going to do it. Jack works long hours, I reminded her. You don't. Call and make an appointment! But she insisted that Jack would take care of everything.

Then she told me that she had seen a different doctor she liked in Carmel Valley; he was more understanding. She said that he suspected she had liver cancer and had done a biopsy. She promised to let me know the results.

Into a Dark Tunnel

One evening about a week later, Jack called. Scott answered the phone and I knew immediately that it was very bad news and that it was about Katy. I remember stifling a scream even before Scott held the phone aside and said Katy is dead. He looked stunned.

Jack told us that he became concerned when Katy didn't return his calls, even though we all knew that she sometimes didn't answer the phone. But it had been almost two weeks since he had actually seen her. He went to her condominium and saw her car there. When there was no answer to his knock, Jack let himself in with his own key.

What Jack described to Scott and me has created an image I know I will never erase from my memory, nor will I ever again speak of it to Jack for I think that he is already haunted by it.

I saw what I thought was a black garbage bag on the kitchen floor and saw long hair stuck to dried blood and realized what I was looking at. He called the police and as he waited outside for them to arrive, my grandson, having heard the sirens, came up the stairs. Jack, in shock himself, would not let him inside to see what he himself had seen. After all the trouble Katy's son had caused over the years, Jack still protected him. My grandson was hysterical.

His Reno grandmother, now divorced from the husband who spent time in federal prison for conspiracy and fraud, flew in from Reno as soon as she heard of Katy's death. From that point on, my grandson avoided speaking to Jack, Scott or me. We did not know where Katy's body was. I called the coroner and learned that she had been taken to a certain mortuary and when I called there, they were very terse and refused to tell me anything. It appeared that parents, siblings and ex-husbands have no rights. I knew that Katy was fearful of cremation and wanted to be buried in a pretty place beneath trees. Nevertheless her son and her former mother-in-law expedited her cremation. Jack rescued Jazz-Purr, abandoned for the second time by death. How did he survive all those days as Katy lay on the kitchen floor?

Scott and I requested copies of Katy's death certificate. There were two: the first certificate, under cause of death, stated Pending Coroner Investigation. As a result of further autopsy, the second certificate stated Subject choked on food while eating in a state of intoxication.

I wrote to the corner for more information and he replied in detail. Katy's blood alcohol level was 0.47 and she had taken Diazepam and Nordiazepam as well. He went on to describe the progression of decomposition. It was tough reading and I will not repeat it here. The death certificates stated that her body was found March 28th. However, the coroner said, the exact date of death was undeterminable but she probably died four or five days earlier. She may even have died the same night that I spoke to her.

When the police questioned my grandson, he said he had not seen his mother for two weeks that they had smoked marijuana and argued about both their lifestyles and work status. The police report describes the state of Katy's condominium in detail, neat except for a partially filled laundry basket and clothes scattered across the living room floor. In the bedroom, which the police report describes as being set up like a living room, the television was turned to QVC, a Post-It shopping list stuck on the screen. An open can of diet Coke and an ash tray with a cigarette burned all the way down – the police determined it had been freshly lit but never smoked – sat on a table next to Katy's easy chair.

What baffled Scott and me was the fact that, according to the police report, no evidence of alcohol - not even empty bottles or glasses - was found in Katy's apartment, and no prescription drug containers of any kind, only a note on the refrigerator that said Valium. In addition, the report states, her purse was missing along with all identification - they identified her by letters they found, addressed to her. Jack explained that he and my grandson had cleaned up the apartment later but that was days after the police had thoroughly examined the scene and written their report. How could Katy, so debilitated, go down the steps to the trash area and dispose of alcohol and prescription bottles, come back up the steps then wash drinking glasses? No one has ever explained this to my satisfaction.

Months later, hoping for answers, Scott and I met with the Monterey detective assigned to the case. We told him of my grandson's supposed threats to his mother but he dismissed us. Case closed. We had to let it go.

Scott called the grandmother and tried to persuade her to tell us where Katy's ashes were scattered - if they ever were - but she refused. When Scott told her of her grandson's abusive attitude toward his mother, she exclaimed, But he's my baby! Actually, he was thirty-two. Scott told her what he thought of that and hung up.

Scott called local marinas about boats that may have carried her ashes out to sea but learned nothing. My grandson published her obituary with an old photograph from her wild blonde years. In her obituary, he – or his grandmother - wrote that she liked animals, antiques and good desserts. Good desserts?

During this time, Scott and I were still living in the studio on Marine Avenue. I think of that time as being trapped in a black tunnel, no light at the end, no escape. My brothers offered to pay my fare to Sydney but Scott, depressed and upset, said he would feel abandoned. It was too soon.

We drove to Monterey to help Jack. He told me that when he called Donald to tell him that Katy had died, he said, Yeah, she left several messages; I figured she just wanted something. Actually, a few weeks before she died, Katy had told me that she had reached him and that he had told her he had just been released from the hospital and that he might have to have his legs amputated. She called me and sobbed that she was so scared for him. I didn't say what I was thinking, that her concern for him was more than the man deserved.

On Good Friday, Jack, Scott and I held a simple little memorial service of our own under the old cypress tree on Carmel Beach where they had renewed their vows years earlier. We scattered tiny rosebuds from the rocks and watched them float away. The next day Scott returned to the beach and gathered buds the tide had returned. I still have them.

I walk by that tree almost every day and to me, it will forever be Katy's tree. I wrote a note without rancor – it took some restraint – to Donald, inviting him to our little ceremony but he declined with a postcard that said Sorry. Give me a call sometime, Kid. (He had often called me that.)

I published a memorial for Katy in Newport newspapers as well as in Monterey. It was a way to let her old friends in Newport know but we never heard from any of them. I used a photograph as she was near the end of her life, dark hair pulled back, little makeup, somber but beautiful. She might be unrecognizable to those who knew her as a blonde.

When I called the Carmel Valley doctor and asked him about Katy's biopsy results for liver cancer, he was surprised. He told me there never had been a biopsy or any indication of liver cancer, that he had treated her only for anxiety and depression.

Later, Jack learned that Katy had run up a tab at a local liquor store for over a thousand dollars and that it was her son who usually ran her errands, as he had done when he was nine years old. We realized that

Katy had resumed drinking after she and Jack divorced. My grandson, an alcoholic himself, encouraged her. Alcohol, cigarettes and drugs – marijuana at least – became their common purpose. But the face that Katy presented to the world on those rare occasions when she left the house was modest and sober. I don't think she was being intentionally deceitful – I think she wanted to think of herself as a very good girl, a perfect girl. She wanted others to see her that way too.

Back in Southern California, in June of 2003, Ruth drove me to Fountain Valley for a checkup with the ophthalmologist I was seeing at the time. As Ruth waited outside, he told me I was legally blind in my left eye, two-thirds blind in the right. He told me not to waste money on prescription glasses; they would not do any good. I felt numb. In the car, headed south on Brookhurst Avenue, I told Ruth what the doctor had just told me.

I will forever regret that I opened my mouth at that moment. Shocked, Ruth turned briefly to look at me and in that instant, hit a motorcycle. I think it had pulled out onto the divided road unsafely – neither of us saw it coming. We got out of the car and went to the rider's side, a man probably in his late fifties. He said he was all right, even though he had bounced off the hood of Ruth's car. His motorcycle was wrecked. Police cars, a fire truck and an ambulance arrived promptly and he was quickly on his way to the hospital. Ruth seemed to be in shock; I had chest pains – perhaps I had hit the dashboard on impact. A medic checked us both and declared we were fine. We called the hospital later but the man had already been released, so we knew he could not have been seriously injured. Later, he claimed back injury and poor Ruth had to deal with legal implications for about three years, at risk of losing her home. Still, she never blamed me, although I blamed myself. In the end, when it was discovered that the motorcyclist had suffered a previous back injury when his dune buggy overturned in the desert, the matter was promptly settled.

The ophthalmologist referred me to a retina specialist in Newport Beach. In his waiting room, an old man told me, I looked in the mirror and I wasn't there. Wet ARMD had damaged his central vision. The retina specialist described to me a process called photodynamic therapy. He cautioned that if I had this therapy, I would have to cover up like a mummy afterwards, before I left his office, and remain indoors in the dark for several days. If I ventured outdoors or even close to a sunny window, I would suffer third degree burns. It sounded like an exaggeration to me but he insisted that one of his patients had experienced this outcome very recently and was now in a hospital burn unit. Fortunately, after examining me, he decided I was not a candidate for PDT. I don't think I would have done it anyway.

In July, Jack called and asked Scott to help him remodel his Monterey house, in exchange for room and board. Scott was happy to go and I was able to book for Australia. I would return to Monterey, away from the studio on Marine Avenue at last, and stay at Jack's until I could find my own place.

In Sydney, surrounded by life – numerous nephews, nieces and cousins – I began to heal. The love and support of my brothers and sisters-in-law pulled me from my dark tunnel at last. Sydney itself uplifted my spirits from the moment the laughter of kookaburras awakened me at dawn. My youngest brother's wife, Marie, invited me to a scholarship awards luncheon at Parliament House, in the Strangers' Dining Room, which struck me funny. For strangers or not, it was an elegant setting with sweeping views of The Domain. After lunch, we wandered through dark-paneled chambers rich with Australian history. I was unprepared for occasions requiring more than blue jeans and Nikes but a hasty trip to Woolworth's for a pair of black slippers, reminiscent of Audrey Hepburn, helped pull me together.

For my birthday, my brothers surprised me with a memorable gift: the Sydney Harbor Bridge Climb. I couldn't convince the others to join me, so I climbed with a small group, all appropriately instructed, suited up, belted and clamped. On a perfect Sydney day, from the top of the bridge, I had a bird's-eye view of the opera house, the harbor and everything else all the way to the mountains. That day I felt I had conquered more than just the climb.

I stayed in Sydney a month then flew into San Francisco where Scott met me and we drove to Monterey, to Jack's house. Meanwhile, I had applied once again for Foundation housing. I had been at Jack's house for less than three months before I was offered an upstairs studio apartment at Norton Court, built in 1987, newer than Haseltine. I moved in November 2003. Eager to have my own space at last, I didn't realize my apartment was one of only two without its own outdoor area, something that I quickly came to regret. I had looked forward to starting each day outside, alone with a cup of tea and my own thoughts, getting in touch with the morning, the sound of birds and sea, the feel of the air. I had looked forward to planting herbs and flowers. While I was very thankful for my little studio, it sits on a busy street that offers the sound of traffic instead of the sounds of nature. Foundation rules, I had not realized, do not permit tenants to switch apartments, not that any were available. Nevertheless, I was lucky to have a space of my very own, and lucky that the Foundation had accepted me a second time.

Meanwhile, the Reno grandmother, realizing that Katy had not revised her will, hired a lawyer. Scott and I went to court in support of Jack and, outside the courtroom, I told the lawyer I was not there to support his client, my grandson, because I considered him to be greedy and unethical, that he had been abusive to his mother. He replied that he would never represent an unethical client. I said, You have a lot to learn.

Because Katy had failed to draw up a new will leaving everything to Jack, as she had intended, my grandson inherited everything that

Jack had worked for to keep Katy safe – her condominium, her Volvo, money. Even my beautiful childhood book from France and several things belonging to Scott or me, were gone. I sent a list to the lawyer but knew he would not respond. I couldn't help feeling angry with Katy, especially on Jack's behalf. But then, I wished that Jack had protected himself.

Scott and I went to Katy's neighbors to ask if they had heard any disturbance during the days prior to her death. While we were there, we saw my grandson hanging new draperies in Katy's window. Jack learned that my grandson and his partner had wasted no time moving in but soon retreated to their own smaller place because my grandson reportedly freaked out sleeping in his mother's room.

I wonder what the lawyer thought when he saw the front page of the Carmel Pine Cone May 7th, 2004?

On that day, I opened the newspaper and saw the front page headline, Speeds hit 60 mph in chase through town. Beneath the headline was a very odd photograph of a car improbably stuck upright between two retaining walls. Curious, I began to read the extensive article and was startled to see my grandson's name. The article went on to describe a 60mph police chase through Carmel that started in the parking lot at Carmel beach and ended not far from the Carmel Mission. Even after the police officer turned on lights and siren, my grandson did not stop and the chase continued at high speeds through town. It was a miracle, the officer said, that no one was hurt. Even though it was Saturday at dinnertime, few people were on the street. My grandson finally pulled over and when the officer approached the car, the motor was still running and my grandson was fumbling to fasten his seat belt. The officer reported that my grandson was obviously intoxicated. He told him to turn off the engine but instead, my grandson accelerated and took off again, never slowing for stop signs. The chase continued at high speeds until my grandson lost control of the car, went airborne as he took a corner and catapulted from one side of the street to the other, wiping out trees and shrubs in the process. He crossed the mayor's driveway, amongst others, and finally hit a big oak tree then somehow wedged his car at a forty-five degree angle between two walls in the driveway of a house belonging to the owner of the Arizona Diamondbacks. Later the mayor related that two family members had been standing in her driveway only moments before. They credited their dog for saving their lives because he wanted to walk in the opposite direction of my grandson's oncoming rampage.

My grandson sustained multiple face cuts and lacerations, the officer reported. He hit the passenger side windshield from the driver's seat. He was ordered to get out of his car at gunpoint and handcuffed face down in the dirt. Someone later commented that they had never seen so many police cars in Carmel at once. He had absolutely no regard for anyone else, the arresting officer said.

My grandson was arrested for felony evading arrest, DUI, driving with an open container and driving on a restricted license. He was treated at the hospital, released into police custody and booked into Monterey County jail.

Scott and I drove to the courthouse in Salinas for the arraignment and sat directly behind my grandson and his partner. We never spoke but he was clearly unnerved by our presence. The Reno grandmother was not there. He was sentenced to six months in County Jail then placed on parole. He was not allowed to drive for three years; a special monitoring device assured this but he simply went out and bought another car. He was required to attend AA meetings but someone told me they saw him parked outside my apartment once, drinking a can of beer. Years later, Scott found three mug shots of my grandson online - one for assault. Recently, I came across an obituary for the Reno grandmother. She died in 2016, in Pensacola.

Scott renovated Jack's house as planned, from a new kitchen to crown moldings. He repaired earthquake damage, installed new windows and doors, smoothed outdated cottage cheese ceilings, removed wallpaper, restored old wood floors, painted the interior and exterior. Scott considered it an eighty percent remodel. At any rate, the house looked beautiful and Jack decided to put it up for sale. The timing was perfect- real estate prices were at their peak and the house sold quickly at a nice profit. Jack invited Scott to work with him in his thriving iron business and they moved into a house closer to work with three cats. Scott learned fast and being a creative individual, a perfectionist at that, he found he enjoyed ironwork. His efforts increased Jack's profits by, Jack claimed, one thousand dollars a day, although he paid Scott only fourteen dollars an hour. Then, after three years, Jack decided to retire to Florida, where he and Katy had spent happier times and where he might be closer to his own family.

Coincidentally, Ruth was looking at that time for a new roomer at her condominium in Huntington Beach. She'd had some odd ones and liked the idea of having Scott, whom she had known since he was born. She considered the rent she collected extra spending money for the cruises she enjoyed. She and Scott agreed to try this arrangement for six months but it extended into almost four years.

In October of 2005, I drove a friend's car to the DMV to renew my driver's license. I carried a letter from my ophthalmologist intended to help me through a modified eye exam. I scored 100% on the written test but failed the eye test. The patient examiner offered me several test options, with and without eyeglasses, but I failed them all. Clearly, my driving days were over. Another door of my life had closed.

In January of 2006, I returned from a trip to Southern California and opened a letter from HSBC, a Nevada bank, informing me that I might be a victim of identity theft. Because the letter looked like a bad copy, I was suspicious and I immediately carried it to the Carmel Police

Department where an officer confirmed that the letter was legitimate. She surprised me by asking if any family member had access to my personal information? She said that identity theft is often committed by family members.

I immediately called the three official credit agencies to request that a fraud alert be placed on my record. Someone had ordered over six thousand dollars of computer equipment from Hewlett-Packard in my married name, which I had dropped years before. However, they used my current, fairly recently acquired post office box address in Carmel for billing. Because I protect my security diligently and habitually shred, I immediately suspected my grandson who may have had my newer box number but may not have been aware that I had changed my name. The shipping address was in Banning, near Apple Valley where my grandson's father (Katy's ex-husband) had moved when he left Nevada, a fact I discovered accidentally when I happened to see his address in the court papers regarding Katy's will. These facts seemed too coincidental to ignore.

A Carmel detective was assigned to my case and I did some detective work of my own. I Googled a map to see where Banning was in relation to Apple Valley and was not surprised to see they were within easy driving distance.

Scott had just seen a PBS program on identity theft on which a DA from Riverside County was interviewed about an agency called CATCH, which investigates internet crimes. The DA said there was a strong connection between identity theft and meth labs.

I called the DA but he didn't seem to think my case fell into this category, although there was a slight possibility that my identity had been stolen when I booked my airline flight to Southern California online. However, I had booked under my current name, not my discarded married name, which was used in the theft.

I called HSBC and succeeded in getting the address in Banning where the goods were delivered. I wrote to a detective at the Banning Police Department and asked why an officer could not simply knock on the door of that address and find out who lived there or even go in with a search warrant?

The detective told me that my case was the responsibility of the Carmel Police Department because I live in Carmel. However, the Carmel detective told me had no authority in another county. Never the twain shall meet. No wonder these cases are rarely solved. But, as the detective said, the investigating agencies are overwhelmed. After months of getting nowhere, I gave up.

Because I had gone to the police immediately, there was never a question of my being responsible for the bill. If HSBC had bot written, I would never had known that my identity had been stolen. Not all victims are so lucky.

Edge of the Outback

In August of 2006, I returned to Sydney once again. My eldest brother, Bruce, had arranged a first-class train trip for the two of us to visit Helen, the cousin who had published the family book in 1993. According to her postal address, Helen lived in Montefiores via Wellington.

In air-conditioned comfort, we wound through broad sweeps of sun-scorched land, past country towns marked by little quintessentially Australian train stations, unchanged in years but for fresh, bright paint. Then up into the Blue Mountains, down into the flatlands toward Wellington.

Wellington is the second oldest town west of the Blue Mountains, 357 kilometers north-west of Sydney. It sits at the junction of the Bell and Macquarie Rivers and has a population of less than six thousand.

Helen met us at the station and drove us directly to her property, where we met Patrick for the first time. Helen's first husband had died and she had since married this big bear of a man, who had never been married. They seem well suited; Helen is gregarious, Patrick not given to small talk.

A prolonged drought had turned red soil to dust in which nothing grew; Helen told us that they'd had to sell off most of their cattle. Flocks of hungry cockatoos had taken to pecking the Christmas light cords that Patrick had strung on a tree by the house.

The next day we went into town for provisions. Helen gave us a tour of the local Historical Society where she and Patrick volunteer. The musty smell of that old building – the smell of the 1800's - reminded me of an historic hotel in California's gold country where I had stayed years before.

Not far from town we visited the Wellington Caves. Helen waited above ground as Bruce and I climbed into the depths of the majestic Cathedral Cave - so spacious and towering that even I did not feel claustrophobic. Its dramatic stalactites prompted a memory of the Jenolan Caves in the Blue Mountains, where my grandmother had taken my cousins and me as children.

We picnicked on private property that belonged to some absentee friends of Helen's. Beneath weeping willows by the Macquarie River, she laid a feast on a card table spread with a red checkered cloth, as Patrick's two Australian shepherds ran free. The heat intensified the lovely pungent aroma of gum trees.

The morning we were to leave for the train station, my brother wandered out to the fence that marked one edge of the property and found a very young kookaburra caught in the barbed wire. He called to me to find Helen, who came with gloves and wire cutters. As my brother held the bird still and I stroked its head feathers, Helen deftly twisted and snipped through the wire tangle. The kookaburra stayed quite still, as though it sensed we were trying to help. As Helen cut the last wire, she held the bird firmly to prevent it from flying away. She secured it in a sack and went back to the house to call the local Wildlife Rescue.

By now we were running late for our train. Helen told the rescue worker where to find the bird by the fence and we left. I was worried that a snake or fox might find it but as we turned from Helen's long driveway onto the road to town, the Wildlife Rescue truck approached and the ranger acknowledged Helen's wave toward the section of fence where the kookaburra lay.

A few weeks after I returned to California, my brother called to say that Helen had reported a happy ending to our little story. The kookaburra had recovered and had been returned to Helen's property, to an old gum tree that was probably home to its family. Helen said that the day after the youngster was reunited with its flock, she and Patrick were sitting on their verandah when two adult kookaburras flew to a nearby tree and called out as though to say thank you.

Reclaiming my Heritage

In 2007, the Australian Citizen Act was passed, restoring citizenship to those – mostly war brides - forced to relinquish it when they moved to America, which has been historically intolerant of dual citizenship.

My Australian friend Ella had been a war bride and was eager to regain her citizenship. I was excited too; like Ella, I had relinquished mine because I had no other choice at the time. I applied and easily qualified, by descent if nothing else. On March 7th 2008, I was awarded my Australian citizenship, thus becoming a dual citizen. There is a small irony to this – I had traveled to America in 1946 on a British passport – apparently there was no such thing as an Australian then, according to Mother England!

Reclaiming my Australian citizenship has little practical value but it was a loose thread, now properly re-woven into the fabric of my life. An Australian passport allows me to stay there longer and return on my American passport. Scott can apply by descent and I hope he will, if only to mentally expand his geographical options.

Later that spring, a neighbor- a good friend- died. She was a tough, no-nonsense woman impatient with small talk and trivia, whose tiny deck overflowed with flowers. She loved to drive her immaculate old car and insisted on driving me anywhere I needed to go. She was very fond of Scott, who liked her too - we always knew where we stood with Mildred. She died of cancer at home, tended by her caring family. She decided against chemotherapy, having experienced it years before.

Ruth

In November of 2008, I flew to Southern California to stay with Ruth. She had been fighting cancer for several months and was undergoing chemotherapy. With typical Ruth humor, she said, I'll kill you if you don't come to see me! She had joked in that way as long as I had known her. I knew she meant it affectionately.

How can I best help? I asked her and she said she really wanted me to organize her household. I had done this many times for her over the years and enjoyed it. Ruth was a moderate hoarder, I am a moderate minimalist. I knew that after I left, she retrieved half the stuff I had set aside for Goodwill.

I did not tell her that I was having some physical problems myself – I had suddenly developed osteoarthritis pain in my sacroiliac that put an end to walking even a block, let alone to the beach, at least temporarily. I could not see how I could climb into an airport bus or plane, carrying luggage. How would I maneuver Ruth's stairs? There was no question that I would go. To get me through the next twelve days, my doctor prescribed Prednisone. The Prednisone modified my pain but made me frenetically intense. To make matters worse, it kept me awake at night.

I arrived in Orange County in a ferocious heat wave that lasted the entire time I was there. Devastating fires dominated the news, black mushroom clouds loomed over the mountains, thick smoke choked the air.

Nothing could have prepared me for the odor of sickness when I walked in Ruth's door or the changes in my old friend. Despite the heat, she huddled on the sofa, wrapped in a wool shawl over sweaters, mittens and wool cap. The thermostat was turned up, windows shut tight. No longer able to manage the stairs, she'd had a chair escalator installed. I chose not to use it – I conquered the stairs quite easily on my hands, knees and bottom.

While Scott still lived in her condominium and helped her with everything he could, he couldn't be there all the time. I saw that he was kind and patient with Ruth and I knew that she was genuinely fond of Scott; she told me more than once that he was the son she'd never had.

But it was clear that Ruth needed professional nursing care, at least part time. More than once, I caught her in mid-air as she fell without warning and Scott told me he had found her lying on the bathroom floor twice. I was astonished that her daughter, who lived a few blocks away, did not recognize her mother's plight, but Ruth protested her daughter was far too busy. Had her daughter climbed the stairs to her mother's room, she would have seen the untended portable toilet Ruth kept by her bed because she was too weak to walk to the bathroom. She would have seen the uncharacteristic jumble of clothes strewn across the floor and towels smeared with excrement. Scott never ventured near Ruth's room – she had told him very firmly not to – although he could guess at conditions behind the closed door, having found it necessary to routinely clean up their shared bathroom. That first day I threw out the towels and washed seven loads of Ruth's laundry.

She did not complain. To complain would be to admit she needed help and that would mean loss of independence. I understood. When I suggested hiring a nurse part time she was resistant but finally agreed to two half-days a week. I made arrangements through Medicare but Ruth cancelled them the next day. She told me that her doctor had suggested Hospice to which she defensively retorted, I'm not dying! I assured her I knew that but couldn't look her in the eye. She had lost her hair to chemotherapy but, when she went to see the doctor, she wore a wig, which I told her was becoming, a style to adopt once her own hair grew back. I knew that it wouldn't grow back; it was clear my old friend was dying.

Her daughter sometimes stopped by after work and brought Ruth food from McDonald's. Scott and I shopped at Trader Joe's for healthy soups and juices but Ruth only picked at them. She had always joked that she wanted to be as thin as I am but it was no joke now – she was disappearing day by day.

I began to organize her household. I tackled the refrigerator, so deplorable that Scott avoided using it. It took two days to read faded expiration dates, to empty out rotten food and Styrofoam containers. In the process, I plugged up the garbage disposal and sink – of course I should have known better – and Ruth had to summon her handyman. Next I reorganized kitchen cupboards for easier access then tackled the laundry area, storage shed and patio - all jammed with boxes and barrels and buckets half-filled with...what? I felt overwhelmed. I retreated to the little front garden, which I had sometimes tended over the years because I enjoyed gardening and Ruth did not. Fires still raged and still dominated the news. Now, despite lingering smoke and ash, I found it downright therapeutic to be outdoors, hands in soil, hot sun on my back.

The next week, I cleared a spot in the spare room and sat Ruth in a chair to supervise. The room was clogged with odds and ends accumulated over the years but piece by piece, we made piles – to keep, to give to her granddaughters, for Goodwill and so on. We scarcely made a dent but at least created a pathway across the room to the showroom racks packed tight with clothes that Ruth would never wear. More than anything, she wanted to find comfortable pull-on pants that would not fall off her frail frame. This explained the clothes strewn haphazardly about her bedroom: she had been trying to find something to wear, not from vanity, but necessity. I found several pairs, which I washed and ironed and hung on a low rack she could easily reach. Such a small thing, so greatly appreciated.

Ruth had fallen and broken her shoulder a couple of months earlier.

In a way this was a blessing because she could no longer drive – something she had always loved to do. Once a good driver, she recently had had several small accidents, to the point that she was about to lose her insurance. Not wanting her daughter to know, she asked Scott to repair damage to her van and a neighbor's car, which she had backed into twice. Sympathetic, Scott did so but told me he did not want me to get into a car with Ruth at the wheel ever again and I agreed - I had suspected for some time that Ruth's judgment was impaired.

Now she was becoming increasingly unreasonable and demanding – not the Ruth I knew. When her insults accelerated, Scott defended me, pointing out that I had paid my own way to fly almost five hundred miles to help her. I don't want to remember what she said because I knew it was her illness talking. But I realized she was severely dehydrated and that it was affecting her ability to think clearly.

Scott and I bought Smart Water at Trader Joe's and waited while she drank at least a little. I found myself becoming increasingly frustrated with her family, who seemed so unaware. I also knew that Ruth was partly at fault – I felt she had always overindulged her daughter and grown granddaughters and expected little in return. Finally, prompted by that demon Prednisone, I told the daughter that Ruth had to have proper help. I did not handle it well. I was not diplomatic, and the daughter responded by threatening to evict Scott from his rented room so that a nurse could move in. (The spare room was still cluttered and had no space for a bed.) Fortunately, Ruth's doctor delivered an ultimatum: Ruth needed to be hydrated daily at the hospital or be placed in a nursing home.

After twelve days I flew back to Monterey, exhausted and drained. I threw out the last of the Prednisone. I had been there when I was needed but wished I had handled it better. I predicted to friends that it would all fall apart within weeks. When I talked to Scott a few days later, he said everything I had done was undone, that it was as though

I had never been there. He tried to keep up with kitchen and bathroom messes as well as the constant piles that Ruth's senile poodle left all over the rugs, no matter how many times he was let outside.

Shortly afterwards, Ruth entered a nursing home. I called her there and she told me they are taking good care of me. She sounded lucid and peaceful although cancer was spreading to her brain. She said she expected to be home within a week or two, something I knew was unlikely. She died on Christmas Eve. I don't think she ever came to terms with the fact she was dying and I don't know if that is good or bad. Still, when Scott visited her toward the end, she said, if anything happens to me, take care of Mouse, the timid little snowshoes cat she had once rescued, who had attached herself to Scott, and only Scott, like a barnacle.

****

Soon after I returned from Orange County, the lovely English woman I had net a year earlier in exercise class was diagnosed with leukemia. She was eighty-four, her American husband ninety-seven. Such an irony, she told me; she had always expected to care for him in his final days. It was a shock to all of us who knew her – so vigorous, smart and positive. She had an indomitable spirit – she had survived the London Blitz, her sense of humor intact. In a short time, we had become good friends and I wished I had known her all my life. She tolerated hours of daily chemotherapy at the hospital for about a year and suffered, as my old friend Muriel had suffered years before, as Ruth had done so recently. Her memorial, held in a beautiful Carmel garden on a sunny day, was a fitting celebration of her life, joyful and sometimes funny, as her longtime friends shared anecdotes over tea and scones, just as she might have done.

The Sum of a Man

That same month, a letter arrived in a hand-addressed ordinary envelope, from a woman I didn't know. She had found my address on the note I had sent to Donald when Katy died. Now she was trying to locate Scott, to inform him of his father's death in October. Donald was dead. I felt something almost like relief.

The woman who wrote the letter asked that Scott meet with her. To prepare himself, Scott talked to an old family friend, a retired lawyer.

As Scott approached her front door, her neighbor told him, Be careful; she's a user. Scott found her pleasant enough, an unsophisticated woman in her seventies. She claimed she had taken care of Donald in his final days and was executor of his Will. She asked Scott to come back another day for a few personal items he night want. He mentioned that he would especially like to have the oil painting of the family castle in Germany that had hung on his great-grandfather's wall when Scott was a small boy. Their meeting was civil.

She did not offer Scott a copy of his father's Will and our lawyer friend advised Scott to demand it. When they met again, she gave Scott a check for two thousand dollars and some old family photographs; she promised to have a copy of thc Will later that week. Our lawyer friend was certain that the check was all that Scott could expect from his father's estate and he advised Scott to cash it immediately.

The Will reminded me that Donald had been married four times but had no children other than Scott and Katy; all marriages but mine were short-lived. Katy had told me once that one wife, whom she and Scott liked, had to pay Donald $35,000 in their divorce settlement. None of those women made me happy, he told Katy, as though that were their job. I don't think it ever occurred to him that he may have been partly responsible.

We were not surprised to learn that he had cut his son and daughter from his Will. He didn't leave it at that: he scrawled rambling, hateful notes to each of them - just as his own father had done to him years before - and had his lawyer type them into the body of the Will. Our lawyer friend said he had never seen such a thing in all his years of practice. Donald accused his children of trying to use him (Remember, I was a cop for 28 years and I know all the games). To Katy he wrote, We could have had a good relationship but you were so cold. I was glad that Katy, who had tried so desperately her whole life to gain her father's attention and approval, would never see these words. To both children, he blamed me – Your mother! I believe this ranting was really directed at me, because Donald had always known he could get to me through Katy and Scott. He had never forgiven me for divorcing him because he had lost control over me. This was his revenge. It's ironic that Donald, in his hatred of his father, became his father.

Donald had named two different executors in his Will, several years apart. The first executor was a former girlfriend, the second: the woman who claimed to have taken care of him in his final days. In the end these two women inherited Donald's mother's priceless antiques and jewelry that her father had brought from Europe, Donald's car and truck and his condominium, as well as cash. Scott never again saw the gloomy oil painting of the castle to which only he is heir (if only for the privilege of living there, since, under German law, it can never be sold).

Scott went to Hoag Hospital, where he himself had been born, and requested hi father's recent medical records. He wanted to know the exact cause of his father's death and what genetic factors he should be aware of. The records begin June 2, 2007 and end October 8, 2008. These records tell the story more eloquently than I ever could.

D.M. is an 83 year-old male, a morbidly obese (close to 280 pounds) diabetic with hypertension, coronary heart disease, who presents with dyspnea (labored breathing) in a setting of heavy tobacco use, who is currently smoking. He has managed his type 2 diabetes poorly.

The list goes on: chronic kidney disease, lower extremity edema, abscesses, ulcers, staph infection, pulmonary edema, missing teeth, dementia. The records mention that he was abusive to staff. His death certificate lists causes of death on October 10 as cardiopulmonary arrest (minutes) and coronary artery disease (years).

Anyone can get diabetes type 2. However, according to Web MD, People who smoke, have inactive lifestyles, or have certain dietary patterns, have an increased risk of developing type 2 diabetes.

This describes Donald. I also believe that his lifelong negative attitude contributed to his state of health. I believe he self-destructed.

Consider this: he wrote those vindictive notes to his children forty years after he abandoned them. They were eight and eleven at the time. They never forgot his words: When I divorced your mother, I divorced you. In order to justify his own emotional abandonment of his children and to protect his own self-image, he blamed them (and me). Basic psychology calls this projection. The individual expels feelings he finds wholly unacceptable or shameful or dangerous by attributing them to another.

I remember what the Newport psychiatrist told me forty-five years earlier: If he looked into himself, he might very possibly attempt suicide.

For a while, I was angry on Scott's behalf because he did not deserve his father's vengeance. Scott and I had always agreed to question the validity of any Will his father might leave rather than simply accept it. With the help of our lawyer friend, and the opinion of two other attorneys that Donald's neighbor-helper might have influenced

Donald in his state of dementia, Scott did pursue options for a month or two. In the end, unwilling to spend more time, emotional energy and money on a negative cause, Scott and I agreed to deny Donald what he had so long striven for - that we should suffer.

My greatest regret in life is that I married Donald, because in my youthful ignorance, that union produced so much unhappiness. Donald convinced himself he was the victim and in his conviction, convinced a few others as well. They should not judge: they did not live with him or raise his children or suffer his abuse. His final medical records state his occupations as engineer and police officer. How many knew he was not an engineer, but an assistant technician, had never been past twelfth grade, that he was not a trained police officer, but a volunteer reserve officer who had never been psychologically tested? I think he convinced others because he had convinced himself.

Florida, the Unexpected

In October 2010, Scott left Southern California. Jack had asked him to come to Pensacola to remodel his house once again in exchange for room and board. Jack intended to sell the house quickly and pay cash for another in Las Vegas, where real estate prices were low. The goal was to set up a decorative iron business, in which they would be equal partners. Between the two of them, they had years of experience and creative ideas; iron was profitable. The risk was minimal.

With the promise of a more stable work future in sight, Scott seized the opportunity. With funds limited, he reluctantly sold his VW convertible and shipped his vintage work truck to Florida. He moved all his belongings into storage in Monterey and stayed with me for two weeks before we both flew with Mouse to Pensacola.

I was ready for a break, away from the unsettled atmosphere that had prevailed at Norton the past year for reasons that had nothing to do with me personally. But as on-site manager, I was affected. It was a stressful time for both of us, trying to accomplish too much in too little time with limited funds. Fares were high, even with lengthy layovers and plane changes, complicated by the fact that Scott's little cat, Mouse, was flying with us as carry-on luggage. Some airlines claimed they could not guarantee that Mouse could fly with us until we got through security at the airport! We finally gave up trying to book online and did so in person at the Monterey County Airport, where American Airlines guaranteed that Mouse would fly with us. We flew out of San Jose because that was where Scott had to drop off the rental van, which was gobbling money in daily rental fees and gas. We made our flight with little time to spare because a security guard insisted we pay another hundred dollars for Mouse. There was no time to argue or dig into our luggage to produce a receipt. By the time we got on the plane we were exhausted, only to be moved to different seats – the airline's mistake – with a window entirely blocked by an engine. Two months later, American Airlines refunded the hundred dollars.

Pensacola

We were shocked, when we first arrived in Pensacola, to see that Jack had gained so much weight; he shuffled and had difficulty breathing, although he claimed to be in perfect health. Clearly, Scott would be the principal craftsman in their partnership, which suited Scott, who, being a perfectionist, prefers to work alone.

From the very first humid morning, I carried my tea into Jack's big green backyard, screened from neighbors by trees and flowering shrubs. I watched birds darting everywhere - cardinals, orioles, mockingbirds and little brown birds that chattered non-stop. A woodpecker tapped a palm tree as one scarlet cardinal flew so low over my head that I felt my hair lift with the rush of its wings. The air was filled with bird sounds, and now and then the low whistle of an unseen train that made me think of Tennessee Williams.

Florida surprised me, or rather, Pensacola, since that is where I spent most of my time but for a day's drive to Panama City and a brief sojourn into Alabama. I immediately felt an almost tangible drop in the general stress level, like a drop in barometric pressure...it was in the air. Traffic seemed to move at an easier pace than in California; I found people friendly and helpful, from the man behind the post office counter to thc knowledgeable workers at Joe Patti's Fish Market. The local supermarkets and Walmart were larger than any I'd ever seen - well stocked, well organized and spotless. (On the minus side, we found a notable absence of quality bakery goods except for excellent fresh-baked Italian and sourdough breads at Joe Patti's, or home-baked muffins at a little market in Jack's neighborhood; restaurants seemed to deep-fry everything.) Everywhere, litter seemed non-existent. Churches were predominant, for Pensacola falls within the Bible belt. Perhaps that explains the lack of litter: cleanliness next to Godliness.

The heritage business district, with its architecture reminiscent of New Orleans, was pristine, its historic buildings faithfully restored. Apparently, after Hurricane Ivan in 2004, federal money poured into Pensacola - having a governor related to the President may have helped. Roads were in good condition, pedestrian crosswalks were brick-paved, laid well ahead of stop signs and signals for extra margins of safety. Three-Mile Bridge, which Scott and I drove across almost every day to reach Gulf Breeze, spans Pensacola Bay. It is relatively new and wider than the original bridge, which was destroyed by Ivan, along with the adjacent fishing bridge, also rebuilt. Much shorter, it parallels the main bridge. For a fee of only one dollar, people can drive onto the fishing bridge day or night (it is well-lit) and drop their lines. A toll bridge, one mile long, connects Gulf Breeze and Pensacola Beach. Basically sand spits, they were effectively cut off from Pensacola's mainland during Hurricane Ivan. There are sandbars everywhere in Pensacola - the water is mostly shallow. I remember that about Collaroy as a child – and how funny it seemed to see someone standing knee-deep so far out in the water.

Pensacola is flat, very flat. So I shouldn't have been surprised when a tornado warning flashed across our television screen one evening. From Mobile, it was headed directly toward Pensacola but changed course slightly and missed us. It turned north, causing record damage, especially to North Carolina. Two days later we watched the San Francisco Giants win the World Series on Jack's big screen television. The local media paid little attention. In fact, it took two days for us to find out if Jerry Brown would be California's next governor.

Scott and I walked along Pensacola Beach, beyond the pier and waterfront restaurants and bars, to see the unusual round white house that had appeared over and over on television news reports during Ivan. Because of its unique architecture, it was one of the few homes to survive. Originally costing well over a million, it was now up for sale for $495, 000. I liked its innovative contemporary design. Nearby, more traditional homes had blown away, leaving orderly formations of fortified steel pylons thrusting up from the sand like tin soldiers. Common wood pylons had crumbled under the force of the winds and a thirty-foot storm surge tossed them miles away. There were more vacant lots than any evidence of houses. A few optimists, believing Ivan was a rare hundred-year storm, had rebuilt on the sand. At Starbucks, Scott and I met a woman named Sherry, in her early sixties, who had lost two homes on Pensacola Beach. Originally from New Orleans, she had moved to Florida as a child. She had experienced the wrath of Ivan in 2004 but missed the horrors of Katrina in 2005, although Katrina did strike a glancing blow at Pensacola that caused moderate flood damage. Jack was spared: he had done his homework and bought his brick house above the flood plain. Sherry told us she swam in the gulf waters every day in a wetsuit, a knife at her ankle for bull sharks.

I was struck by the size of Pensacola homes in general: large houses on large lots, like pillared Southern mansions, set on sprawling green lawns. Some might have been transplanted from Beverly Hills to manicured lots at the edge of blue bayou or bay. Unlike California, lots are large in Florida - land is cheaper. There is much undeveloped forestland and swamps that house alligators. Pines and grand old live oaks abound: the first oak tree farm in the United States was developed in the Gulf Islands in the early 1800's, for shipbuilding. Live oaks can grow to fifty feet tall and live as long as 300 years. They are all over Pensacola, in parks, in forests, canopied across neighborhood roads. No wonder Pensacola was proclaimed Tree City over twenty years ago.

Standing in one natural reserve we felt we might have been in Point Lobos but for the lack of rocky coves and crashing surf. Instead there was that great, flat expanse of blue water, edged with blinding-white sand beneath a flawlessly clear sky without a hint of smog or haze. Be careful, the blind forest ranger told us. Someone saw a coral snake and a cottonmouth on the wooden trail the other day.

We opted for the narrow strip of white sand, keeping a wary eye on the undergrowth inches away. As we walked in the midday heat, we dipped our hands in the tepid water and found shells that housed live sea creatures. Over a couple of hours, we saw only two other people. On that great expanse of bay, we spotted just one boat, at anchor.

Besides the natural reserves, there were neighborhood parks everywhere, some with walking trails, tennis courts, baseball diamonds, basketball courts or putting greens. At one, we saw a fenced dog park at the water's edge with four showers so that dogs could go home sand-free. Everywhere, beneath young trees, pine straw served as mulch.

Every park and recreation area had well-built restrooms, often with granite counters and polished floors, always spotless and well equipped. Perhaps because it was October, most recreation areas were deserted. At Shoreline Park, besides a pair of white swans nearby on the beach, we had the best of Gulf Breeze to ourselves. Late in the afternoon we happened across the impressive modern entrance to what appeared to be a large steel and glass house, set among tall trees on a private point. We were curious.

We had to wait until the following day to attempt to reach it by ducking under several private piers along the narrow beach. We don't know whose house it is – obviously someone very rich who values seclusion. Its location may be the best in the Gulf, on a near-inaccessible point with broad water views from every part of the house. Its setting is entirely natural – white dunes and sea oats and native grasses and shrubs. There is a guesthouse as well, a smaller replica of the main house but still oversize. Some might think it too commercial-looking but Scott and I, with our love of the modern, appreciated it.

Across the bay, even Pensacola Beach was deserted as far as the eye could see - a picture perfect postcard of endless white sand and sea oats laced with an occasional stake fence curved artfully into the dunes. As if to complete this idealistic scene, a sea turtle paddled in the pale clear shallows. We saw no oil from the terrible BP spill in the Gulf a few months earlier, although another day, further along the coast, we did see crews with machines digging deep into the sand, raking and sifting. Thankfully, I saw no creatures in distress although I tried to not look for them.

We swam in the warm water at Pensacola Beach one day, although swim is hardly the word for it. The yellow caution flag was up but that didn't deter us. The water was shallow and looked calm enough but there were obvious diagonal rips. I didn't mind that either. But while Scott plunged right in, I found myself toppling like a bowling pin over and over again. The sand was so silky fine and soft that it simply kept slipping from under my feet. I'd topple over to the right, bounce upright, topple again. I felt ridiculous and couldn't help giggling while Scott earnestly demonstrated the right way to plant my feet, to no avail.

The warning flags on Pensacola Beach were the same as those I'd seen in California but for one additional flag: purple, indicating Dangerous Marine Life. We were told that might include bull sharks (we saw one from the pier) barracuda and stingrays as well as jellyfish. We saw an abundance of those on the beach, much smaller and milder than Sydney bluebottles.

Scott and I drove beyond Pensacola Beach to Fort Pickens, along an empty road that cut through a narrow sandbar flanked on both sides by white dunes and blue water and space. Fort Pickens is an historic brick fortress, dating back to the Civil War, where Geronimo was once imprisoned for eighteen months with sixteen other Apache men, isolated from their families. We explored the fort then went to the visitor center, where I bought a fife, a harmonica and a tiny iron cannon paperweight. Amid a swirl of monarch butterflies, we walked on top of the seawall that surrounds much of the fort and saw people reeling in their easy catches from the fishing pier and beach.

Jack, Scott and I spent a pleasant day at the Great Gulf Coast Arts Festival in the park near Seville Square in the heritage district. An annual three-day invitational event, it represents some of the best artists in the country. Ethnic foods were abundant, the Pensacola Symphony Orchestra exuberant. A quartet of young sisters in blue jeans entertained passers-by, switching effortlessly between cello, violin, banjo and guitar to create an impressive range of sounds from classical to country to bluegrass. The festival is a lively event and it's free except for parking, and if one should want that, the nearby tiny historical wood cottages have surprisingly large backyards which owners open up for parking during the festival. We paid just five dollars to park all day while a homeowner made a little extra cash.

I left Pleasantville, as Jack calls Pensacola, and flew back to Monterey November eighth via Charlotte, NC and Phoenix. There were things I liked about Pensacola but I have no heart for living there. I am not fond of humidity, hurricanes or tornadoes.

Before we went to Pensacola, I had resolved to avoid stirring unhappy memories of Katy for Jack's sake. But one evening, shortly after we arrived, Jack began to speak of her. Scott and I learned things we hadn't known, that Katy was repeatedly unfaithful, that she had lost one job because she was caught stealing. According to Jack, she had been diagnosed as manic-depressive and possibly schizophrenic as well. Jack told us that my grandson had been diagnosed with both. I asked Jack how many years of their twenty-five years together had been happy and he replied, three. I asked him why he didn't leave her sooner and he said they had managed by leading separate lives. They simply avoided one another as he continued to support her, as he had promised.

Until this conversation, Jack believed, as I once had, that Katy had liver cancer. When I told him that I had called her doctor after she died and learned that it was not true, that he had treated her only for anxiety and depression, Jack shook his head as if to say, Just one more thing.

The conversation was oddly cathartic for me. I finally let go the lingering traces of maternal guilt I'd harbored ever since Katy's death over seven years before. I stopped asking Why? The simple truth is that Katy was mentally ill, delusional in the end. I don't know how, or if, her medical problems as an infant might have played a part; or her experiments with drugs, or even if the genetic thread from Donald's suicidal father might have caught her somehow.

I felt sad for Katy, who always seemed discontent, incapable of joy. Still, one image persists, when Katy was about nineteen. On a hot day at Corona Del Mar beach, we rode the waves together on a rubber raft, shrieking and laughing helplessly like children all the way to the beach.

Best Laid Plans

Scott finished a major remodel on Jack's Pensacola house and readied it for sale. Jack seemed enthusiastic, searching for Las Vegas properties to buy, perhaps two houses, one to live in, one for investment. Scott packed Jack's belongings and offered to drive a moving van alone to Las Vegas, put things in storage then set up an iron shop ahead of Jack. He was anxious to get on with his future; he had been in Florida fourteen months with no income. Then Jack said, Well, Pensacola isn't such a bad place to live.

****

Back from Florida, I sat down to catch up on mail. Reading one notice, I wondered who had made such a poor copy: an inch of type at the left margin was missing. For a moment I experienced whirling white lights in my left eye- the eye most affected by dry macular degeneration. When the flashing passed and the missing type returned, I shrugged it off, but my friend Joy urged me to call my ophthalmologist. When Dr. Rosenblum examined me, he found that nothing had changed in my left eye but that my right eye –my better eye- had signs of bleeding. Wet macular degeneration! This was something I had tried to avoid since my diagnosis in 2005. Dr. Rosenblum referred me to Dr. Del Piero, a retina specialist in Monterey.

In November 2010, Dr. Del Piero scanned my eye with an imaging system called Optical Coherence Tomography (OCT) which has been used in recent years to process detailed images from the retina, with micrometer resolution. It was used originally, among other things, in art conservation, to detect layers of paint.

When Dr. Del Piero expressed surprise to his assistant at the results on the screen (I didn't expect that!), I asked, Is that good or bad? He replied, Well, it isn't good. He told me the bleeding had occurred in my central vision. When I asked how long this might have been going on, he told me no more than six weeks. Counting back I realized that was the exact time Scott and I had flown to Florida. I asked if flying, or extreme stress, might have triggered the bleeding and he replied, Absolutely not. That was a relief: I did not want to think I had brought this on myself.

Family Days

In March 2011, the time of the devastating Japanese earthquake and tsunami, my youngest brother Rodger and his wife, Marie, visited m from Australia. They were well prepared: using a GPS, they drove right to my doorstep. Despite constant heavy rain, they didn't complain and explored nonstop. We visited spectacular Yosemite when there was still snow on the ground and few tourists.

Sometime in June, as I walked up the hill from the beach, I noticed a very slight left foot drag, as though a leaf had stuck to the sole of my shoe. This continued to happen, but so slightly and irregularly that I shrugged it off.

Bryan and Ana came in August. We drove to Big Sur where we hiked, waded in the Big Sur River, then lunched in sunshine at Nepenthe's. Bryan brought old photos I had never seen – mostly me as a child- and letters from my father to his sister-my Aunt Phyllis, Bryan's grandmother. The first letter, dated October 1937, was written at sea, en route from Argentina to America. The second one, dated September 1939, was sent from Massachusetts. Articulate and well-typed on transparent paper, they speak almost entirely of my father's business dealings with Argentina. I can only guess why such details might be of interest to Phyllis.

Scott came in September and stayed two weeks, happy to escape Florida's humidity and the smell of Jack's pot smoke every morning. I did not mention my foot drag because I scarcely thought of it. We hiked in the hot, dry wilderness beyond the Las Padre dam. In Big Sur we talked to a young ranger who had grown up in Southern California. We asked him about the possible risks of mountain lion and bear attacks while hiking in the Big Sur wilderness. He told us, There is little danger because Northern California supports a strong, balanced eco system, which supplies a natural bounty of food for its wildlife. They have no interest in humans, unlike those in the nonproductive eco system of Southern California. Overbuilding has left little natural habitat for wildlife.

One Thursday in late November, as I crossed my living room, I became dizzy and tilted to the left. I called Sue and asked her to be on standby, just in case. I called my primary care doctor, Dr. A.J. but since his first available appointment would be three weeks away, I saw his assistant the following Monday, December 5. She scheduled tests at the hospital for Friday the 9th. But the very next day after I saw her, I was in the hospital. That day, Tuesday December 6, 2011, I was walking with Sue when my speech became garbled. Sue looked at me and said, I'm taking you to the hospital! Incoherent, I tried to protest that I just needed to lie down for a little while. Sue, whom I have known over thirty years, who never raises her voice, shouted at me, You're going to Emergency! Over the phone, Dr. A.J. strongly agreed and off we went. I had suffered a transient ischemic attack (TIA) and spent two days in Emergency, where, a neurosurgeon later told me, I had continued to garble for a full hour as my normally low blood pressure shot up over 180.

Sue called Scott in Florida and two days later he flew with Mouse into Monterey, this time to stay; Jack's Las Vegas plans had gone nowhere and I had to pay twelve hundred dollars to have Scott's work truck shipped back to California. With no income, Scott had no recourse but to stay with me temporarily, against all rules. Mouse was illegal too. I felt like Anne Frank.

After an MRI, an electrocardiogram, a CT scan and carotid duplex ultrasound, I seem to have recovered with no ill effects. All these tests reveal that I am in good health; no one can explain exactly why I had a TIA in the first place. However, according to the Mayo Clinic's website, the main risk factors are age (over fifty-five), and genetics. I believe my father suffered one TIA in his seventies, and, like me, he recovered. However, according to the website, that one single episode presents a risk factor for his children, just as my one episode presents a risk factor for Scott. The best defense is a healthy lifestyle but even that didn't prevent my TIA because I made the mistake of ignoring all the little warnings that came before. Dr. A.J. was adamant: If you experience just one of those symptoms, go to Emergency immediately! While some doctors consider a TIA a warning for a more serious stroke, others, like Dr. A.J., believe a TIA is a small stroke. One TIA increases further stroke risk to forty percent. Sometimes I feel as though I'm waiting for the other shoe to drop.

The day after I was released from the hospital, whenever I closed my eyes, I experienced patterns like interlocked red Olympic rings, spinning, gyrating faster and faster until they tuned into an undulating lavender and green pattern. I dreaded closing my eyes.

Dr. Rosenblum told me I had Charles Bonnet Syndrome- so named after a Swiss scientist of the same name, discovered in the 1700's, although not recognized in the western world until 1982. It produces visual hallucinations: flowers, animals, people – anything. Before it was identified, people thought they were going insane.

During his examination, Dr. Rosenblum discovered a tear – a rip – in the corner of the retina of my right eye. He arranged an immediate appointment with Dr. Del Piero, who determined that surgery to repair the rip would not be practical for an eighty-two year-old woman with advanced macular degeneration. I had already decided I would not opt for such surgery.

In my post-TIA examination, with Scott present, Dr. A.J. told me he did not want me to live alone, for two reasons: the possibility of another stroke, and my degenerating vision. To be honest, if Scott hadn't been there, I would have chosen to live alone. It suits me, I like my independence.

Dr. A.J. also advised me to use a white cane for crossing streets. Mostly for the drivers, not you, he said. I had my initial training session on January 19, 2012. However, since two SUV's sailed through the Carmel crosswalk I was in, I have taken instead to wearing neon colors.

Life Interrupted

In July 2012, Scott suddenly fell very ill. He had enjoyed a three-mile walk that afternoon and we had eaten a healthy dinner together, which I had prepared. Only Scott, however, ate one small bowl of Kellogg's Frosted Mini-Wheat cereal for dessert.

Within two hours, he experienced severe abdominal pain. Assuming it would pass, he delayed going to Emergency but his condition worsened. When he finally reached the hospital, he was misdiagnosed with a stomach virus and sent home.

There, his pain only increased, to the point he felt he was going to die. Eleven days later he returned to the hospital where a cat scan revealed some kind of internal injury. The attending surgeon, Dr. Garza, told me that without immediate surgery, Scott had twenty-four to forty-eight hours to live. At ten o' clock on Friday July 27, 2012 - opening night of the London Olympics - Dr. Garza, having cancelled his vacation, operated and saved Scott's life. He discovered perforations in the colon and intestine and a massive amount of peritonitis attached to all the internal organs.

Two hours later he emerged and explained everything to me very frankly. Scott would have to wear a colostomy until reattachment surgery. I delayed telling Scott this and was relieved when Dr. Garza did so. He said that the second surgery would be more difficult than the first surgery and could not be done until after a lengthy healing process. It could not be rushed; to operate too soon might mean wearing a colostomy bag permanently. Prior to repair surgery, Scott would have a colonoscopy. To date there had been no evidence of Crohn's disease or cancer. No one could explain why a healthy, athletic man like Scott would suddenly need a colostomy. Nor could Dr. Garza explain any possible cause for such extensive internal damage.

I knew Sue was away. I called Ella to let her know what was happening. I paced the empty halls of the hospital, feeling very alone, until I saw Ella and her daughter walking toward me. I knew they hated to drive at night, but here they were. I am fortunate in my friends.

Scott was hospitalized for nine days. I visited him every day but one, via limited bus service. At the hospital, knowing he would need professional care for a while, I asked where he might go to recover, and was told that such care would be unavailable to him because he had no insurance. Nearly six years later, he is still paying off his medical bills.

Scott recovered on a mattress on my studio floor. Visiting nurses came a few times – mostly to instruct him on colostomy bag use.

During his recovery, Scott often sat outside the library on Ocean Avenue. One day he was approached by two police officers; a woman working in a nearby jewelry store – the place for one so inclined to purchase a Rolex- had reported him as suspicious. Such is the paranoia that exists in the vicinity of money!

About two months after Scott's first surgery, we turned on ABC World News and saw a segment about a Kellogg's cereal recall. A dysfunctional machine had mixed wire mesh into the cereal: Frosted Mini-wheats! The dates and numbers of the recalled cereal exactly matched those on the box that Scott had kept in my kitchen cupboard, untouched since the one and only bowl he had eaten hours before his severe pain began.

I immediately went online and found a brief, inconspicuous announcement by Kellogg's, offering consumers who had purchased boxes of Frosted Mini Wheats with specific code numbers, to return the boxes to Kellogg's for a fifteen dollar refund. The FDA remained mute.

We had no doubt now as to the cause of Scott's ordeal.

We contacted several lawyers, few of whom impressed us, some unwilling to take on a major corporation. None would even consider suing the local hospital for malpractice...a separate issue. Then I read online of a big law firm in Texas, with offices in Beverly Hills and Newport Beach, interested in the Kellogg's recall. Scott called them and was told We don't deal in pennies, only millions. For a year they were in touch with us almost daily: text messages, phone calls, faxes, letters, as we provided information as well as detailed copies of the offending cereal box. They charged us nothing all this time, so confident were they of winning, but after a year, unable to locate the specific factory where the wire mesh malfunction had occurred, they had to give up.

The head of the firm in Texas called one day to apologize. He told me, You should have won this case, I'm sorry. But after a year, we just could not continue to invest more time and money into it.

I told him that I had seen no evidence that the FDA had intervened on behalf of consumers. He laughed and said: Oh, the FDA is the lap dog of corporate America!

In early 2017, Scott happened across an item online regarding that Kellogg's recall. The factory in question is in Canada! No wonder the law firm couldn't match that one code number (of several) on Scott's box. (Which he still has in his possession, untouched since that single bowl that almost killed him.)

Unfortunately the statute of limitations prevents justice for Scott and probably others like him. I believe, in the name of justice, this should change.

****

At the end of summer 2012, Jack finally sold his Pensacola house and moved to Las Vegas. The last time I talked to him, he was renting an apartment close to a casino where he likes to penny gamble every day. He told me he had never been so stress-free and seems to have abandoned any plans for work, including the proposed partnership with Scott. Having seen his physical condition in Pensacola, I was not surprised to hear that he suffers from COPD.

Charles Bonnet Revisited

September 2013, my brother John and his wife Cataline, visited. They had been traveling in Europe, out of touch until the Friday night when John called from San Francisco's Chinatown, wondering if there was a bus to Carmel? We had been looking forward to seeing them at their Carmel motel on Monday – the last time we spoke, John had mentioned that he might renew his international driving license. It was too late to call the car rental agency, so Scott went online, and tried to book a van, big enough for the four of us and a likely large amount of luggage. On Monday morning, we took a taxi out to Seaside to pick it up, only to find that no van was available. We waited until one arrived then drove to San Francisco. Things became more chaotic. We hadn't realized that the America Cup yacht races were happening on San Francisco Bay. Traffic was at a standstill, sightseers and police everywhere, no parking anywhere.

We made our way to Chinatown, having alerted my brother to be ready at the curb, then drove back to Carmel. They stayed six days, walking and riding local buses, while Scott returned to his job in Marina.

On Sunday, we drove them back to the Bay Area, this time to Oakland, where they had booked a motel close to the Oakland Airport. We didn't know that the new Bay Bridge had just opened! Cars were jammed willy-nilly at all angles, trying to access the bridge. I clearly remember thinking I'm having a nervous breakdown. I told no one that I had been up at three that morning, my entire visual world bathed in blood, nothing but blood. Fearing vision damage, I had called Dr. Del Piero, who told me to be in his office by eight o'clock Monday morning, before his first patient.

We said goodbye to Cataline and John, having cautioned them to stay in their room until leaving for their flight to Hawaii: Oakland is known for its crime rate. They would relax in Hawaii before going on to Australia. Scott and I drove back to Carmel.

On Monday, when Dr. Del PIero determined my vision was undamaged, Scott came and drove me to Emergency, where I was once again diagnosed with visual hallucinations – Charles Bonnet syndrome - brought on by stress.

****

Finally, all things considered, I applied for a two bedroom apartment in Pacific Meadows, a complex for people over sixty-two, where Scott qualifies as my caregiver and small pets are allowed. Good thing: there was never any question of giving up Mouse.

Unlike Carmel Village, the Meadows is generally quiet and in this expensive coastal California rental market, it is the most affordable. We waited four years for our little apartment to become available.

From my balcony overlooking the forest, I have seen deer, bobcats, coyotes, birds of prey, hummingbirds, Stella jays, acorn woodpeckers and my favorite little juncos, amongst others. At night I hear the hoots of owls. Flocks of resident quail scurry - always in protective groups - into the forest and back, every morning, every evening, chattering sweetly. There are mountain lions too but I have yet to see one.

When management asked for suggestions for new activities, I immediately requested an exercise class and was thrilled when Maryanne, the best exercise instructor on the Peninsula, agreed to come two mornings a week.

****

In early 2017, we lost our precious little snowshoes, Mouse. She was, we guess, fifteen or sixteen. She died at home in the middle of the night, as we watched over her, hands stroking her, until her final, tiny goodbye meow and her last breath. She didn't know she was a cat: never clawed, hissed, bit or growled. She had a rough beginning but knew nothing but love and trust in her life with us. Terrified of people when Scott first met her, she had taken to jumping onto my lap the moment I sat down with my morning tea. Since my robe is soft and pink, we called this the pink lap-sit. And that is how I will always remember Mouse. She was a gift.

The Road Ahead

Unlike the old man in the retina specialist's office years earlier, (I looked in the mirror and I wasn't there), I've had no sudden loss of vision. But I feel a general frustration over things like increasingly fragmented newspaper headlines, or long numbers like those on credit cards, because the numerals at the right simply disappear, like a string of performers leaving a stage. I can no longer read bus numbers or street signs, even when I'm standing right under them. After all, ARMD is a progressive disease.

Dr. Del Piero has told me that laser, the most common treatment for wet ARMD for years, would only cause further damage to my central vision. He has given me several series of Lucentis injections at the hospital, usually once a month for four or six months, but recently switched to Eyelea, because Lucentis was no longer effective. He told me once that these injections might give me a fifty/fifty chance of retaining my vision at its present level.

When I see Dr. Del Piero in his office after the shots, he says, The bleeding is gone. That is always good news. However, when his assistant asks me to read the eye chart, I can see only the top left letter. After a pause, the doctor's assistant says, What about the one next to it? Oh.

I am more aware now of increased blurring in the central vision and I don't recognize people I know until I am face-to-face with them. I told a friend once who thought I was ignoring her as we passed one another on the street: I look at you but I don't <u>see</u> you. As soon as I said it, I knew it to be true.

There are no miracles yet for ARMD but future generations may benefit from stem cell therapy. Given current life expectancies, the disease will affect more and more people over sixty-five since age is the primary risk factor. Genetics rate second. As Dr. Del Piero said, You can blame both your parents! My father had ARMD, and while my mother died too young to experience any symptoms, her sister did; she was blind when she died in her nineties.

When the central vision is affected by wet ARMD, reading and detail work become increasingly difficult and ultimately impossible. Colors, I'm told, become monochromatic. So far, this is not so. A friend thinks, as an artist, I have color memory!

I can still walk briskly – walking is essential to me, not only physically, but emotionally and mentally as well; interacting with Carmel dogs at the beach is a big part of that. Since Carmel is all crooked, I watch the ground a few feet ahead and tell myself: I will not trip! Sometimes I use trekking poles, for balance as well as core strengthening.

Research tells me that patients are usually left with peripheral (side) vision, which some wag described as like having a dinner plate over your eye. Peripheral vision, unlike central vision, does not allow the patient to see a face. I realize now that my father had lost his central vision when I saw him last. He would cock his head and glance sideways in a futile effort to actually look at the person he was talking to. I imagine that peripheral vision might do little more than prevent one from bumping into a wall or being totally in the dark.

I remember something a woman said once during a meeting for the visually impaired. Her family did not believe she had a problem because she could spot a tiny piece of lint on a carpet. I understood. It's a matter of contrast or motion: a black spider on a white wall is easy to spot; the same spider on a dark carpet may be invisible until it moves. I never pick up lint without first viewing it through a magnifier to see if it has legs or wings. One learns, they say, to adapt.

I avoid crossing busy streets now, even with signals. By the time I can focus, the signals might have changed or glare may have rendered them colorless or made them pop unreliably in and out of my vision. She who hesitates might get run over.

While the landscape is becoming an Impressionist painting, I can still see the colors of nature and that, to me, is paramount to the quality of my life. I already have lost more than I care to acknowledge: the pleasures of drawing and painting, reading in bed, recognizing friends' faces from across the street, spotting migrating whales, knowing what bird just flew by me down at the river beach, driving, traveling independently. I want to know that I will see the rosy green wine foliage of autumn next year but no one can promise me that. In the meantime, I try to store the images of nature like old color slides, to view on demand. I look out at the sea and describe to myself the scene in detail: The sea is Winslow Homer Prussian blue, or whitecap-scattered steel green, the sky leaden with aqua slits, the tide low, the beach by the Frank Lloyd Wright house kelp-flung.

Creativity doesn't stop just because one goes blind!

I have willed my body to the University of San Francisco for medical research. Scott will need only to make a single phone call for pick-up. Meanwhile, I have a DNR. Beyond that, I hope for the best.

One thing is certain: you have to laugh at life and especially yourself, although it is not always easy. Even vision loss has its funny side: at the Cherries Jubilee hot-rod show on Alvarado Street in Monterey, Scott pointed out a tiny dog by one of the cars. It looked so forlorn, I told Scott I wanted to go back and pet it. Mom, he laughed, It's a fake dog, peeing on the tire!

Another day, I saw a hand-scrawled sign propped against an abundantly leafy tree in Carmel. Curious, I dug my little magnifier from my backpack and bent to read the sign but had to decipher one letter at a time, which took a little while.

The sign warned: BEE SWARM IN TREE!

Perhaps that's life: learn by trial and error, make the best of it. Sometimes I feel as though I have lived several different lives... perhaps in search of the right fit?

The seventeen year-old in Sydney would never recognize the eighty-eight year-old she has become. Had I been wiser then, I might have tried to weather my grandmother's paranoia and made plans to visit America later, to spend a year or two, perhaps attend college or find a job, then return to Australia and all things familiar, to family.

Or perhaps not.

Without A Script

Finale

At nine o'clock Friday evening, February 2nd, 2018, I felt a distinct lump in my left breast. Being a weekend, there was nothing I could do. First thing Monday, I called the Breast Care Center in Monterey and was told I needed a referral from my Primary Care physician.

I saw Dr. Straface February 13th, then on to the Breast Care Center the same day. It had been eleven days since I discovered the lump. I now had a series of mammograms, ultrasounds and a biopsy and a thorough examination by, the very kind, Dr. Roux.

The next day-Valentine's Day-Dr. Roux called me with results. She told me she was surprised: I had a cluster of tumors. She added: This is the bad guy of a very aggressive cancer.

I appreciated her candor; she knew I wanted it straight. I had already told her *No Chemo!* I am almost eighty-nine, although people seem to think I am younger! I had seen three friends suffer through chemo; they died anyway, with little quality of life.

Dr. Roux referred me to Dr. Ganeles, an empathetic oncologist whom I saw February, 21. She ordered a c-scan for the next day with a follow-up visit later the same day. She told me I probably had two to three months to live and arranged an appointment February 23 with a surgeon, Dr. Stuntz, who shares an office with Dr. Garza, who saved Scott's life in 2012.

After checking the c-scan, Dr. Stuntz scheduled me for a mastectomy at noon March 29, the first available date, which is cutting it a bit close! But I like and trust Dr. Stuntz and intend to stick with him. I was in his office over three hours, and he put things into perspective. I told him I fear brain cancer; I want to be alert to the end. He felt chemo would be my best chance, so I have agreed to four sessions.

As of today, I feel totally well, with my usual high energy. I am taking advantage of that and have cleaned out files, sent clothes to Battered Women and met with the Montage art curator to donate five of my paintings to the hospital.

So... I shall live on through my art!